MANAGING MUSEUMS AND GALLERIES

The current economic climate, coupled with an all-embracing desire for museums to be respondent to 'the market' make a proper grounding in management essential. The 'bottom line' is one of the most powerful measures of management performance. Museums and galleries invariably have a neutral bottom line, they are not set up to make a profit and many of them are constrained by governmental accounting rules and charity legislation. Managing these organisations is difficult and this book tackles the issues that make it easier.

Managing Museums and Galleries examines the highly sophisticated principals and techniques of modern business management from the perspective of museums and galleries and delineates their practical application. The book surveys the day-to-day issues of time management, delegation and recruitment. It also examines the problems of strategic planning and initiating and controlling change. The study incorporates the needs of both the independent and national sectors and discusses the links between the museum and commerce.

Michael A. Fopp is Director of the Royal Air Force Museum, London. He has twenty years of museum experience, of which more than half has been spent directing major museums in the independent and national sector.

The Heritage: Care–Preservation–Management programme has been designed to serve the needs of the museum and heritage community worldwide. It publishes books and information services for professional museum and heritage workers, and for all the organisations that service the museum community.

Editor-in-chief: Andrew Wheatcroft

Managing Museums and Galleries

Michael A. Fopp

London and New York

First published 1997
by Routledge
11 New Fetter Lane, London EC4P 4EE

Simultaneously published in the USA and Canada
by Routledge
29 West 35th Street, New York, NY 10001

Typeset in Sabon by Florencetype Ltd, Stoodleigh, Devon

Printed and bound in Great Britain by
TJ International Ltd, Padstow, Cornwall

British Library Cataloguing in Publication Data
A catalogue record for this book is available from the
British Library

Library of Congress Cataloging in Publication Data
Fopp, Michael
Managing Museums and Galleries / Michael A. Fopp
p. cm. – (The heritage)
Includes bibliographical references (p.   ) and index
(alk. paper)
1. Museums–Management–Handbooks, manuals, etc. I. Title
II. Series
AM121.F66   1997
069'.5–dc20   96–34796
CIP
ISBN 0-415-09496-8 (hbk)
0-415-09497-6 (pbk)

Contents

Contents

Figures

Preface and acknowledgements

My introduction to museums, and particularly their management, came later in life than for most other museum professionals. By the time I started my own career, I had already had 15 enjoyable years fulfilling a boyhood dream of riding horses for a living.

My decision to concentrate on the management aspects of museums was predicated by a mixture of influences. First, I experienced appalling management in my first career and this left a profound impression on me. I have yet to discover why perfectly normal human beings feel the need to act so poorly when they go to work. I cannot, to this day, understand why workers will accept comments or behaviour in a work scenario which would be totally unacceptable to them in their social life.

Second, I found that museums in general were better but by no means adequate in managing their affairs. I was, I suppose, a mediocre historian/researcher and saw an opening in an area which, in my opinion, was lacking. I therefore concentrated on management.

Third, I had tremendous support from a small number of people who had confidence in my ability to research this new area of museum work. Undoubtedly my original mentor was Dr John Tanner, the founding Director of the Royal Air Force Museum at Hendon. It was he who took me to one side some years ago and suggested that I take an academic route which has resulted in this book. I shall always be grateful to him for his faith in me and I am proud at having both justified that faith and succeeded the post he occupied so successfully for twenty or more years. I am also indebted to Professor John Pick and Dr Eric Moody of the City University, London. Both John and Eric knew me only as an ambitious young man with a mission to succeed. They gave me the opportunity to prove myself academically and I am conscious that in so doing they took some risk. I hope I have repaid them after passing on the results of my studies in this book and in teaching their students for almost a decade.

No one has supported me more than my family. My wife, Rosemary and son, Christopher, have had to bear the financial and physical disruption of years spent holding down a challenging job whilst working on postgraduate studies. All those odd jobs around the house and games in the garden which I could not do or which had to wait; all those holidays spent waiting for Daddy to finish his reading or writing.

Finally, I should also thank those many managers who have influenced my life and thinking in two careers spanning over thirty years. I thank those who were appalling almost as much as those who were good because I probably learned more from them. They were truly awful and I hope this book helps to prevent other people, particularly in museums and galleries, being afflicted with their type. Management affects people's lives and should therefore be taken very seriously indeed.

Michael Fopp
London, 1996

Introduction

The concept of management studies and the fact that senior staff within museums and galleries might have management training or qualifications, is a relatively new phenomenon in museums. For the best part of 150 years museums were managed with little or no attention being paid to management training for staff. The view has often been expressed that management training and the resulting techniques are inappropriate to museums and, as such, are irrelevant to the museum profession. The general opinion has been that museums are different from other organisations and this is a view which a large section of the museum profession still retains. This problem is compounded by the fact that employers are not acknowledging the importance of training throughout the profession and for management in particular. Until recently the entry level qualification which had been generally accepted (at least in local authority museums) was the Museums Association Diploma, but its management content was always, understandably, minimal. The Association has itself recently revised the criteria for the award of its Associateship but it, too, still concentrates on traditional 'museum studies' graduates which all too often involves no more than a cursory glance at the skills of actually managing a museum or gallery.

It is time for the museum profession (if that is what it can be called) to acknowledge that curatorial and academic prowess, whilst being essential for the well-being of museums, are not the only areas which need professionalism. Indeed, the museum profession has now come to realise that it is not really a 'profession' at all until it achieves a standardisation of training which lays down acceptable levels of achievement in all areas associated with running a successful and effective museum or gallery. This book is meant to assist the museum professional in his/her gathering of knowledge to achieve a better understanding of the process of management.

During the recent decade or so of contracting subsidies (in real terms) for the arts/heritage generally, and greater competition from an increasing number of museums and other leisure attractions, those working in the museum profession have been forced to acknowledge their shortcomings in the areas of organisational control and management. The many new independent museums, obliged to earn income in a competitive market, have given useful guidelines

1

to the other museum sectors. As a result, the museum profession is, I hope, becoming increasingly aware of the need for greater expertise in the management of their institutions rather than just the collections under their care.

Some explanation is needed for the attitude of members of the profession which has, at best, been circumspect with regard to management until recent years. These attitudes are explained by three significant factors which have a bearing not only on the state of the profession at the moment but also on our ability to 'weather the storm' and move forward into the next century with some kind of confidence both in ourselves and in the future of the institutions we control.

First is the method of recruitment. The profession is almost a sealed box; entry has been severely limited at almost every level except the very lowest with no more than forty or fifty junior curatorial staff entering the profession in each year. The Museums Association, until a few years ago, published an information sheet about careers in museums wherein it stated:

> Opportunities for a museum career are comparatively limited in numbers. Applicants must be prepared to wait for a suitable vacancy and to move around the country. Competition is intense – a post in a national museum may attract over 300 applicants. Promotion within the national museums is gradual and staff tend to develop specialist research within their collection. There is greater mobility of personnel amongst local authority museums to achieve promotion.
>
> (Museums Association, 1979)

It is still the case that, as a result, the widest recruitment of candidates from outside the profession is done at the start of an individual's career. Approximately half of the junior entrants to the profession each year enter without any formal museum-orientated training. Immediately after they have completed their academic education (which is usually to university first degree standard) they then join the profession at the lowest level. In many cases the more senior posts are filled by candidates from outside the museum world. By the time those who can help change the profession have obtained a position of influence they have been in museums for a considerable time. They, therefore, may be pre-eminent in their specialised subject, but their experience of management may, at best, be limited.

The second factor is the actual reason people enter the museum profession in the first place. The qualifications required for entry are generally rather high. An honours degree, often supplemented by a higher research degree is almost the norm. As a result, the profession tends towards the academic in context and outlook. By their nature museums do not offer the same sort of career prospects as many other openings available to graduates with similar qualifications. The perception of the museum profession is probably still similar to that of the museum itself – a rather 'dusty' or mundane sort of existence, of interest only to subject specialist and ideal for the introverted – the home of the 'enthusiast' or 'bookworm'. Such people can hardly be regarded as the most innovative, ambitious or entrepreneurial of the graduates available at the end of each academic year.

It is inevitable that subject-specialists, as they progress through the museum grades, find themselves increasingly divorced from the purity of research and become involved in departmental or institutional management. The profession is, as a result, well endowed with experts in the specialist areas of curatorship (there are few trained and experienced managers) working with the wrong attitude but unable (and ill equipped) to do anything else. This factor has drawn the attention of the outside world in the past and I recall an interesting piece published in the *Guardian* in 1986 where Waldemar Januszczak summed up his views about the recent unveiling of ambitious plans to turn the Tate Gallery into one of the largest museum complexes in the world by its then Director:

> This then is the ramshackle institution which today unveils its grandiose plans for the future. We do not know where the money for the new museum complex is coming from. We do not know when it will be finished. We do not know how it will be administered. All we know for sure is that a landlord who cannot keep a bedsit in order is planning to build a palace.
>
> (Januszczak, *Guardian*, 25 September 1986)

This sort of criticism of the basic management ability of the most senior museum directors of the country has continued, off and on, ever since. However, it is but a microcosm of the problem throughout the profession and is not just reserved for those at the top of the nation's principal institutions.

The third factor is the quality of members of the profession itself. Museums tend to have experts in their subject field who, on promotion, often find management difficult or incomprehensible. This may be a generalisation but one which should be recognised more openly by those who may be able to address the problem. I know that I will attract criticism from colleagues in even raising the matter, but the whole career within a museum, its development and training, is geared almost exclusively to the specialist subjects within which individuals work. Very little attention has been given to developing broader skills so that museum specialists of the requisite calibre – and some will wish to remain scholars all their days, to the enrichment of their museums – can also become innovative and effective managers. These people will, with wider thinking, new techniques, improved administration, revitalised financial systems and greater collaboration between institutions and public, be able to transform old fashioned museums into vibrant and popular centres that are an integral part of the community's educational and recreational lives. This problem is real and threatens museum employment status as a profession. More importantly, it threatens the whole museum framework.

The attitude of the museum profession to the available training in management subjects was less of an impediment in the past than it is today. After the late 1970s museum provision was a relatively secure part of public funding whether national, provincial or university based. The museum was recognised as being a place of learning, research and conservation. The changes that have taken place during the past decade have altered not only the place of museums, but also the way in which they are perceived by their funding bodies.

The greatest change has been the burgeoning independent or private sector, where museums are generally being created to fulfil some specific and defined purpose. From the start their aims and objectives have been pretty clear. In contrast many of our greatest and most long established museums and galleries have forgotten their defined purpose, or that purpose has been eroded or altered by years of change. The independent museums have a powerful incentive to attract visitors and provide a display that invites inspection; they are obliged to earn income to pay all or part of their expenses. They have had to attract an audience in order to survive, something totally new in the public sector. This approach to the whole concept of running a museum has had a profound effect on the management techniques that are required of senior museum people in the independent sector. The independents have shrugged off the dusty image of museums by providing the general public with eye-catching and informative displays; as a result museums have moved forward from being purely academic institutions to becoming venues that combine education and leisure. This new environment has encouraged the public to visit them, and they have done so in large numbers. The size of the audience and the number of people visiting museums has had a much more serious impact on museums that charge admission than those that allow free admission, for visitors generate the income necessary to run these institutions and, therefore, these have been visitor-orientated places and have shown the way.

The changing role of such museums has had an effect on the attitudes of the public; the visitor now has greater expectations from museums than once was the case. Skills in design, in earlier years an inconsequential subject, are now as important to a museum as conservation. Designers have provided innovative and exciting displays; they have turned previously dull subjects into lively entertainment. Television has provided the public with a much keener awareness of shape and form; visitors are not satisfied with a meagre standard from museums and have responded accordingly – often with their feet. Museums have changed on an even broader base, including increases in the number of appointments to posts concerned with this external image; these appointments have included marketing specialists and educationalists as well as designers and interpreters. A wish to know more about museum visitors and their attitudes has been achieved through visitor surveys and has required a commercial or marketing expertise that did not exist before.

Not only has the outward appearance of museums changed, the internal areas of work have been changed as a result of these external influences. As we approach a new century, museums are in a very different position to a mere fifteen or twenty years ago. They are now required to find an audience to entertain and enlighten, and to give value for money whilst retaining all the other skills and specialisations that go to make up an academic institution which preserves collections. Allied to this requirement is the more stringent approach to funding which has resulted from world-wide economic factors. In this climate, the management of museums has become more complex and demands academic status *plus* those skills associated more with business and commerce. The complication arises when it is realised that there are fundamental differences between the type of senior manager in commerce or industry and the type needed in museums. The industrialist may well be highly qualified in a specialist subject connected with his/her industry, but will probably have accepted that, to become a senior manager, specialising in the techniques of management is necessary. In museums, virtually without exception, the senior manager is a specialist and a curator. However, traditionally the arena in which he or she worked did not require the same management techniques as needed in the commercial sector, so the acceptance of having to add management skills to an already long list of academic achievements has met with resistance. This inexperience has had other effects on the profession; the skills required to motivate a team of employees whose intellectual and academic gifts span the whole range of human achievement, from the lowest to the highest, requires profound skill which cannot always be found without specialist training.

The purpose of management training is to enable the individual to be more effective; management systems are aimed at deploying resources, whether financial, human or material, in the most economic and effective way. Because priorities are likely to alter as policies change, management systems should be designed so that the necessary adjustments can be made as and when required, within the resources allocated. The learning of techniques to help cope with the changing environment and culture of the museum framework is fundamental to the successful future of our museums. This book explores those areas of management which have been practised for many years and puts them into the museum context. It looks at management techniques for the individual and how museums can realise greater effectiveness. The museum framework as a whole is examined in the context of organisational theory (particularly relating to structures of museums) to study how basic concepts can be applied to the organisational problems of museums. This is not a textbook designed to accompany a rigidly structured course of study. It is, in some cases, quite light-hearted, but its messages are serious and clear. It seeks to help the reader to become a more effective manager with an understanding of the importance of curatorship and the differences between the museum/gallery and the commercial sector. It is written by a person who has, I hope, experienced the process of management at the bottom, the middle and the top – both the good aspects of management and the bad.

I am a committed manager within the museum profession making decisions in the context of curatorship – and this is the crucial point – unless we learn the skills of management they will be inflicted upon us by others less able to recognise that there are intervening factors which must always be considered in our judgements about our institutions and their collections and these can, in many cases, be incompatible. 'Curatorial Sympathy' are my watchwords and it is this (uniquely museum-related) trait which must be part of the management process, without compromising the effectiveness of what we do.

It is impossible for managers who have not worked in museums or galleries to acquire this trait easily and for that reason we must learn to be good managers as well as expert curators.

I hope that you find this book useful and that it provides you with a tool kit which will assist you to become an effective museum/gallery manager.

1

The history of management and the museum context

Before we can move into the practical area of acquiring skills which will assist us to be effective managers it is appropriate that we first look at the theories of management and how they have been explained over the past century or so. We will follow the chronology of management thinking and how that thinking has affected museums and galleries for very few museum professionals have had specific management training, but their empirical solutions to management problems have been described by theorists over many years.

The study of managers at work has been undertaken for nearly a hundred years in an effort to distil the principles and practices of good management, and thereby improve the average manager if not to the highest level, then at least to a better level than he/she would otherwise achieve. From such studies have emerged several schools of thought concerning management, each with its own characteristic view of what management is about. The value to the museum profession of being aware of these different approaches is that they provide an alternative perspective on the way museums may be managed, and point to possible solutions for the problems that museums are more frequently being called upon to face.

SCIENTIFIC MANAGEMENT

'Scientific Management' is the term used to describe the principles relating to the management of production work and the theories behind these principles were formulated by an American engineer, Frederick Winslow Taylor (1856–1915). His view was that a manager should:

1 Develop, through scientific analysis and experiment, the best methods of performing each task.

2 Select and train workers to use the best methods.

3 Co-operate with workers and view management and productive work as two equal components in an enterprise.

Taylor described his theory as: 'The principle object of management should be to secure the maximum prosperity for the employer, coupled with the maximum prosperity for each employee' (Taylor, 1947, p.31). Taylor's views were extended and developed by his colleague, Henry Lawrence Gantt (1861–1919) famous today for the charting process which is used for project planning, and by the industrial engineer Frank Bunker Gilbreth (1868–1924) and Lillian Evelyn Moller Gilbreth (1878–1972) who laid the foundations of the modern science of 'work study'. Work study is the activity or process of systematically examining, analysing and measuring methods of performing work that involves human activity in order to improve those methods. This has often been termed 'time and motion study'.

Taylor's theories were first presented in 1903 when he wrote a paper 'Shop management', for the *Transactions of the American Society of Mechanical Engineers*. The name 'Scientific Management' seems to have been coined in 1910 during discussions between Taylor and others about decisions to argue before a tribunal that American railway operators should not be allowed to raise their fares because they were so inefficient. It was argued that if the railways followed Taylor's methods of 'Scientific Management' they could save $1 million a day. The case aroused enormous public interest and, in 1911, Taylor published a book called *The Principles of Scientific Management* and thereafter his theories were part of the foundation of management studies. His work was also known as 'Taylorism'.

Taylor's quest seems to have been the pursuit of the fundamental principles of efficiency and underlining his search was a belief that there was 'one best way' of doing any job. He insisted that it was management's task, using careful experimentation and observation, to identify the one best method, and to develop standardised procedures and standardised tools for implementing it. Managers should select the workforce very carefully choosing only persons entirely suited for the job and then train them to use only the best method. In this way, production could be improved and costs reduced. Workers would share in the resulting benefits by being rewarded for a fair day's work, their assigned goals being carefully determined by stopwatch study. Taylor acknowledged that this could lead to higher wage costs, but he argued that management should be concerned less with labour costs than with the overall cost per unit, and that his methods would lead, through increased output, to a reduction in unit costs. He called upon management to improve working conditions and to reduce physical effort and fatigue, in order to increase the output per worker.

Many listened to, or read of, Taylor's theory and believed his principles to be sound; however, some considered that his view was dangerous and that he attempted to reduce men to the status of machines. It is not likely that the total concept of Scientific Management has ever knowingly been practised by the museum and gallery profession for it is much more suited to businesses concerned primarily with production than the service-orientated areas within which museums operate. His theories are relatively simple yet they form an imperfect solution to a very complex problem and in isolation they may seem to have a great many benefits. They over-simplify quite intricate issues by suggesting that extra money alone will motivate many to work harder and they ignore the inevitable conflict of aims between the labour force and management. Indeed, the variety of human relations, goal-seeking and role elements of everyday life within museums and galleries would seem to run counter to nearly all of Taylor's theories, particularly the rather authoritarian attitude which may have been acceptable at the beginning of the century.

However, it is appropriate to break down Taylor's theory into its component parts; museums have incorporated some of his philosophy but, as is the case throughout management, have also taken substantial elements from others. Taylor's desire to improve efficiency is a concern held by most managers, not least those who work in museums. His wish to achieve the one best way of doing a job is not to be dismissed as an impossibility in museums. For many years the profession has been encouraging its own form of regulated training for curators. Whilst this could never achieve the robotic results wished for by Taylor, it was and is an attempt to standardise training to an extent where all will have had the same professional start. Indeed, the Museum Training Institute is now developing standards for the whole museum profession, from its lowest level to its highest. Taylor's view that selecting the best person to do the job is as valid today as ever it was and his pioneering comments regarding conditions of work still hold great weight. His theory does not take into account (for how could it) the vast changes in the attitudes of workers and the higher standard of general education. The biggest flaw in seeing any useful parallel in museums for the furtherance of Taylor's theories is that his single-minded attitude, and lack of flexibility could not work in the open, educated, task-motivated world of museums. Nevertheless, there are still a few examples of museums being run by authoritative managers in a way somewhat similar to that proposed by Taylor. Museums have to look to other methods of describing their approach to management – the 'scientific approach', using Taylor's theories, does not seem to be the ideal. Taylor should not be dismissed as an ogre, for his ideas have left a legacy of principles and beliefs, some of which are still implemented today.

THE QUANTITATIVE APPROACH

During the 1960s and 1970s the Quantitative Approach to management gained strength and grew into what is now generally known as Management Science. In its simplest form it can be described as the application of scientific techniques, research and results to the problems of management. It is virtually synonymous with 'Operational Research' (OR) which is the activity, process or study of applying scientific methods to the solutions of problems involving the operation of a system. It is sometimes suggested that Management Science is concerned with general theories whilst operational research is concerned with solving particular problems. The reliance on detailed study and experimentation point this approach towards Taylor's theories of Scientific Management and there is no doubt that the Quantitative Approach can be traced back to those principles. However, a more recent antecedent has been the implication of quantitative techniques to the analysis of wartime operations (hence the name of one of the main ingredients – operations research) which led to similar techniques being applied to the business problems of peacetime. This approach has gained impetus from the increasing availability of computers to handle the storage of data in management information systems and to manipulate the complex mathematical models which are used to simulate business activities and predict outcomes. Whilst this approach has little relevance to the broad spectrum of management problems, it has profound effects on our ability to organise and make decisions which then have a greater chance of being pragmatic, particularly those decisions that relate to financial information or project planning.

Museums have, unwittingly, been adopting the Quantitative Approach in their decision-making for many years for it is in the nature and training of the curator to be scientific in his/her approach to the management of a museum's collection. It is doubtful, however, whether these principles have much to offer senior museum staff primarily exercising a management role. The Quantitative Approach does have merit in evaluating options in a scientific way; there is little doubt that this element of the overall theory is helpful to the museum profession. In areas of financial decision-making, coupled with the availability of low-cost computer hardware and software, museum staff can now apply quantitative techniques that would have demanded considerable time and expertise a few years ago.

The principle task with the Quantitative Approach is to build a mathematical model of a situation using data that is readily available. This model is then input into a computer and the likely outcomes of a variety of options can be calculated quickly. As we become more aware of the power of these methods and the relative ease with which computers can be used to perform immensely complicated manipulations of a model, then the Quantitative Approach will have a place in museums and galleries. That place will never be of prime importance as an overall system, for the Quantitative Approach has serious limitations as an all-embracing set of management principles. However, there are now, and always will be an increasing number of museums who use the application of quantitative techniques. It is generally known that spreadsheet, project analysis and financial applications are existing software packages used by managers within museums throughout the profession. They therefore apply quantitative techniques, examples of which are:

1   *'What if . . . ?' problems*
    With a suitable computer model, one can quickly answer the 'What if . . . ?' type of question. What if funding levels change? What if visitor targets are not achieved? What if costs escalate? One can vary these parameters and leave the computer to calculate the likely effects on performance. Naturally, the accuracy of the model will influence the reliability of its

predictions but these calculations are being used (or should be being used) in museums at present.

2 *Sensitivity problems*

In a very similar way, one can identify those parameters to which a proposed course of action is most sensitive. The computer might reveal, for instance, that a large variation in visitor numbers would have little effect on earned income while a relatively small variation in salary costs might have a dramatic effect on revenue costs. Sensitivity tests of this kind could alert managers to those aspects of an operation which they most need to monitor so that corrective action can be taken as soon as it is needed.

3 *Goal-seeking*

The manager specifies the results he/she wants to achieve (e.g. a level of admission income) and the computer model will work backwards to determine, for example, the levels of admissions (including ratios of specific admission categories) that are needed to achieve it.

4 *Mixing problems*

Linear programming is a mathematical technique for determining the best possible mix of factors to attain the required outputs and is used, for example, in the petro-chemical industry to calculate optimum mixes of very complex resources. It is only relevant to museums with significant project or resource problems. Linear programming could conceivably be used to plan a major refit or the introduction of new systems for, say, the cataloguing of collections.

5 *Bottlenecks*

Models can be developed to represent, for instance, new shop or exhibition layouts. By running the model one can detect where queues and bottlenecks tend to occur, and one can test alternative options to find the best solution.

Some managers in museums are already using techniques of a quantitative nature for solving 'what if' problems and the step forward to other techniques is not far away. Training is the key, particularly in these management techniques and in the use of computers not merely as information storage devices, but also as complex calculating machines. Once again, it is difficult to see the Quantitative Approach being relevant as a complete management system either in business or commerce or within the museum and gallery context. There are elements of the approach that do have a place, but in the limited ways already described.

THE CLASSICAL APPROACH

Classical management has its roots in the writings of Henri Fayol seventy years ago. Fayol's analysis of the functions of management still form the basis of one of the most frequently adopted views, so much so that it has been called the Classical Approach. It is also widely known as the Process School because it uses management as a process and examines the component parts of the process separately.

Fayol defined management along the following lines: 'To manage is to forecast and plan, to organise, to command, to co-ordinate and to control' (Fayol, 1949, p.22). He developed a framework for a unified doctrine of adminis-tration that he hoped would hold good wherever management was exercised. He was one of the first to stress the importance of the organisation chart, which, with his insistence on job descriptions, still remains a chief instrument of business management. He was a firm advocate of the view that management could and should be taught; this was a revolutionary idea in 1908 when he first put it forward.

There have been many attempts to improve on Fayol's theory. For example, the idea of a manager 'commanding' has a strangely old-fashioned ring about it and it has often been replaced by words such as 'directing' or 'leading', though even 'leading' can sound dated in the modern world with its concern for ideas of participative management and industrial democracy. The word 'motivating' is often preferred, perhaps because it sounds less militaristic. This is certainly the case in museums and galleries where a consultative approach to management is employed in the most successful organisations. However, top-level museum professionals are still called 'Directors' and museums and galleries are still 'directed' rather than 'managed'. There is no doubt that Fayol's analysis retains a widespread popularity as a way of looking at manage-ment. Museums are employing many of the functions which Fayol attributed to management yet they do so without realising that they are operating under his Classical Approach.

Museums and galleries along with other businesses may have modified Fayol's original list of functions, but they nevertheless employ the process described by him. The principles of his analysis are that managing consists of four major activities: planning, directing, organising and controlling.

Henri Fayol's approach provided a concept of managing for managers at any level. His original analysis of attributes has been developed so that managing can be described as planning, directing, organising and controlling the activi-ties of subordinates to achieve or exceed objectives. Defining the various ele-ments of his original definition has exercised the minds of many over the past seventy years, but established definitions of these elements are now common-place and are listed below because they form an important part of our under-standing of how museums have been managed empirically in the past. They also give us guidance towards a preferred way of management for the future:

1   *Planning*
    Determining what needs to be done, by whom, by when and in what order to fulfil one's assigned responsibility:
    (a) Objective: A goal, target or quota to be achieved within a certain time.

12

(b) Programme: Strategy to be followed and major actions to be taken to achieve major objectives.

(c) Schedule: A plan showing when individual or group activities or accomplishments will be started and/or completed.

(d) Budget: Planned expenditures required to achieve or exceed objectives.

(e) Forecast: A projection of what will happen by a certain time.

(f) Policy: A general guide for decision-making and individuals' actions.

(g) Procedure: A detailed method for carrying out a policy.

2 *Directing*
Implementing and carrying out approved plans through subordinates to achieve or exceed objectives:

(a) Staffing: Seeing that a qualified person is selected for each position.

(b) Training: Teaching individuals or groups how to fulfil their duties and responsibilities.

(c) Supervising: Giving subordinates day-to-day instruction, guidance, and discipline as required for them to fulfil their duties and responsibilities.

(d) Motivating: Encouraging subordinates to perform by fulfilling or appealing to their needs.

(e) Counselling: Holding private discussions with a subordinate about how he/she might do better work, solve a personal problem or realise his/her ambitions.

(f) Communicating: Exchanging information with subordinates, associates, superiors and others about plans, progress and problems.

(g) Decision-making: Making a judgement about a course of action to be taken.

3 *Organising*
Arranging and relating the personnel and the task to be completed so that the work can be performed most effectively by the people involved.

(a) Developing organisation structures: Identifying and grouping the activities performed so that they are carried out in relation to their importance with the minimum of conflict.

(b) Delegating: Assigning work, responsibility and authority so that subordinates can make maximum use of their abilities.

(c) Establishing relationships: Creating the conditions that are necessary for a mutually co-operative effort of people.

4 *Controlling*
Measuring progress towards set objectives, evaluating what needs to be done and then taking corrective action to achieve, or exceed objectives:

(a) Standard: A level of individual or group performance defined as adequate or acceptable.

(b) Measuring: Determining through formal and informal reports the degree to which progress towards objectives is being made.

(c) Evaluating: Determining causes of and possible ways to act on significant deviations from planned performance.

13

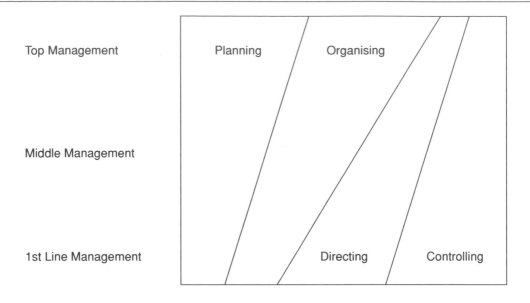

Figure 1 The emphasis on tasks according to position in the management hierarchy. (Based on a handout issued to management trainees by INCOMTEC)

(d) Correcting: Taking controlled action to correct an unfavourable trend or to take advantage of an unusually favourable trend.

It must also be noted that the nature of the managing part of the job changes too. Not only is it necessary to monitor the proportions of time spent doing the job as against getting it done through other people, but it is also necessary to be aware of the relative attention given to the different functions of management. The Classical Approach points out that, as an individual moves up the management ladder, the time and attention given to planning and organising must increase relative to that given to directing and controlling. This can be illustrated by a simple diagram (see Fig. 1).

It can be seen from Fig. 1 that Fayol's original list of functions remains fundamentally the same but has been slightly modified and that management is presented very much as a process in which the component parts can be laid out systematically. It would seem at first glance that most serious attempts at good management employ the techniques illustrated in this Classical Approach. Staff in museums exercise the skills of classical management in many ways; some museums have senior staff who have attended management schools, whilst others have people who have entered the museum profession following other careers. Those that exercise these techniques knowingly are few, but the Classical Approach is founded on logic and good sense. As a result the empirical 'seat of the pants' methods of management so often used by managers in museums, are nearer to this theory than others. Indeed, it is such an ordered and defined method that its component parts find great favour with people in the museum and gallery profession. However, whilst it forms the basis of traditional management thinking, it is by no means the optimum system. The Classical Approach was particularly popular following Henri Fayol's published work at the beginning of this century and continued as such until its decline in the period between the two world wars. There was a resurgence of interest in his methods between the early 1950s and the end of the 1970s, but even though it may well be used in museums to this day it is in decline generally elsewhere.

THE HUMAN RELATIONS APPROACH

The Human Relations Approach developed strongly during the 1940s and thereafter, partly as a reaction against the seemingly impersonal features of Taylor's Scientific Management, but mainly because research studies conducted during the previous two decades had demonstrated the importance of good human relations and the influence of social factors on workers motivation. The primary research undertaken became known as the 'Hawthorn studies'; named after a long series of observations of people at work. This was carried out by the Western Electric Company at the Hawthorn factory near Chicago between 1927 and 1932. The Hawthorn plant was large, employing about 29,000 workers and producing telephone equipment. The studies are regarded as a milestone in the evolution of management theories. During the period a group of young female workers who assembled telephone equipment at the Hawthorn plant were the subject of a series of studies undertaken to determine the effect on their output of working conditions, the length of the working day, the number and length of rest pauses, and other factors relating to the 'non-human' environment. The young women specially chosen for the study, were placed in a selected room under one supervisor and were carefully observed.

As the experimenters began to vary the conditions of work, they found that with each major change, there was a substantial increase in production. They decided, when all the conditions to be varied had been tested, to return the girls to their original, poorly lighted, workbenches for a working day without rest pauses and other amenities. To the astonishment of the researchers, output rose again, to a level higher than it had been even under the best of the experimental conditions.

At this point, the researchers were forced to look for factors other than those which had been deliberately manipulated in the experiments. For one thing, it was quite evident that the workers developed very high morale during the experiment and became extremely motivated to work hard and well. There were several reasons for this:

1   The girls felt special because they had been singled out for a research role; this selection showed that management thought them to be important.

15

2 The girls developed good relationships with one another and with their supervisor because they had considerable freedom to develop their own pace of work and to divide the work amongst themselves in a manner most comfortable to them.

3 The social contact and easy relations amongst the girls made the work generally more pleasant.

A new kind of hypothesis was formulated out of this preliminary research. The premise was that, motivation to work, productivity and quality of work are all related to the nature of the social relations among the workers and between the workers and their boss. In order to investigate this more systematically, a new group was selected. This group consisted of fourteen men; some were wiring equipment which others then soldered and which two inspectors examined before labelling it as completed. The men were put into a special place where they could be observed around the clock by a trained observer who sat in the corner of the room. At first the men were suspicious of the outsider, but as time wore on and nothing special happened as a result of his presence, they relaxed and fell into their normal working routine. The observer discovered a number of interesting things about the group:

1 Though the group felt its own identity keenly as a total group, there were nevertheless cliques within it roughly corresponding to those in the front of the room and those at the rear. Men in front felt themselves to be of a higher status and they thought that the equipment that they were wiring was more difficult than that of the group at the rear. Each clique included most of the wiremen, soldermen and inspectors in that part of the room, but there were some people who did not belong to either exclusive group. The two cliques each had its own special games and habits, and there was a good deal of competition and mutual banter between them.

2 The group as a whole had some norms, certain ideas of what was a proper and fair way for things to be done. Several of these norms concerned the production rate of the group and were based around the concept of a fair day's work for a fair day's pay. The group had established a norm of how much production was fair and this was a figure which satisfied management. However, it was well below that which the men could have produced had fatigue been the only limiting factor. Related to this basic norm were two others; no member of the group should produce at a rate too high relative to that of the others in the group, and a person should not produce too little relative to the others either. Being different in either respect engendered rebukes and social pressure from others in the group. Social ostracism followed if a person did not respond to the pressure. The men were thus colluding to produce at a lower level and in so doing they restricted their output.

The other key norm which affected working relationships concerned the interface between the inspectors and supervisors of the group. In effect the norm required those in authority not to be officious or to take advantage of their position of authority. The men attempted to uphold the assumption that inspectors were no better than anyone else and that, if they attempted to take advantage of their role or if they acted in a superior manner, they were violating the group norms. Incidentally, one inspector did feel superior and showed it. The men were able to play tricks on him with the equipment to ostracise him and to put social pressure upon him to such an extent that he asked to be transferred. The other inspector in the group and the supervisor were very much a part of the group and were accepted for this reason.

3   The observer discovered that the group did not follow company policy on a number of key issues. For example, it was forbidden to trade jobs because each job had been rated carefully to require a certain skill level. Nevertheless, the wiremen often asked soldermen to take over wiring while they soldered. In this way, they relieved monotony and kept up social contact with others in the room. At the end of the day, each man was required to report the amount of work he had done. The supervisor was supposed to report for all the men, but he had learned that the men wished to do their own reporting and decided to let them do it. What the men actually reported was a relatively standard figure for each day in spite of large variations in actual output. Actually however, the output within the group varied greatly as a function of how tired the men were, their morale on the particular day, and many other circumstances. The men did not cheat in the sense of reporting more than they had done. Rather, they would under-report some days thus saving up extra units to list on another day when they had actually under-produced.

4   The men varied markedly in their individual production rates. An attempt was made to account for these differences by means of dexterity tests given to the men, but these test results did not correlate with output. An intelligence measure was then tried with a similar lack of success. What finally turned out to be the key to output was the social membership in the cliques. The members of the high-status clique were uniformly higher producers than the members of the low-status clique, but the very highest and the very lowest producers were the social isolates who did not belong to either group.

Evidently, the individual output was most closely related to the social membership of the workers, not to their innate ability. The output rates were actually one of the main bones of contention between the two cliques because of the pay system; each man received a base rate plus a percentage of the group bonus based on the total production. The high-status clique felt that the low-status one was cheating and continually expressed this view to them. The low-status group felt insulted to be looked down upon and realised that the best way to get back at the others was through low production. Thus, the two groups were caught in a self-defeating cycle which further depressed the production rate for the group as a whole.

These, and similar studies, were the foundation of a theory in which a person's needs were assumed to be largely satisfied and determined by the norms of the work group. Elton Mayo (1945), who was associated with the Hawthorn studies for part of their long duration, concluded that:

1 A worker is basically motivated by social needs.

2 As a result of the rationalisation of work, meaning has gone out of work and must be sought in the social relationships of the job.

3 The focus of the workgroup will do more to influence behaviour than the incentives and controls of managers.

4 A supervisor will only be effective to the extent that he/she can satisfy his/her subordinates social needs.

This approach had an impact on management theory and practice; especially as it was so contrary to the presumptions of Taylorism. The impact was so big that the cult of the group began to dominate management theory. The importance of the group definitely needed to be rethought, but like many of these approaches, group theory suffered from an over-generalisation and it, too, has now fallen back into its proper perspective.

In the years following the Second World War further research was conducted into groups. Rensis Likert carried out some studies which seemed to show that departments with low efficiency tended to be managed by people who were job-centred; by managers and supervisors who regarded their main function as being to get the job done and who viewed people as being just another resource provided for this purpose. Such managers tended to adopt the attitudes which stem naturally from Taylor's Scientific Management; they tended towards keeping their subordinates busily engaged on prescribed work, done in a prescribed way, and at a prescribed pace, determined by time. Such methods, it was noted, could achieve high productivity, but they were inclined to create very unfavourable attitudes towards the work and the management, often resulting in strikes and stoppages as well as a high wastage of material and poorly manufactured goods.

Management, according to Likert (1959), is always a relative process. To be effective and to communicate, a leader must always adapt his/her behaviour to take account of the persons whom he/she leads. There are no specific rules which will work well in all situations, only general principles which must be interpreted to take account of the expectations, values and skills of those with whom the manager interacts. Sensitivity to these values and expectations is a crucial leadership skill, and organisations must create the atmosphere and conditions which encourage every manager to deal with the people he/she encounters in a manner fitting to their values and expectations. We will discuss this more fully later.

Likert's studies also showed that, in contrast, work groups with the best performance were often managed by people with genuine concern for the well-being of their subordinates, and who sought to build effective groups with high achievement goals. Such employee-centred managers and supervisors regarded people as people and not just as another resource. They saw their managerial jobs as being concerned with individuals and with helping them to do their work more efficiently. Such managers exercise a much looser form of control, but they compensate by setting very high performance targets and by motivating people to meet them. There is much to recommend this philosophy in management by museum professionals, particularly in curatorial and research departments.

Douglas McGregor is best remembered for his 'Theory-X/Theory-Y' ideas (McGregor, 1960) which explored the assumptions underlying the two contrasting styles of management which we have already noted in Likert's research. In the 1950s, McGregor described two sets of propositions and assumptions about man in the organisation:

Theory X

1   The average person is by nature indolent and works as little as possible.

2   He/she lacks ambition, dislikes responsibility, prefers to be led.

3   He/she is inherently self-centred, indifferent to organisational needs.

4   He/she is by nature resistant to change.

5   He/she is gullible and not very bright.

6   The implications for management are:
    (a) Management is responsible for organising the elements of productive enterprise – money, materials, equipment, people – in the interest of economic ends.
    (b) With respect to people, this is a process of directing their efforts, motivating them, controlling their actions, modifying their behaviour to fit the needs of the organisation.
    (c) People must be persuaded, rewarded, punished, controlled, their activities must be directed.

Theory Y

1   People are not by nature passive or resistant to organisational needs. They have become so as a result of experience in organisations.

2   The motivation, the potential for development, the capacity to assume responsibility, the readiness to direct behaviour towards organisational goals are all present in people. It is a responsibility of management to make it possible to reorganise and develop the human characteristics for themselves.

3   Management is responsible for organising the elements of productive enterprise in the interest of economic ends, but their essential task is to arrange the conditions and methods of operation so that people can achieve

their own goals best by directing their own efforts towards organisational objectives.

The studies of Likert and McGregor may seem rather simplistic when current advances in psychology and sociology are taken into account. However, they are the foundation of more soundly based approaches to management which have a relevance today. The human relations approach is totally relevant to museums, in that it deals with the individual rather than the person as a robot. It also has less of an element of production within it than other theories such as Taylorism. Fundamentally important in the context of museums is the ability to manage a wide-ranging group of people who have different academic and intellectual abilities. The museum professional in a management position is required, on the one hand, to negotiate on day-to-day administrative problems with exhibit cleaners and, on the other, to discuss, motivate and control work at a high academic level. The human relations approach is appropriate to this style of management and is suitable for adoption throughout the museums and galleries profession. However, it is not a panacea that museum professionals can take on board to solve all their management problems. As we shall find out, there are other theories and there are even more ways of using them.

THE SYSTEMS APPROACH

Whilst not as old as some management theories the Systems Approach has been steadily evolving since the 1930s. Systems thinking developed concurrently with Management Science and Organisational Behaviour and emerged strongly in the 1960s and 1970s. More modern theorists of management are increasingly persuaded that there is wisdom in applying the *status quo* where this is still appropriate (often referred to as the 'wisdom of the appropriate'); of the match of people to systems, the task to be done and the environment in which the organisation operates. The interrelationships between these four elements (people, systems, task and environment) are what has been called the single 'systems' approach to management theory. The Systems Approach emphasises the interrelatedness and interdependence on the parts in any whole. It is not unique to management, having been applied to problems in many scientific fields, but it provides a helpful way of looking at many management problems, particularly those concerned with organisations. The approach entails an overall study of the situation in question, whether it is a biological system such as the human body or a socio-economic system such as a museum organisation. In other words it avoids a piecemeal approach and considers the whole, rather than the parts in isolation as is the case with so many other theories. An important aspect of systems theories is to understand and analyse the way the constituent parts behave under different conditions.

With each system there are likely to be sub-systems, each a separate entity but each forming an integral part of the whole. Systems thinking is particularly concerned with the interdependence within the sub-system. One of the key teachings of the System Approach is that any managerial tampering with the sub-system will inevitably have repercussions throughout the whole system. Hence the need for managers to understand the interrelationships and inter-dependence between their own sections and all others.

In any organisation one very important sub-system is usually the social sub-system. A broad Systems Approach draws attention to the importance of the human element, stressing that in most organisations it deserves as much attention as the technical sub-system. This is particularly critical in the museum context for, whilst the technical sub-system is important, by far the greatest emphasis should be placed on the skilled professional element. This is an obvious link between the Human Relations Approach and the Classical Approach.

A boundary is regarded as existing around each system or sub-system defining it and separating it from all others. A single 'closed' system is one which functions entirely within its boundary, and is totally unaffected by anything outside itself. An 'open' system (by far the most common) is one where flows occur across the boundaries. There are likely to be factors which are outside the boundaries of the system but which will affect it significantly, and these factors are called the 'environment'.

This concept of boundaries is important to a manager because many of the managerial problems arise at the boundaries of the system that is being managed, and boundary management is likely to occupy much of the manager's time and effort. Similarly, he/she must be aware of the changes in the single 'environment' which may affect the single 'open' system that he/she manages.

In a museum library, for example, a system might be seen which transforms newly acquired books into properly catalogued library items, available to the public and researchers. The system would transform uncatalogued and unaccessioned items into a shelf of properly catalogued reading material.

For the system to function, the necessary resources must flow through it. The idea of resources flowing through a system (or organisation) captures the essentially dynamic nature of the process rather than some other ways of looking at organisations which see them as rather static entities. Systems thinkers focus on flows of materials, flows of human resources, flows of money and flows of information through an organisation. In many businesses, information is not always recognised as being a vital resource; museums rely so totally on information that this resource is always high on the list of any museum employee's priorities. The Systems Approach elevates information as a resource to its rightful place. It assumes that managers find their job impossible without an adequate flow of data.

This approach, particularly in museums, is relevant when projects are cyclical in nature. That is, they can be anything from projects that range from six-monthly updates of work to full-scale departmental reviews which may only take place every few years. The usual method of dealing with such projects

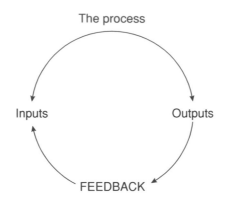

Figure 2 The feedback or control loop

is to undertake time-consuming work of fact-finding and analysis each time the project is tackled. If a Systems Approach is adopted much of this effort should be eliminated.

So, how does the Systems Approach work? The first step is to identify those elements of the system that, when varied or altered, will affect the other elements of the system. The most obvious are the inputs. They will affect the process, the outputs, and the feedback mechanism. The idea of feedback is an important systems concept as is the feedback loop (or control loop) (see Fig. 2) which detects any deviations from some pre-determined normal plan, and feeds back the information so that corrective action may be taken. The feedback or control loop is a hugely important management tool and we will come back to it time and time again.

The concept of an 'open system' and the control loop can, for example, be applied to a museum's exhibit loan processing system, where loan forms are processed. Depending on the size of the museum, the system may originally have been set up to process perhaps only ten loan forms per week. If (as a result of a temporary exhibition or some other reason) that figure was to increase to fourteen loan forms per week, the input of the system obviously increases, but what happens to the other elements? If the process was designed to handle ten loan forms a week it is unlikely to be able to deal with a 40 per cent increase and will become out of phase with the input; a bottleneck will occur. In this specific example the output will remain the same, as the process can only deal with ten loan forms per week. If the control loop were only recording the quality and quantity of the output, then no adverse conditions will be reported. Thus this example serves to illustrate that a system can be analysed into its component parts and the relationship between those parts established to determine what affect they have on each other (i.e., how the inputs change, the effects the changes have on the process and the outputs) and the effectiveness of the feedback element to the control of the system which will make it sensitive to any changes.

22

Once the key variables likely to affect the system have been identified, the system as a whole can then be designed in such a way that any changes in one part of the system are reflected in necessary changes in the other parts. Therefore, by periodically checking (controlling) that the key variables are still relevant and that the system as a whole is responding to deal with any changes, a large proportion of time-consuming and repetitive work can be avoided.

The Systems Approach may be simplified under a variety of headings:

1 Analyse the system to identify its component elements; inputs, outputs, processes and control/feedback mechanism.

2 Consider how the component parts interact with each other. This involves observing what effect changing one part of the system will have on the other part. Once the cause and effect relationship have been discovered the key variables will be identified.

3 It is unlikely that key variables will change from time to time. The careful design of reporting documentation will help to identify any changes. These changes may be outside the control of the users of the system, i.e., environmental changes such as the economic climate, changes in legislation and (in the museum/gallery context), a very important element – visitor/tourist statistics. It is therefore important to be attuned to the environment in which the system operates so that changes can be predicted and dealt with.

4 Select the criteria for the feedback/control mechanism. All systems have purpose and the feedback/control mechanism should be designed to make sure that the purpose is achieved.

5 Consider the needs of adjacent systems. The output for one system may often be the input to another, therefore care should be taken to ensure that outputs are of the required quantity, quality and frequency. This point also underlines the fact that the Systems Approach entails an overall examination of the situation rather than a piecemeal one.

6 Once the stages have been completed the system can then be designed, together with any reporting documentation.

7 In addition to designing the reporting documentation, listing data concerning the behaviour of key variables, the frequency of any report and the control of this have to be decided. The control limits will indicate to those monitoring the system, when it needs to be reviewed. By recording trends in the key variables, it is possible to predict when the system may be going out of control and reappraisal is necessary.

There are a variety of uses for the Systems Approach within museums and galleries, but in order to examine a simple system and how it might operate an analysis is suggested of the possible co-ordination of research enquiries within a small museum. In this example, the system would need to be analysed into its component parts:

1 *Inputs*
  (a) Copies of requests from the public/researchers for information.
  (b) Information received by way of books, documents, photographs etc.
  (c) Call by staff for particular reference material.

2 *Processes*
  (a) Receiving requests and delegating researcher with task.
  (b) Updating reference catalogue.
  (c) Ordering material required by staff against requisition.

3 *Controls*
  (a) Checking facts in draft reply.
  (b) Checking material required and requisitions not already duplicated by information received.
  (c) Ensure requisition correctly entered.

4 *Outputs*
  (a) Reply to enquirer.
  (b) Make new reference material available to staff and/or public.
  (c) Order sent to supplier.

Fig. 3 describes this situation in diagrammatic form.

The key variables that will affect the operation of this system are the frequency, volume and size of the orders made by staff for new reference material and the number of requests for information received by researchers. In addition, the other departments of the museum (library, archives etc.) will anticipate a

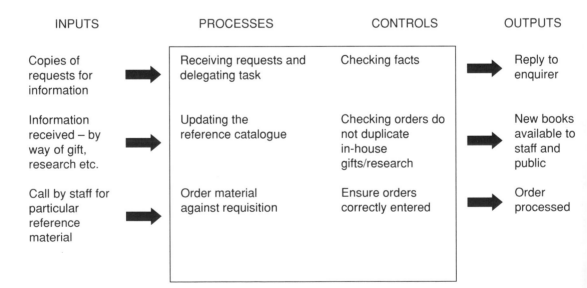

Figure 3 Research department: enquiries co-ordination

certain level of service in as much as they will expect to receive the material they order within a time-scale after requesting it.

It is possible that external and environmental factors may affect the system outside the control of the co-ordinator. For example, if a new television programme was produced and broadcast on a theme connected with the museum it is possible that the number of enquiries received from the general public in response to the programme could be overwhelming. This type of situation may require extra resources, both financial and human. By deciding what the control limits are to be for the key variables, the extra resources and staff requirements can be predicted and provided in time for the change, rather than after it, which is so often the case in existing established systems.

The adoption of the Systems Approach to projects can have a profound, and immediate, influence on the effective management of the museum, particularly in those areas relating to the processing of time and costing of resources. This is particularly so when a system replaces regular detailed fact-finding, such as the annual review of a department's work or regular reviews of work done to provide information for management. Introducing the Systems Approach can release capacity to enable new and additional projects to be carried out. It also has a beneficial effect for the departments using the systems; by reporting changes on a regular basis their systems are continually under review. Major reviews can then be undertaken where necessary, rather than when scheduled and, if the system is well designed with key variables accurately identified, these should be at less frequent intervals.

It would be wrong to assume that systems theory actually provides answers to problems. It can be very helpful in revealing where problems are likely to occur and this is the first step towards dealing with them. Systems thinking is an attempt, in itself, to simplify and present processes which are, or can be, quite complex. Its place as an overall approach in museums is probably limited, but a systematic process to provide methods for dealing with projects or repetitive elements of work can have beneficial results and leave resources available for other things. Museums have always inclined towards traditional methods of tackling repetitive tasks. With the introduction of computers and the contraction of resources, the thinking of museum managers must be diverted more towards ensuring that their resources are used to the greatest effect. Senior management should be capable of monitoring, more effectively, the key variables that will affect the operation of any systems introduced. As a result it is likely that this approach may well become a useful method of providing more effective uses of resources and greater flexibility within our museums today.

CONTINGENCY THEORY AND THE SITUATIONAL APPROACH

Towards the end of the 1970s, the Situational Approach to management was beginning to take hold. In essence, this view acknowledges that things really have a tendency to depend on the circumstances. Circumstances can be totally different from one situation to another, and the Situational Approach recognises that it is impossible to prescribe any single solution that will be best in all circumstances and situations. In contrast to Taylor's Scientific Management, the Situational Approach does not claim that there is one 'best way of doing things'. What has emerged is known as Contingency Theory, and this argues that there is no one right way in structuring the operating of an organisation. The structure is contingent to the circumstances. This theory proposes that an organisation will be more successful if it consciously adapts its structures and its administrative arrangements to the tasks that need to be done, the technology that is used, the expectations and the needs of the people performing the task, the scale of the total operation and the complexity of the amount of change it has to deal with in its environment.

Large and complex, museums and galleries seem to have disparate organisational structures for dissimilar parts of themselves, because the circumstances vary in different parts of the organisation and because of the call for distinct answers. The results can become untidy, pragmatic, temporary and even confusing to those who look for a more ordered view of things. Contingency Theory attempts to provide a set of rationales to help make sense of this diversity.

Different researchers have focused on different parts of the contingency situation. The variation of organisations, in relation to function and environment, is the subject of one of the more important modern British works on organisation theories (Burns and Stalker, 1971), which is based on researches in the electronics and other manufacturing industries in the mid-1950s. The authors were concerned with organisations, both as social systems and also in respect of their appropriateness for different kinds of industry – those where the technological and market conditions were changing, and those where they were stable.

The results were a classification of systems of industrial organisation into 'mechanistic' and 'organic' types, or rather complete opposites of forms which such systems can take. The authors arrived at this classification partly by research based on interviews with managers and partly through analysis. The lengthy classification of the characteristics of the two types of systems may be summarised as follows:

1 *Mechanistic*
   (a) The differentiation of functional tasks is based on specialisation and every functional role is defined in terms of the rights, duties and technical methods attaching to it.
   (b) Hierarchic structure of control authority and communication; lines of internal communication are mainly vertical.
   (c) Working methods prescribed in instructions.
   (d) Emphasis on loyalty to the organisation and to superiors. This assumes that omniscience, gender, internal or local knowledge and skill are

valued more highly than other factors derived from broader or external experience.

2   *Organic*
   (a) Individual's responsibilities to the organisation are broad and not precisely defined; evasion of personal responsibility discouraged.
   (b) The presumed common interest of all employees in the survival and growth of the business is relied upon as the principle sanction for individual conduct rather than a contractual relationship between the employee and the impersonal corporation.
   (c) Omniscience is no longer ascribed to the head of the concern. Knowledge and points of initiative may be located anywhere within the organisation.
   (d) Internal communication is lateral rather than vertical, ignoring differences of rank. Information, consultation and advice are used rather than command. Readiness to co-operate with others in promoting the purposes of the organisation.
   (e) A commitment to the tasks of the organisation and a 'technological ethos' is more highly valued than loyalty and obedience.

Mechanistic and organic organisations have some similarities with McGregor's Theory-X and Theory-Y people but they are not the same and neither are they good or bad types of organisation, in the same way that neither Theory X or Theory Y was a good or bad type of person. Nevertheless, this classification (mechanistic and organic) although representing something of an advance in management theory cannot be final or exhaustive, particularly in the context of museums and galleries. The analogies are too simple. Probably the single most significant contribution that this theory has had is that it identified the need for a different structure where the technology of the market is changing.

Other researchers have discovered the importance of the flexible nature of the Situational Approach. Many management theorists have demonstrated that, even within manufacturing industry, there is not one rigid theory or single set of rules which applies to the overall practice of management. Management must vary according to environment, purpose, function, technology and other circumstances. Hence one must expect, I believe, even greater variations outside manufacturing industry, particularly in the field of museums and galleries. The Contingency Approach brings all the factors of the various theories associated with the Situational Approach together as a whole, which becomes the Contingency Theory. At one level this theory seems like common sense, but is very difficult to test whether it is true. Most organisations are adapting to several contingencies at the same time. This makes it hard to disentangle the affects of one adaptation from another going on for a different purpose. Furthermore, some factors, such as performance of competitors, are more important to many organisations. Museums do not have a monopoly (except for, perhaps, some of the national collections) but if they had, they could possibly afford to ignore the pressures for change that come from the market-place. However, even small museums have a little niche in their own 'local market' – as much of a niche as a national museum does in the national context. To date, it has not been possible to prove that the various proportions of Contingency Theory really work, but there are a number of theorists who believe that they correspond to what may 'feel' to be true. The real point of Contingency Theory is that it forces the manager to do a systematic analysis of the situations facing his/her organisation, instead of managing by intuition and the art of the possible, and it is a commendable approach for museum professionals for it gives them the guidance needed to turn their backs on the intuitive approach which serves them ill.

So, let us summarise the examination of how management thinking and theory has passed through its several stages for this will give guidance to all in the museum profession who have not had any formal management training. Management theory has developed thus:

- Classical and Scientific Management were concerned with structure.

- Taylor analysed activities and individual jobs and showed the 'one best way' to do them.

- Fayol grouped individual jobs into organisations by applying management principles.

- The Human Relations Theories were concerned with people.

- Systems Management was concerned with the relations between structures and people to use as a system of inter-dependencies and it is thought to show that some of these relationships might be better discharged with the aid of quantitative methods.

- Contingency Theory and the Situational Approach uses all these insights, and it takes us back to the particular problems faced by managers and individual situations.

In museums the professional curator has a management and administrative role to play which is an essential, though different, job from that for which he/she is primarily employed. The emphasis on management and administration often increases in direct proportion to the level of seniority obtained.

I think it is probably appropriate here to explain the difference between the word 'administration' and 'management'. There are a lot of misconceptions over these two words and they are often joined together, people believing they are one and the same thing – they are not. Let us have a look at their formal definition. It is beyond the scope of any dictionary to give the full flavour of the former's meaning in its various contemporary context. 'Administration' is certainly not quite synonymous with 'management', although this impression may be gained from reading the meticulous histories of the two words in the *New Oxford Dictionary*. The derivation of 'manage' from any other language does not seem entirely clear, although it has a similarity to 'menage' –

suggesting a household or physical collection of things, people or animals which can be subject to some sort of rudimentary control.

'Administration' has a Latin parent, *administrare* which can mean 'assist' as well as 'direct'. 'Administer' in various contexts seems to have application with 'minister' which can mean 'serve' or 'servant'. Some of the early meanings of both 'manage' and 'administer' can be summarised as 'looking after things' or 'taking charge of' and one simple modern definition of both would be 'getting things done'. Yet 'administration' has a rather more subtle and extended series of meanings, it is more usually found in the public sector than the private and in general, carries an implication, not of ultimate sovereign control, but of directing and (more importantly) co-ordinating things on behalf of other people or authorities. It is often connected with some notion of service, and in the context of museums, rewarded accordingly and badly.

The term 'management' usually carries a rather different, more commercial flavour. There are various styles of management; some are very sophisticated and some are even permissive, but the most commonly used style often carries rather more than a suggestion of authoritarianism. This aspect of management style is particularly noticeable in museums; and in the more popular use of the word (in museums) tends to reflect the authoritarian management theories of the last generation, described when we discussed Taylorism (see pp. 7–9).

Management can sometimes be referred to in an almost mystical sense as an abstraction – 'the prerogatives of management' and so on – and this can be confused with the notions of the 'management revolution'. On the other hand, good management, in the sense of a practical process of getting things done effectively, is a common need of all types of organisation. Some people prefer to use the word 'administration' in situations that are complex and where there is no single criterion of efficiency. It is thought that an all-embracing term is descriptive of a mass of preparatory and supporting work for higher-level decision-making. Whilst there is little doubt that there is a key place for the administrator within museums, the overall management must be retained by those whose background is curatorial (in the broadest sense). The distinction here is based on policy. Policy is a decision as to what to do; administration is getting it done. Administrators can, and should, be concerned with serving and assisting the policy-making process but managers make the policy decisions. If managers are unaware of the processes or the techniques for dealing with policy they are disadvantaged. Preparation for management needs, first and foremost an appreciation of the need to be equipped professionally to undertake the role. The perception of this need in museums is more likely to be understood by the administrator than the curator thus providing a mismatch in the decision-making process which currently makes the museum professional vulnerable. There are many examples of the inadequacy and fallacy of a purely administrative perspective; the worst was certainly Hitler's 'Final Solution', which may have seemed logical from a purely administrative point of view, but was a disastrous policy made out of the basest of motives and ultimately incapable of implementation.

Professional management in museums must evolve as an extension of the academic nature of the curatorial function that we all have to perform. This is, perhaps, harder for the curator to understand than for his/her equivalent in other industries. Management has a somewhat uncertain status in museums, both as an academic discipline and as a basis for practical action – few museum curators are proud of being good managers. In universities management often tends to be a poor relation of the general theory of academic administration, artificially separated by faculty boundaries, and too concentrated on institutional structure. The rise in the number of business studies faculties and business schools has shown that the demand is increasing, but none of these has yet fully targeted the museum profession. With the growing influence of the Museum Training Institute and the burgeoning 'new' universities, let us hope that, soon, appropriate management courses for the museum profession will be available. National and local government institutions have facilities for training their staff but these tend to be a patchwork containing bits of undigested doctrine of business management, some of it outdated and much unrelated to the needs of the museum profession. Management in museums is as much a 'science' as any other discipline. Science, properly so called, must surely always include not only formulating systematic hypotheses, but also linking and testing them by controlled experiment and/or measured observation – experiments or observations which can be independently replicated and tested. All this is accepted in the natural sciences and in large areas of the social sciences. Museum management, however, is in a constant state of flux, sometimes observable only from within, sometimes only from a distance. It never stands still to allow replicated and controlled experiments, and the amount of measured observation that can be carried out is very limited. Theory is needed to make sense of what would otherwise be chaos, but much of this theory must necessarily be based on somewhat abstract reasoning, although allied with practical, but never comprehensive, observation and experience. I do not apologise for the theory that we have had to trudge our way through in getting to this stage of the book for it is necessary, particularly for a profession which generally has so little knowledge of the subject in the first place.

The previous pages of this book have laid out a mix of theories and concepts which are relevant, in part, to the museum world. Taylor's theories may seem particularly outdated and his authoritarian approach may not seem to be appropriate in the intellectual environment in which we, the museum profession, live. His approach is also rather peripheral, dealing with some of the subsidiary technologies of management rather than with real issues. Whilst his theory was conceived to be of use to the worker as well as the manager, there is little doubt that its most influential effect has been the misleading centring on the authoritarian doctrines of control and motivation.

The Quantitative Approach applies scientific techniques and follow-up research. Museums are themselves places of research, but I seriously doubt their inclination to apply research techniques to their management problems. Perhaps this approach is visible in some museums with a strong scientific or military bias but I would not expect any museum's overall management strategy to be based on it.

Classical Theory has merit in itself but gives no clue as to which basis is preferable in any particular circumstance. Hence, its principle of unity of command is also ambiguous. This shortening is due to inadequate diagnosis of situations and definitions of terms, and to the lack of detailed research into real situations. However, Fayol's basic tenet of management is particularly valid. Museums may have modified the Classical Approach to their own needs but it is likely that their use of it has been minimal except in such a way as to be an experiment of expression of their own education, background or empirical judgement. This theory provides a logical and ordered method for managers but is lacking substance when dealing with anything more than philosophical situations. As a framework of good practice it has much to commend it, but as a definitive proved system it has been overtaken by more modern theories and practices. Fayol's thoughts also have a place in other theories, particularly the Human Relations Approach which added scientific research to reinforce a dissatisfaction with traditional management techniques. Careful observation of individual workers in different situations (albeit they were predominantly in production-related jobs) showed illuminating results and greatly changed managers' understanding of the workers under their control. It seems strange today that painstaking research and observation had to take place before it was realised that people's productivity, quality of work and motivation to work are all related to the nature of social relations amongst the workers, and between the workers and their bosses. Other researchers have provided testimony to the vagaries of human nature and in so doing fuelled the fire of controversy by giving managers a choice of their view of workers. Nevertheless, these contributions whilst valid seem rather simplistic and are not always substantial enough to deal with the sociological diversity within the average museum or gallery. The value to the museum manager is the knowledge regarding the individual which is gained from these studies; the Human Relations Approach is more likely to succeed in the museum environment than authoritarian or dictatorial approaches. The mix of ability, intellect and status is so broad within museums that the task of managing must lie closer to the Human Relations Approach, for this studies the needs and reactions of people. It is particularly appropriate when managing groups with different academic and intellectual ability, the sort of scenario we all experience within the museum profession.

Whilst I believe this style is adopted quite widely in museums I am also aware that this is so by accident rather than by design. Indeed, the whole process of management in museums is based on empirical judgement. However primitive the techniques of management that are actually used on a day-to-day basis, they are rarely considered as anything more than peripheral to the real function of curatorship. A combination of the Human Relations Approach and the Systems Approach would, at first glance, seem eminently appropriate to the museum world. The disciplined consideration of an organisation as a whole, rather than parts in isolation should receive a sympathetic view from museum curators.

31

The concept of 'systems' and 'sub-systems' underlying an ordered environment is the type of approach favoured by those whose training has prepared them for academic research. The understanding amongst the majority of museum people that any managerial tampering with a sub-system will inevitably have repercussions throughout the whole system has yet to be learned. There is a case to be made for museums to adopt this approach in part, but in concert with other approaches. This method also brings order to complicated processes; it insists on monitoring and feedback to ensure success. Libraries, archives, exhibit loan departments, and a host of other museum functions can benefit from analysis of their performance, compilation of a model and implementation of a system. Many museums already operate similar techniques covered by this approach but it is doubtful to what extent the principles are applied as a result of specific knowledge of them and how much is done purely by virtue of need or common sense.

Probably the most used and relevant approach is found within Contingency Theory, for this is an adaptable method which can take account of varying situations. It is an integrated method which allows for a wide variety of styles and yet also ensures continual diversification and adaptability. The changes in culture and environment which are having such a profound effect on museums are forcing forward changes which already necessitate effective management, and upon this will be based the survival of museums. The Contingency Theory is one of the most suitable methods to cope with such changes. The importance of the management function in maintaining a balance within an organisation, of internal communication systems (particularly feedback) are the strength of the theory. We should also remember the concept of 'appreciation', for when this is coupled with sympathetic decision-making, it can change the people and organisations that make them. These two processes coupled together have enlarged the outlook and scope of activity of individuals, their mutual confidence and hence the shape and orientation of the institution as a whole. Only the Contingency Theory gives such flexibility; the kind of compliant system necessary to the changeable environment of museums. It is possible that this concept, when added to Contingency Theory is most appropriate in the museum context.

Whilst Contingency Theories are the most likely systems for the museum environment, it would be wrong to assume that such a subtle, delicate and elusive subject as the management of museums can be easily equated with business management. The final picture must be a mix of approaches. Museums are a developing complexity, an enigmatic network of disciplines with a diffusion of authority and administrative functions. This inescapable fact results in an increasing number of individuals in museums being actively involved in the management process, sometimes without being fully aware of it.

The development of management philosophy has followed a defined path, which is similar to the development of individual managers. It's interesting to consider how managers are developed generally but also, how they are created in museums. Put very simply, the untrained manager grows in experience and maturity and, in so doing, passes through the same stages of development as management thinking has over the past century or so. Managers start by looking for universal principles and ideal solutions then realisation comes that the best they can really hope for is a fine balance between the needs of people and demands of the system. Only an awareness of the theories and principles can speed up the assimilation of this knowledge and that is why we have spent some time going over these theories thus far.

The problems facing senior museum managers are likely, therefore, to follow this development; this will only change when more managers are made aware of the principles of management theory and its application to their own distinct environment and duties. I have already said that management training is accorded relatively little priority in museums. If this is the case, even senior managers in museums have minimal training in their management function. Whilst they may be highly experienced subject-specialist they will usually be extremely immature managers. As such there is little surprise in the assumption that they should intuitively (and unknowingly) opt for Taylor's Scientific Management methods – probably the most inappropriate for the work they are expected to do. They should be looking for much more, for their own survival, the survival of their institutions, and the benefit of all those who work for them. Complacency with regard to management and the resulting drift towards dictatorial or authoritarian styles is neither appropriate nor deserving of the museum of today. Therefore, having disposed of the theories of management we will now turn our attention to the practices.

2

Managing yourself: the 'player manager'

We are usually promoted because of our ability to do the job properly and well. Our expertise at scoring goals somehow qualifies us to become manager of the team. This means that, sometimes for many years, we have conscientiously carried out an operations function within our organisation; this might be cataloguing books in a library, accessioning items, doing research and all the other tasks which go to make up a modern museum or gallery. Having been so good at this for so long we eventually achieve promotion and we go home on a Friday evening very pleased with ourselves, knowing that when we return on Monday morning we will be a 'manager'. That is how it happens. A relatively simple change you might think. Not a bit of it, the transition from being an 'operator' to being a 'manager' is fraught with danger and the first way of dealing with this change is to recognise that it is going to happen, or is happening, to you.

It is ironic that the very skills that have helped you as an individual to achieve promotion may now prevent you from being an effective manager. You will find that you will naturally attempt to retain some of the roles at which you had formerly excelled as an operator; this can be detrimental to your effectiveness in your new role. There are plenty of grey areas between operating and managing – you will need to decide what is a managing or an operating function. This is not always easy, particularly if your responsibilities only include the supervision of a small group of people. However, you should, at the outset, be able to distinguish whether you are still fulfilling your previous role as an operator or have made the transition to an effective manager. You should not expect this transition to happen easily or in a short period of time. Nevertheless, with some thought, you will be able to appreciate the differences and react accordingly. You will find work is full of anomalies and there are many cases where you will know that you are acting as an operator rather than a manager but, nevertheless, it is essential that you do so.

Let us distinguish between operating and managing. The operating function includes purely technical aspects of the work, which may be routine or following procedures which have already been laid down. You may even be operating when you fail to use the abilities of those operators who are subordinate to you. We will deal with the matter of delegation later but, the newly promoted manager often finds it very difficult to delegate to people who he/she worked side by side with prior to his/her promotion, and whom he/she probably thinks will take longer to do the required task than he/she would. These are traps which are laid in front of the aspiring manager and considerable thought is necessary before an assessment can be made to identify whether the function being carried out should be a managing one, or delegated as an operating one.

The following hypothetical situations serve to illustrate the distinction between operating and managing and are presented in the form of a quiz, the answers to which are given in the notes at the end of this chapter. You should go through these and determine whether, in each instance, the subject is an operating or managing function.

1 You are visiting a local museum with a member of your staff to give advice on the conservation of an exhibit.[1]

2 You are required to sign an authorisation for routine expenditure.[2]

3 You are conducting an initial screening interview of a job applicant.[3]

4 You are giving one of your experienced staff your solution to a problem before you have asked for his/her recommendation.[4]

5 You are giving your solution to a recurring problem one of your new staff has just asked about.[5]

6 You are conducting a meeting with your staff to explain a new procedure.[6]

7 You are telephoning another department to request help for one of your staff in solving a problem.[7]

These simple examples illustrate the complexity in distinguishing between the operating and managing functions, and if they do no more than set your mind thinking about this crucial aspect following your transition to management they will have done their job. There are very few hard and fast rules in the early stages of this transitional period and you must carefully assess what you are doing to determine whether you are reverting back to the role from which you have been promoted. I would emphasise that managers *do* operate. However, you must be aware if you start to slip back into the operating mode from which you have recently been elevated. This is particularly appropriate when workloads become high and you fall into that insidious trap which lies in wait for untrained and inexperienced managers – stress.

STRESS

Inevitably on promotion into a management function you will be required to undertake a different type of work. This may well include elements of the work you have already become successful at and which have resulted in your promotion to management. In the case of curatorial work in museums and galleries it is often the case that promotion within a curatorial department requires the manager to continue his/her curatorial function but have added to it, an element of management. An immature manager will attempt to continue to fulfil both the operating and managing roles and this will result in overload, something we have all experienced at one time or another. Two types of overload can occur, one causes pressure, the other causes stress.

Pressure is motivating. Stress is debilitating. Pressure is something which good managers apply to themselves and their staff in order to motivate them and to achieve results. Effective application of pressure (whilst watching carefully for signs of stress), will ensure more effective management of resources and an institution which is progressive rather than regressive. However, there is a fine line between pressure and stress and, whilst the manager should be watching carefully to ensure that the one does not become the other in his/her subordinates, he/she should also have a weather eye on his/her own workload with a view to ensuring that it is confined to a motivating element of pressure rather than a debilitating downward spiral of stress. In many cases it is easier to recognise the signs of stress than it is to identify those of pressure. Pressure has an uplifting affect and is personified by high morale and the achievement of targets. Stress has rather insidious symptoms which include:

1 Lowering of performance. A person who had previously been able to carry out his/her duties suddenly seems to have the weight of the world on his/her shoulders. Things are not done and excuses are constantly being made.

2 Over-busyness. People suffering from stress, because of their lowering performance, tend to put on an act of being extremely busy. This is characterised by an untidy desk or office, a diary full of meetings, working long hours and spending time on seemingly minor matters.

3 Insecurity. As the lowering of performance and the over-busyness seem to have little affect on the workload a person becomes insecure and unwilling to make decisions. They also become frightened that work, for which they have a responsibility, will only be done (and done properly) if they personally take charge of it from beginning to end. They often make more work for themselves in an attempt to assure all those around them that they are needed and necessary.

4 Unwillingness to delegate. Their insecurity and their belief that only they can do the job properly precludes them from sharing or passing work to others.

5 Irritability and short temper. It is hardly surprising that, when all these symptoms accumulate one upon another, people become short tempered and irritable. A 'short fuse' is often a sign of a person under stress.

6 Panic reactions. Because of their unwillingness to delegate, their insecurity and their lowering of performance, work gets left until the last minute and then panic reactions set in. Decisions result from panic rather than careful thought.

7 Reliance on tobacco, alcohol and drugs (i.e. tranquilizers). The untidy office of an over-busy chain smoker who has a short temper and is not producing results is probably the clearest example to any manager that a person is suffering serious symptoms of stress.

A great deal has been written about stress in the past few years and it's discussion has become almost a fashionable thing. However, its affect should not be underestimated and effective managers should be able to recognise the symptoms in themselves and, most importantly, in those who work for them. However, there is a fine balance between successfully motivating staff through putting manageable pressure upon them and overdoing it by introducing stress into their lives.

Stress in the workplace is one thing, stress at home is another. The symptoms are often the same but the solutions may be different. An open system of staff appraisal and counselling can help with both, and careful monitoring of performance will identify the onset of stress or the success of applying pressure when it is necessary.

One of the key areas which produces stress both in the manager and in his/her subordinates is the inability of an individual to manage time.

TIME MANAGEMENT

The rise in popularity of personal organisers, both paper and electronic, is but one part of an ongoing trend which acknowledges that time management is important. The majority of people in museums and galleries probably have a problem with the management of their time. For the manager attempting the transition from operator it is crucial that the management of time is not only a high priority but also an understood and developed part of everyday working life. There are two aspects of time management which are important. On the one hand there is the need for the organisation to achieve the highest productivity and most effective use of its most valuable resource, the staff. On the other hand there is the need for individuals to be able to reduce the chances of becoming stressed and failing to meet individual productivity and performance targets. If a manager is both able to organise his/her own time effectively and ensure that those who work for him/her are also managing their time, he/she will be significantly more effective. I shall therefore deal with the subject of managing time in two elements, the individual management of time and the manager's management of time within the organisation.

Management of time: the individual

There are three areas which we can look at which will assist us in managing our own time.

Work-shedding

Eighty per cent of our results can generally be attributed to 20 per cent of our effort. This is the 80/20 law and has been part of management philosophy for nearly a century. If you think about it you can probably illustrate many examples where you have finished a day's work and looked back at exactly what you have achieved during your working period. There will be some days where you have a list of achievements but there will be many more where you ask yourself the question, 'What did I achieve at work today?' This illustrates the point that no matter what happens a large proportion of your time will not produce results. If we understand this we can identify, in advance, those elements of our work which are achievable and those which are more properly delegated or even discarded. The achievable elements of our work can be grouped into key activities, that is, those activities which will produce results allied to our purpose of being effective managers. With regard to delegation if you have a problem over being able to delegate bear in mind your cost to the institution and the cost of the person you are delegating work to. To do this you should know (and communicate to all the people who work for you) the cost of a minute of your time. This can be calculated using the following formula:

	£
Annual Salary, say	10,000
Add allowances (London Weighting etc.), say	1,000
Add 25 per cent (pensions, national insurance etc.)	2,750
Add 100 per cent (overheads including office, heat, light etc.)	13,750
Total	27,500
Divide total by 220 (working days per year)	125
Divide result by 8 (hours per day)	15.63
Divide result by 60 (minutes per hour)	.26
Total	**26 pence per minute**

Therefore a minute of time of a person earning £10,000 per year is over 26 pence per minute. This is a salutary reminder to you as a manager, and to those who work for you, of your cost to your museum or gallery.

So, when you have identified the key activities which will produce results, hopefully you can convert the 80/20 law into a more advantageous ratio which will provide you (as an effective manager) with a higher percentage of results from your efforts. In delegating you should assess these key activities to attribute work which could be done by a person earning a lower salary and therefore at a lower cost to your institution. A typical example of this is the simple task of photocopying. If a person earning £25,000 per year spends fifteen minutes photocopying a document which could have been done by a person earning £10,000 it does not need a mathematician to calculate that the museum or gallery within which that person is working is losing a considerable amount of money as a result of ineffective management of time. By understanding this simple principle the new manager finds that the barrier to delegating to subordinates with whom he/she previously worked can be significantly reduced.

Time saving

Obviously if you can save time in carrying out the tasks that you have identified as key activities you will make further inroads into being more effective in your use of the time available to you. In order to do this you must ask yourself a number of key questions:

1 Am I doing work which should be done by others?

2 Am I giving enough time to my key activities?

3 Could I reduce the time taken to do certain activities?

4 What else should I be doing?

5 Where am I wasting time?

6 Am I spending time operating rather managing?

7 Do I need training?

Having got over the initial reluctance to delegate the first of these questions is probably the only one which is regularly asked by managers. However, the others are important and having asked them, savings in time are almost inevitable. There is a common failure within museums and galleries to carry out work in a routine fashion regardless of its importance or whether it will achieve the required result. We tend to work in a situation where there are inputs and we have little regard for the results – our output. The accumulation of work and the lack of experience in managing time produces what may, in many cases, seem an extremely efficient system which is invariably wholly ineffective. Our purpose as good managers is to be effective, and efficiency and effectiveness are not always the same thing. You can be extremely efficient at what you do, but if you are not doing the right job your efficiency will not produce effective results. Saving time by asking these key questions and acting upon them will assist you to establish the effectiveness of your work and, having done that, you can ensure that those key activities you have identified are carried out efficiently.

Time planning

There are many proprietary methods on the market to assist us with time planning. Most of them take more time to carry out than the job they are designed to streamline. However, they may be relevant and are worth exploring. Depending on you as an individual, or the people who work for you, day planners may be useful for setting yourself key tasks during the day. Actually writing 'to do' lists is a useful exercise particularly when you are a young or immature manager. However, do not fill up your day planner early in the day, leave gaps for the inevitable interruptions and additional tasks which will be laid upon you.

Understand, once again, how much a minute of your time costs. Make your staff aware of their cost to the organisation and that they should be carrying out work which can show an outcome. Put your work into priorities, use any tool available to you and which, in your case, might help. Day planners are one method, computer software has been developed which carries out a similar task and there are now powerful pocket-sized electronic organisers. A personal system is required and, therefore, it is difficult for anyone to lay down a model which will work for everyone. Whichever method you use, whether it is a formal written-down planning sheet, computer software, personal organiser or any other method, remember to leave time to rest. Part of a manager's function is to think and you will find it very difficult to think while you are constantly applying yourself to key activities which have been worked out in a rigid fashion using an inappropriate planning method. There is nothing wrong in stopping everything now and then during your working day, and simply leaning back in your chair and staring out of the window for ten minutes. This is not only rest, it is also thinking time which, in spite of our knowledge of how much a minute of our time costs, is, in fact, a key activity.

Management of time: organisational

Having therefore become the ultimate individual time manager you can turn your attention to ensuring that those people who work for (and with) you are also aware and able to manage their time more effectively. This can be done by personal counselling and advice to individuals, particularly if you see they have a problem. It can also be done by instituting changes in the workplace which will avoid time-wasting. You will find many examples of where this can be done and I merely illustrate the point with one or two which on the surface may seem trivial but in practice can be quite important.

We have already talked about the delegation of photocopying and this can be allied to all sorts of routine tasks within our museums and galleries. However, if you place your photocopier, fax machine, book binding equipment (or whatever) in the wrong working area, similar time management problems will result. For example, you have quite rightly delegated the photocopying of a document to a person who earns half your salary. That person then goes to the photocopying area which has been sited within a department surrounded by workstations – the person you have sent to do the photocopying enjoys a gossip. The result – a five-minute photocopying job turns into a twenty-five minute conversation about what was on television last night. It is not possible (or desirable) to totally eliminate social contact within the workplace, neither would you as an effective manager wish to do so. However, you should be aware that non-working contacts between staff will inevitably produce time-wasting and resultant reductions in productivity. Being aware of this will provide you with options to provide solutions which can subtly increase the individuals' ability to manage their time more effectively. A further example is the way in which tea breaks and meal times coincide to allow groups of staff to socialise together during working hours. I am not advocating that staff be kept rigidly separate in order to ensure such contact is not made but if you, as a manager, supply a tea room which is outside of eye and earshot of management and allow staff to congregate for set periods of time in the morning and afternoon for the purpose of taking tea together you will find that your fifteen-minute tea break extends to forty-five minutes and time is wasted in large chunks by whole groups of people. A similar result will be evident if you allow members of staff to start and finish work without proper control over times. It is human nature for people to take advantage of weaknesses in management and this is particularly evident if the managers themselves are abusing the system. If managers arrive at work late and leave early it is only natural that their subordinates will do the same. If there is no system in place to control and monitor the working hours of members of staff they will waste time by arriving late and leaving early. Similarly, the proper recording of annual leave (and time off in lieu) must be introduced; each person is allocated an amount of leave but, if this is not properly recorded, they may take days off which are unauthorised.

All this has a bearing on the amount of work that can be carried out by a group of staff for which you, as a manager, have responsibility. If you are not able to identify where weaknesses in the system might lie your ability to manage your team will be compromised. This may seem a rigid approach to dealing with people whom you would consider to be honest and hard working. It is a fact that natural human behaviour at work is inclined towards doing a fair day's work for a fair day's pay. However, if your organisation or group of staff is not properly managed, they will revert to an unmotivated set of individuals with low morale, working not for the organisation, but solely for themselves. This will result in low productivity, poor morale and an inevitable ineffectiveness in the work you are trying to achieve through them. People respond much more positively to fair and equitable management. They like to know exactly where they stand and that those who work with them are required to perform to an equivalent standard and 'pull their weight'. There is a natural tendency for the lowest common denominator to become the norm and this requires not only firm, but fair, treatment and a positive and outward example of good practice from management.

DECISION-MAKING

Planning and control

Because decision-making is part of every effective manager's function you should have very clear in your mind, either at the point of transition from

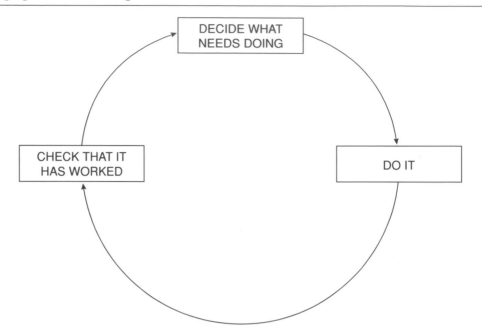

Figure 4 The problem-solving control loop

operator to manager or at any time you are in a managing situation, exactly how the decision-making process is capable of being controlled. You will have heaped upon you, day by day, a succession of minor, moderate and major problems. Some will require immediate snap decisions, others can be carefully considered and a reasoned judgement given following consultation and/or analysis. Whatever the speed at which you have to decide, or the scale of the problem which is to be solved, there is a process which must be understood. A lack of this basic understanding is commonly one of the failures of inexperienced or untrained managers. Quite simply the problem-solving process involves three simple elements. First you must decide what needs doing, then do it and then check that it has worked. These three rudimentary things may seem to be a gross over simplification but it is a fact that the inexperienced manager, when faced with decision making, tends to leave out the third element of checking which is so essential to ensure that the job is done according to the standards set. This process is illustrated in Fig. 4.

This circular process is characteristic of many management principles which are, by their very nature, circular. The manager constantly returns to a point to assess his/her judgement/decision/target to ensure the original objective is still capable of achievement. In the problem-solving process, before the first element of this control loop can be implemented, it is necessary to analyse the problem. This will help you look, in detail, at the individual stages of the decision-making process.

Analyse the problem

There are various ways that problems can be analysed, both mentally and diagrammatically. There is nothing new in this, how many of us have produced lists when trying to decide which model or make of new car we should buy? It is quite common for us to put the pros and cons of different products down on a piece of paper to analyse in our minds, before making the decision to buy, exactly which is the product that best suits ourselves and our pockets. Exactly the same process can be used in analysing work problems. There are more sophisticated methods using decision trees, cause and effect diagrams, networks, matrices, and all kinds of project planning software. However, the key is to understand that before any decision can be made thought should be given to the actual content and composition of the problem. We are still not yet ready to attempt the process of solving the problem until we have added to our analysis the task of setting clear objectives. Setting objectives is not only relevant to solving individual problems but should be part and parcel of our work as effective managers – as individuals, working in groups, and within organisations generally.

Ideally, every organisation should have clear objectives. People within the organisation should know precisely what they are trying to achieve and management should communicate those objectives to the people whose responsibility it is to achieve them. This is the function of management, and it is the function of individual managers to set objectives for the tasks they are trying to carry out themselves and those that they wish their subordinates to carry out on their behalf. You, and the people who work with and for you, should know the objectives of your department/museum/gallery and they should, where possible, be in writing and displayed where everyone can find them. You, and everyone who works for and with you, should know who determined the objectives and what arrangements there are for reviewing them. The higher up the management tree you climb the more of a part you will have in formulating these objectives. So, in the problem-solving process at an individual manager level similar criteria should apply. There are tactical and strategic decisions which need to be made.

Tactical decisions are those which affect the day-to-day work of the organisation and are usually made as part of an evolving process of management. Strategic decisions are made for the future policy of the institution and will determine what is to be done next, rather than how, why and what is being done at the present.

Setting criteria

Having analysed the problem and set objectives the next stage is to set criteria. The criteria will determine the boundaries within which the objectives can be dealt with and achieved. For decisions at a strategic level your criteria might state that the solution must:

1 Contribute to the overall strategy of the museum or gallery.

2 Show a return on investment (not necessarily financial).

3 Be at an acceptable level of risk (which should always be defined).

4 Take into account the needs and expectations of the visitors/customers.

5 Make use of, or reinforce, organisational strengths.

6 Not rely on weaknesses.

7 Exploit major opportunities.

8 Avoid, reduce, or mitigate main threats.

9 Accord with moral and professional codes or practices.

10 Be consistent with other major strategies.

11 *Be capable of implementation.*

All these criteria are also relevant to your own decision-making process, with the last the most important of all. There is little point in an effective manager embarking on a process for which he/she has made the decision when it is inevitably going to be incapable of implementation. Put quite simply, we should not be in the business of attempting the unachievable. This is particularly important in museums owing to the time-scales in which we work. There are very few other professions which work and make decisions which will have an affect in hundreds or thousands of years in the future. Many of the curatorial decisions we are called upon to consider mean that our judgement over whether they will be capable of being implemented is extremely important.

Options

Having analysed the problem, set our objectives and looked at the criteria, we should then have assembled in front of us (or in our mind if we are happy to, and capable of, going through this process mentally) a list of options. I advocate two methods of selecting the option most likely to be successful:

1 The rational technique is the empirical way we ordinarily decide which option we would take. We simply go through the options and choose the one which looks most likely to be capable of implementation.

2 There is a less rational technique which is to look at the options and to choose the *least worst*. This may sound rather odd, at first glance, but it is often the case that none of the options seem particularly appealing but, having analysed the problem, there must be a way of achieving the objective. In this case we need to understand that even though none of the options look very good we should be prepared to take the least negative of the options we have in front of us. There is often a tendency in inexperienced

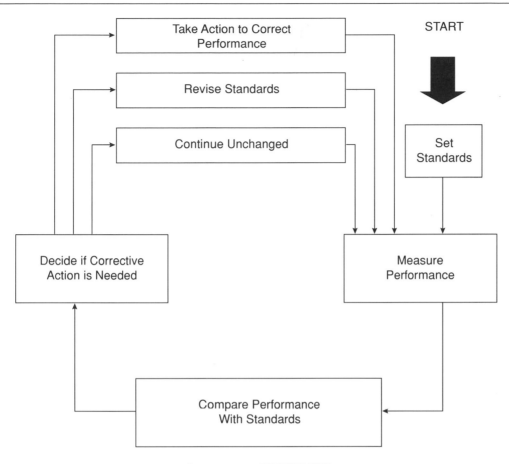

Importance of FEEDBACK

Figure 5 The complex control loop

managers to fail to make a decision because none of the options seem worth while. By looking at them in this rather opposite sense, a preferred option often becomes clear.

Having been through this process we can look again at the control loop on page 42 and add elements to it to ensure a more reliable or sophisticated approach to the problem-solving process. Fig. 5 illustrates this more clearly.

As can be seen from Fig. 5 the start of the process requires that standards or targets, objectives, goals etc. are clearly set and specified. The effective manager will always do this to ensure that his/her objective is properly and clearly communicated to those people with the task of implementation. Having set these standards the next stage is to measure the performance. This, obviously, will be done after the process has started, but needs to be actioned reasonably quickly to discover whether any changes need to be made. Having measured the performance and having set clear standards the manager can compare the two and decide if any corrective action is needed. He/she then has three options: whether to take action to correct performance if the standards have not been achieved, to revise them if they are not appropriate or (and this is hardly ever the case) continue unchanged if corrective action is not necessary. The process does not stop there. Whatever option is chosen, performance should again be measured and around the loop we go again. Only when the objectives have been achieved can the process for that task stop. When activities aimed at achieving a standard or goal have taken place, there must always be *feedback* of information before any corrective action can be taken. This is essential, not only in the decision-making or problem-solving process, but feedback generally is a necessary and imperative part of a manager's work.

Using these relatively simple processes will allow the manager to think more clearly when faced with decisions and problems. This will assist in the transition from operator to manager by giving a structure to the young or immature manager in his/her decision-making or problem-solving areas of work. I may seem to be merely adding to the manager's workload by expecting empirical things such as decision-making to be structured and given a routine. This is certainly the case for the experienced and well trained manager and he/she would hardly ever go through these processes in the rigid format in which they have been written here. However, for the new manager it is useful to know the process by which the trained manager is able to make his/her decisions in a more structured or useful way. That is all I am advocating here – that thought is given to the process, for it is a serious and essential part of effective managership.

These, then, are the essentials for your transition from operator to manager. The basic skills which will not only enable you to start managing from day one, but also skills which will give you confidence to take on a management role. You will make the transition into management knowing some of the problems that will face you, the factors which will influence your effectiveness, and the differences between operating and managing, You will be aware of the benefits of pressure and the effects of stress; how to manage your time and solve problems in a structured way. All these subjects are factors which can make a difference to your ability to make a smooth transition and become an effective manager more quickly. However, these skills are mainly addressing your management of yourself – as you now know, one of your main tasks will be to manage other people and that is the subject we are going to look at in the next chapter.

NOTES

1 Operating, this is a purely technical aspect of your work which, though probably necessary, is not actually a management function.
2 Operating, there are probably procedures for such routine elements of your job and this illustrates how a manager can also be an operator.
3 Operating, the initial screening interview could be delegated, the management function is fulfilled when the final interview which selects the person for the job is undertaken.
4 Operating, because you are failing to use the abilities of your staff, a common occurrence during the transitional period to management.
5 This can be managing or operating depending on the situation but, since you are dealing with a new member of staff, you may consider it part of your training function (i.e. management).
6 This is management, your function is to communicate policy and new procedures are invariably a part of that.
7 This could be operating if you were trying to find the answer for your subordinate but managing if you were easing his/her access to the other department.

3

Managing other people

Management of people is probably the single most complex and difficult aspect of management. There are four particular skills that are necessary and which should be borne in mind by all aspiring managers. The first of these is *awareness* of what is going on in your relationships with other people, why they are behaving in a particular way and what your influence is having on their behaviour. *Motivating*; you need to know what motivates people to work and what demotivates them to stop working, in order that you can use one and exclude the other from your day to day management. *Communication*; if you find it difficult to communicate or your communication skills are not well developed, your effectiveness as a manager will be all the more difficult. Being able to communicate at varying levels is an essential skill which needs to be acquired from the outset. *Style*; your style, and your ability to adapt your style to circumstances will be a significant contributor to your success.

We will look at all four of these skills but they all hinge on an initial awareness of how people behave, both as individuals and in groups. There are no simple answers as to how you may deal with people. We are going to look at how we may better understand other people so that we can see why they act in ways that may seem quirkish, pig-headed or even obstructive. We will also look at the equally intriguing question of why people usually are prepared to behave co-operatively and work cheerfully, sometimes in very unpleasant conditions. This is not meant to just be about the 'manager/worker' relationship. An awareness of what is going on with your relationships with other people should also give you an insight into your own feelings and aspirations. Let's look at difficult or obstructive behaviour first and to do this I will illustrate with two examples. Your Head Attendant asks:

> 'See that photocopier in the Archive Department, I'm not allowed to use it because we are not part of the Curatorial staff, but we have to use it to provide rosters and reports for the Admin Department. Now and then, when I get really fed up with this job I don't hand my reports into the Admin Department. They get hopping mad but I just tell them I'm not allowed to use the photocopier, am I?'

How often have we heard similar responses to what people often see as petty rules? Some people, because it is in their character, will do everything they can to operate within rules and to make those rules an end in themselves. Others will consider them to be obstacles put in their path and usually will circumvent them or even become obstructive.

There is also perverse behaviour. An example of which might be the recently appointed Design Manager who is put in charge of a new exhibition with a strict time-scale. This person wants to impress his/her employer by finishing a couple of days before the opening, even though all the planning indicated the work would take until the opening day to complete. He/she therefore works his/her staff flat out in a two shift system where one group comes to work at 7.00 a.m. and leaves at 3.30 p.m. and the other group comes on at 10.00 a.m. and works until 6.30 p.m. Often the two groups work on particular elements of the job which require total effort during 10.00 a.m. to 3.30 p.m., when everyone was available. Both groups were annoyed at the manager's attitude and the way in which they had been 'forced' to change their working hours. As a way of getting back at the manager the groups leave work for each other, this means that the project falls behind; in some cases the groups would even destroy their own work and start again, to ensure the project was delayed.

What explanations can there be for behaviour which is not just uncooperative but actually makes life more difficult for people who are behaving badly in the first place? Immature or inexperienced managers will tend to believe that perverse or obstructive behaviour is something quite normal which has to be dealt with almost as a routine. They will give various reasons why people behave like this:

1 It is in their nature to behave like this.

2 It is in their upbringing and experience.

3 It is the way they see things from their position in the organisation.

4 It is the kind of behaviour managers should expect of people.

5 It is the pressures on them from their colleagues.

6 It is their response to the way they are treated.

7 It is because of the rewards which they expect (or know not to expect) to come their way.

8 It is frustration and powerlessness.

These points may seem rather simplistic and can hardly be a comprehensive explanation of human behaviour. However, one or two may seem to fit the bill in some situations. But we need to understand that there are very complex reasons for perverse or obstructive behaviour. It is most important to know that, occasionally, an explanation of unusual behaviour is misinterpreted as a defence of such behaviour. We often explain something rather than condone it. We should not try to explain or justify perverse or obstructive behaviour; we should go out of our way to understand when it is actually happening and take steps to alter that behaviour. It is particularly important to note that none of the explanations we are to consider are about faults and neither are they total explanations in themselves. The theories I am now going to explain deal with behaviour, not just of people you work with, but your own – so you may judge how closely they fit your behaviour and experience.

It is human to behave strangely but the worst thing we can do is to regard people who *appear* to us to be behaving irrationally as somehow stupid or perverse because they are not seeing things in the same way that we do.

A management psychologist has said:

> If there is any common human relations mistake made by organisational superiors in their relations with their subordinates, it is the mistake of assuming that the 'real world' is all that counts, that everyone works for the same goals and that facts speak for themselves.

(Leavitt, 1972)

There are three erroneous assumptions in this quotation, they are closely linked and will serve to illustrate what we need to know about human relations and our dealings with groups of people who work for (or with) us.

1   The real world is the only one that counts (the real world being the world as we, the managers, see it).

2   Everyone works for the same goals (and those are the organisation's goals).

3   The facts speak for themselves (and give the same message to everybody).

We intuitively know that these assumptions are false but, nevertheless, many managers (possibly most) base a great deal of their managerial activities precisely on the assumptions we know to be incorrect. Let's look at these false assumptions in greater detail for they have a bearing on the way in which we can be more effective.

THE REAL WORLD IS THE ONLY ONE THAT COUNTS

We tend to act on the basis of what we perceive to be reality. The problems arise because we do not all see the same reality, i.e., one man's lock-out is another man's strike, or one man's rationalisation of business is another man's threat to employment. Some facts are generally accepted as being beyond dispute but hard facts in business and management are few and far between, and a lot of opinion masquerades as fact. So, what is the real world? Quite simply, for each one of us the real world is what we believe it to be.

We tend to regard people who hold a different view of reality to our own to be wrong. Generally we prefer people with beliefs similar to our own. This might seem theoretical but it is important. The fact that people hold different views, and that they act according to what they believe to be reality, might make them (from our point of view as managers) awkward, difficult or, even, dangerous. However, it does not necessarily make them perverse fools, however irrational their actions might appear from our point of view. We must be aware that it is wrong to fall into the trap of assuming that only one reality (our own) counts. The first step in avoiding such problems is to recognise that other realities exist and need to be taken into account. To do this we have to ask why people see different realities, for it is rare to find a total conflict of view on every issue and even rarer to find total agreement. The skill of the effective manager is to constantly look for this compromise and to always realise that the other person's point of view is as relevant and meaningful to them as ours is to us.

EVERYONE WORKS FOR THE SAME GOALS

We are still trying to understand why people behave as they do. We have already seen that most people behave in ways which, to them, seem totally rational. The fact that we might not see their behaviour as being irrational is because we have a different view of reality. We see things from our own point of view.

In politics, religion, sport etc., we accept the differences between people as a fact of life. When it comes to work, however, managers often fall into the trap of assuming that everyone in the organisation is working (or should be working) towards the same goals – namely those of the organisation as conceived by management. Intuitively we probably know that this is a fallacy, but the danger exists that a lot of decision-making will take other people's reactions for granted. We expect everyone to see our reality and take it for granted that they will then co-operate willingly.

Very often, the real reasons why people co-operate (that is, work willingly) have nothing whatsoever to do with achieving the organisation's goals and everything to do with achieving their own goals – fortunately, in many cases, the two are not incompatible.

The art of effective management of people includes the ability to ensure that personal goals and organisational goals match as near as possible so that both may be attained simultaneously. To achieve this happy state we need to know something of the goals that people are seeking to attain by working, and some of the needs that push people to work willingly in conditions that, in some cases, can be quite intolerable.

Goal-directed behaviour

Most human behaviour is aimed at achieving a goal. Things don't just happen they usually have a purpose. Our behaviour is thus needs driven. Therefore, as managers, we should be acutely sensitive to the needs of our team. There is little point in our offering rewards or incentives which do not match the needs of the people who work for us. A reward can only be a reward if it matches some unsatisfied need.

Role-based behaviour

Having emphasised the fact that human behaviour is aimed at the attainment of personal goals and the satisfaction of personal needs, another way of explaining behaviour is to recognise that, for most of the time, we are 'acting' our role. To be more accurate, we are acting several roles and, more particularly, we are acting in a way that we understand is expected of us by our subordinates, peers and superiors. Most of the time we are trying to fulfil the expectations that people have of us in our particular role. We are acting out a part that has probably been created for us by others. To illustrate this, ask yourself how often you feel able to tell your boss (or colleague) all about your real feelings? How often can you really be yourself? Have you ever experienced how odd it can feel to be in the presence of two people who have different expectations of you, for example, a close social friend and your boss. This can often be an uncomfortable experience, for your friend knows you as an almost totally different person than that which you 'act out' to those people with whom you work – particularly your boss. It is worth remembering that everyone else is also playing their roles as they feel they ought to be played and sometimes they are over-playing them.

Learned behaviour

This is quite noticeable and obvious to us all for we learn things and behave from experience – it is especially noticeable in children. How many of us have seen a screaming child given a sweet/candy to quieten him/her down? The result is usually a child that screams even louder, even more often, in order to obtain yet another sweet/candy. This learned behaviour carries into adulthood, a good example of which is the speed at which trade unions will use the threat of industrial action if they believe the negotiations they are having with management may be prone to delay.

Conflicts of interest

If we recognise that individuals' goals differ we may be able to find a compromise so that the organisation's goals and the worker's goals coincide. Unfortunately, there may still be conflicts of interest. It is important to realise a few facts about these:

1   We should not assume that co-operation is normal, healthy and proper, and that conflict and opposition is pathological or deviant behaviour.

2   We should not assume that conflict arises from error, and those opposing are somehow mistaken, led into error, confused or evil. The other person usually believes his/her position is as reasonable and as rational as we believe ours to be.

3   Organisations, like other social institutions such as families and small groups, contain both co-operation and conflict as a natural course of events.

Effective management rests not on the eradication of conflict (which is, in most cases, impossible anyway) but on the ability to identify it and face it. Indeed, as effective managers we need to be able to use conflict constructively.

THE FACTS SPEAK FOR THEMSELVES

One of the most common mistakes we can make is to assume that the facts always speak for themselves. Usually the facts that we give have a totally different message to different people. The actions of both workers and managers are just as likely to be misinterpreted and our job is to be aware that such misinterpretation is more than likely to happen and to avoid it at the outset. We must develop skills which include an ability to explain, in the most appropriate fashion, the facts as we see them in order that the people we are communicating with understand them as fully as we do.

How can we ensure that conflict resulting from misunderstanding is reduced in our own organisation? This leads us on to management sensitivity, a term which is most reviled as being an insincere attempt by managers to explain their actions. This should not be the case and it should be taken seriously by all who aspire to be effective managers.

Management sensitivity

Up until now I have talked about a very broad subject; collectively of 'the management', 'the workers' and 'human relations'. These may seem rather abstract as for all of us the problems are much more personal and immediate. What we need to know is how to deal with individuals and groups. At the level of dealing with individuals, it makes more sense to talk specifically about 'you', 'the people you work with', and 'interpersonal relationships'. Fortunately everything we have discussed so far, about human relations in general, applies to relationships at the individual level as well as at the group level. We must always bear in mind the need to look at the causes of behaviour, not just the symptoms. We need to take account of other peoples realities. We need to acknowledge others' goals and objectives and recognise that the facts do not speak for themselves. We have to communicate freely and handle people with understanding and sensitivity. This latter requirement is perhaps even more important in the face-to-face circumstances of interpersonal relationships than in the collective relationships of management and workers.

There is no doubt that the quality of your own personal relationships (both as a manager and as an individual) have a direct bearing on your effectiveness. Individual skill and sensitivity in this area is vital. Good interpersonal relationships are closely linked with good communication, and a sensitivity to the nuances not only of the spoken word but also to non-verbal communication, something we will deal with later.

As part of our management sensitivity we need to understand how we can create job satisfaction and, in so doing, motivate people to work. Only improvements in the actual tasks which constitute the job and, in particular, improvements in the level of responsibility (as seen by the worker), can increase motivation to work better. For a reward to affect a person's decision to exert effort, that person must believe that his/her effort will increase the probability of obtaining the reward. Thus we can see that there is a link between effort and reward and that this link is extremely important. From effort comes performance which produces greater outcomes and those outcomes can be affected by either reward or punishment depending, for example, on whether targets have been met, or productivity maintained/exceeded. The links between effort, performance and outcomes are important. They should be clear and strong for they provide powerful motivation for a positive result. If there are no links, or the links are weak, the outcomes will have little power to motivate. Effective managers understand that if the outcome is to have any effect the person must either want the outcome (the reward) or not want it (the punishment).

This brings us neatly on to the matter of incentives which are a tool used by management to encourage higher performance and positive outcomes. There are various systems used in business which are either financial or non-financial. Many of them may transfer into the museum and gallery world but most are based on sales or production, i.e., the manufacturing process. Incentives which can be of use to the manager within the museum profession are mainly non-financial. It is easy to consider the payment of performance-related pay or financial bonuses as an effective way of motivating staff. This, on its own, is not so. Financial incentives work only in the short term at and around the time when they are initially given; thereafter, they become a norm and are treated by the worker as an expected part of their overall salary package. Performance-related pay has a similar effect although it can be a useful tool to reward improved or high performance by offering a financial incentive. It is important, however, to separate these awards from the regular staff development/appraisal systems which, if used sensitively can be powerful motivators. However, financial rewards should not be given an importance they do not warrant.

Other incentives are less obvious and more difficult to impart. This is not because we find it hard to provide non-financial incentives, it is simply that they are often intangible, transient and not seen directly as incentives at the time. However, they are fundamentally important. By intangible incentives I mean, at the simplest end of the scale, a verbal 'thank-you' to people for doing good work. A recognition that a person's value to the organisation is understood by management, the involvement of a person in satisfying elements of work which might include foreign travel, invitations to opening receptions, acknowledgement by governing bodies of good work etc., can all be used to improve morale and motivate staff. They will work better than financial incentives and last a great deal longer.

As an effective manager you should be constantly motivating your team and this is best done by having an awareness of what is going on, caring about the people who work for you and taking the trouble to know about them (their families and their problems), letting it be known openly that you are happy to encourage career advancement at all levels in your organisation, and a willingness to communicate freely at all levels with the people who work for you. I once heard a comedian say that 'sincerity is the hardest thing to fake'; this joke has a strong element of truth. If your staff believe you to be insincere (which they will if you are) you will have little chance of motivating them to perform well. Your task as a manager is to achieve results through people and to do this you must understand the intricacies of human relations. You must also be able to choose and develop a team to work for you.

4

Choosing your team

Most of us are quietly confident that we can assess people. We like to believe that we are good judges of character. Unfortunately, it is a fact that we tend to judge people on the basis of characteristics that we actually invent for them. This is human nature for it is often difficult for us to stand back and view individuals impartially, and without making judgements which are based on our own experience and learned behaviour. Because of this the traditional method of choosing people is flawed. The method commonly used is to advertise, sift applications, interview, select and appoint.

All these elements are a necessary part of recruitment but they are notoriously unreliable and can be an ineffective way of choosing a team. We should look at any areas that might be refined to offer us an opportunity of recruiting the best possible person. For this we must have a systematic approach for choosing people who will, hopefully, become the 'tools' of our own effectiveness.

Normally, when a vacancy occurs we merely advertise the fact based on the work done by the previous person occupying the position. If you do this you miss an important opportunity to redefine the task and think afresh about the job that needs to be done. The first part of the recruitment process should not be to dash off a job description, advertise the position and wait for responses. To be effective we should attack the problem of recruitment of our team in a more structured way.

RECRUITMENT PROCEDURE

Decide what the job needs

The first question we should ask ourselves is whether the job is actually necessary at all. This is particularly important in museums and galleries where a job has been occupied for many years and a person retires. It may well be that the job, as it has been done for so long, is no longer appropriate. If this is the case we may wish to change the direction of the financial resources we are currently putting into the employment of the person filling that position and create something totally different which has a greater relevance to the work being done by the museum today. So, the question of whether the job actually needs to be done should be the first thing we ask ourselves. If not, we can then think of a different job to apply the resources to, or consider whether we can apply the resources to something else within the museum which has equal or more priority. If we decide that the vacancy or another job actually needs to be filled the next step is to analyse it. For this we should analyse the job systematically and there are various checks we can carry out to achieve this:

1   *The key words approach*

    We should ask ourselves:

    What is done?

    When it is done?

    Why it is done?

    How it is done?

2   *Responsibilities*

    Responsibility for subordinates, equipment, plant, materials and money.

3   *Working relationships*

    Relationships with superiors, colleagues, other departments and the public.

4   *Job requirements*

    Required standard of performance and results, skills and experience, intelligence, education and training, physique and health, motivation and social skills.

5   *Working conditions*

    Physical conditions and surroundings, social conditions and the working group. Economic conditions, including pay.

6   *Check-up*

    Check back with the job holder and the job holder's superior.[1]

Having used this checklist we should have a comprehensive appreciation of exactly what the job is supposed to do for our organisation, how it is done, the manner in which it is done and the relationship it has with the organisation in general. We can also sketch out in our minds the type of person best suited to the job. Alternatively there are psychometric and other systems available which will analyse the job and characterise the ideal job holder for us scientifically.

Describe the job

Having analysed the job it is then (and only then) necessary to write a description which looks at the tasks, responsibilities and accountabilities that comprise the job. Job descriptions are an essential administrative tool of management and, whilst they should not be too detailed, they should include all the important aspects of the job which can be used to assess performance against requirements. Every organisation should have a master list of job descriptions which describes the jobs of every person employed. This should be regularly examined and updated according to changing circumstances – always in consultation with the people doing the job.

Describe the person for the job

Having analysed and described the job we now need to look at the sort of person who will be appropriate to fill the vacancy. This person may then be recruited internally or externally but, in either case, we should know as much as we can about the sort of person we need before we go through the process of selection. There are two helpful models available to us to compile the personnel specification. The first is the seven point plan.[2]

1 *Physique, health and appearance*
   (a) What are the requirements in terms of physique and health?
   (b) Are height, build, hearing, eyesight and general health relevant, and in what way?
   (c) What are the occupational requirements in terms of appearance?
   (d) Are factors such as looks, grooming, dress, voice, relevant?

2 *Attainments*

   These refer to the knowledge and skills required to do the job covering such factors as:
   (a) The level of general education required.
   (b) Any specific job training that is necessary.
   (c) Any experience of similar work which is relevant or required.

3 *General intelligence*
   (a) What levels of mental ability are necessary?
   (b) Can these be defined with specific accuracy by the use of relevant intelligence tests?
   (c) Are general definitions of quickness, accuracy, comprehension etc. sufficient instead of (b)?

4 *Special aptitudes*
   (a) Does the job demand any special factors and, if so, to what extent?
   (b) Is mechanical aptitude desired?
   (c) Manual dexterity?
   (d) Verbal ability?

(e) Numeracy?

(f) Are there tests available which are relevant to this post and which could be used to assess these special needs?

5 *Interests*

(a) How far are any leisure interests relevant to the job? These could include intellectual activities, practical interests (building, repairing, physical activities, sports etc., social interests (public speaking for example) or artistic interests (music, drama, painting).

6 *Disposition*

(a) How acceptable should the successful candidate be to other employees and at what levels?

(b) What capacity is required for leadership, or influencing and persuading others?

(c) What importance is attached to steadiness and dependability, and to independent thought and action?

7 *Circumstances*

Could the personal circumstances of the individual be relevant to the job?

(a) What domestic commitments are there?

(b) What degree of mobility is there?

(c) How near does he/she live to work?

(d) Would he/she be ready/able to work irregular hours?

The second is a model personnel specification an example of which is shown in Fig. 6.

We now know what the job is (the job analysis) what it entails (the job description) and the sort of person we require to fill it (the personnel specification). We should also look at the context (or environment) in which the job will be done. This is that part of the museum to which the job is attached and the people who already work in it. The person you select must not only have the skills and attributes to do the job well (or the potential to acquire those skills and attributes) but should also fit comfortably into the working context. You should not ignore the context. Consider how the person will fit into the organisation before the interview in order that you have some idea of the type of person that is needed. Inviting potential interviewees to attend the museum to 'look around' does not only furnish them with information about your organisation but will also give you an insight (from the comments of the staff they meet) as to their suitability with regard to fitting in.

Advertising for the job

Having got this far we can now go about the process of recruitment which traditionally has meant placing an advertisement in professional journals and other publications. However, this is not the only way of obtaining candidates

A.   **Physical Attributes**

Minimum:
Good health record
Few absences from work
Tidy appearance
No significant disabilities

Desirable:
Excellent health record
Smart appearance
Creates good impression on others
Capable of working for long hours under pressure

B.   **Mental Attributes**

Minimum:
Top 30% (A/B Grade) for:
General intelligence
Verbal ability
Numerical ability

Desirable
Top 10% (A Grade) for:
General intelligence
Verbal ability
Numerical ability

C.   **Education and Qualifications**

Minimum:
5 GCSE subjects (including grade C in Maths and English)

Desirable:
1st Degree in Science
Diploma in Management Studies

D.   **Experience Training and Skill**

Minimum:
5 years' experience in museum or gallery, including responsibility for up to £50,000 budget.
2 years' experience of supervising a small office or section.
Ability to write good reports and to understand basic financial information.

Desirable:
10 years' experience in a similar job, including responsibility for up to £150,000 budget.
Successful record of supervising qualified staff.
Good social skills.
Successful completion of a reputable management training course.
Ability to plan, organise, co-ordinate and control work under pressure.

E.   **Personality**

Minimum:
Motivated to achieve middle management status.
Stable personality.
Career record shows ability to adjust to normal circumstances.

Desirable:
Motivated to achieve senior management status.
Mature and stable personality.
Socially well adjusted.
Able to communicate at all levels.

F.   **Special Circumstances**

Minimum:
Aged between 28 and 55 years.
Able to work overtime and at weekends.

Desirable:
Aged between 32 and 50 years.
Willing to work long hours when required, and travel throughout UK.

and is often too expensive for the smaller museum to undertake. There are other ways apart from advertising. You should, of course, look at internal candidates although I would recommend that internal applicants should always be put into competition with people from outside, otherwise standards within an institution can slowly drop over a period of time. You should look at introductions and personal recommendations and your own data bank of previous applications which should be kept up to date. Job Centres should not be forgotten and the Appointment Boards of universities, and further education colleges, coupled with careers counsellors may be consulted. All these alternative methods to the highly speculative advertisement process (which is so favoured) should be considered.

Having decided to recruit, and the method by which recruitment should take place, we should construct an advertisement and an information sheet. If you have little experience in putting together recruitment advertisements there are a number of pitfalls you can fall into; read the advertising pages of, say, the *Museums Journal* to see where mistakes have been made. The following is a list of elements which you should consider for inclusion in any advert you place for a vacancy in your museum.

1 Job title.
2 (a) The name of your museum/gallery.
  (b) The nature of its collections/themes etc..
  (c) The location of the job.
3 (a) The nature and responsibilities of the job.
  (b) The title of the person to whom the job holder would be accountable.
4 (a) The qualifications required.
  (b) The experience expected.
5 The age range (if relevant)
6 (a) The salary or salary range.
  (b) Any fringe benefits.
7 Genuine promotion prospects.
8 The manner in which the application should be made (e.g., write or telephone for an application form etc.).
9 The closing date for the application.

You may not wish to include all these elements in your advertisement but I am sure you can pick out those that are essential. It is often very helpful to insist that potential applicants write to the museum requesting an application form to which you can add further details of the job. This information sheet can be more comprehensive as the constraints of advertising space do not

Figure 6 Example of personnel specification

have to be taken into account. Remember that the information supplied in the advertisement, and in the information and/or application form, can form part of the employment contract and, therefore, you should not exaggerate or make the job out to be something which it is not. Do not forget there is legislation to which you must conform when recruiting and employing personnel. You should also remember that your recruitment process is also providing a very public arena for your museum. If your approach to recruitment is professional it will show, if it is shoddy it will damage your museum's reputation and probably put off potential applicants for the job.

THE SELECTION PROCEDURE

The paper sift

It is common for vacancies in museum curatorial jobs to be heavily over-subscribed and recent experience has shown that for a single such vacancy it is not unknown to receive hundreds of applications. You should therefore have a process set up to deal with the initial sifting of applications and some form of pro forma (such as the personnel specification referred to earlier) which will allow you to methodically process the applications to a short list. Your position in management will determine whether this job is delegated or is carried out by you personally. This decision will also depend on your need to ensure your team is built up effectively, particularly in the initial stages following your transition from operator to manager. It may well be in these early stages that you would wish to take part in the complete selection process of all members of your team until the team is established and you can delegate appropriately. If this is the case, you will understand that this element of your management task is an essential operating function for the time being.

The sifting of applications can be a laborious job but it is important and you should understand that there are a number of factors which will influence you, both positively and negatively, towards a candidate; some may not be relevant. The neatness of the application: you may immediately be put off by an application which is illegible or, conversely, you may be wholly impressed by an extremely well prepared application with a copious curriculum vitae attached in a professionally bound folder. It is natural to be swayed towards one and away from the other, but do persevere through even the illegible applications for the content may reveal just the sort of person you are looking for. The presentation is important but the lack of it may not necessarily signify a low quality application. It will not always be possible to sift down an enormous number of applications to a manageable figure for interview purposes but you should endeavour to shortlist no more than six people for final interview in a single day with, perhaps, a further six as standbys should candidates drop out.

THE SELECTION INTERVIEW

Getting ready

Preparation is all important. Some weeks prior to the interview you should select those people who will assist you on the interview panel. If you are the line manager with direct responsibility for the person being appointed you should be present at the interview and you should ensure there is an independent person (i.e. not in your department) to assist you. If the work requires specialist knowledge you should have a specialist present who can judge the candidates accordingly. The ideal number of people present for the interview is three. Each person should have, in advance of the interview, full details of the applicants (their application forms, CVs etc.), a copy of the personnel specification, and some form of rating sheet (see p. 66) which should be devised to assess candidates uniformly and impartially during the interview. I will return to this sheet for it is important. All these documents should be in the hands of the interviewers in advance and they should use them to prepare any questions or areas of questioning they wish to put forward at the interview itself. You prepare the venue to ensure that both the interviewers and the interviewees are comfortable, that the timetable for the interviews is manageable, and the interviewees are properly hosted and kept apart. Interviewing for jobs, in most cases, is confidential and it is not appropriate for the other interviewees to meet the people with whom they are competing. Refreshments should be available for the interview board and these should be timed to coincide with a break in the interviewing. Time should be set aside prior to the first interview for the board to discuss the format of the sessions, and at the end to discuss their decisions. The layout of the room should be carefully considered to convey either a formal or informal interview situation. Using a table and chairs or, conversely, armchairs or a sofa conveys a totally different impression to the interviewee and, whilst one is no more appropriate than the other, you must decide which is the most appropriate for your purpose.

When the interviewers meet, the Chairperson should brief them on the format of the interview and ask them for any areas which they wish to cover with the candidates. You should also have prepared a series of administrative elements which the Chairperson must ensure are conveyed to the candidate. These will usually include salary (or salary range, which could be a point of discussion with the candidate), terms and conditions of service, annual leave, period of notice needed to be given by the candidate if the job is offered to him/her, and other aspects of purely routine or administrative purpose. The Chairperson should inform the other interviewers that he/she will conduct the interview in a specific format and will call upon them to ask questions when appropriate, and agree with them the content and format of their questions. Each person should know what the other is going to ask and which areas they are going to cover. The Chairperson's responsibility is to ensure that all the necessary factors which need to be drawn out to assist the candidate in 'selling' themselves are undertaken. As soon as everything is clear and the interviewers are properly prepared the first candidate can be brought in for interview.

Conducting the interview

The Chairperson should immediately attempt to put the candidate at ease but interviewers should understand that, invariably, candidates are nervous of this rather unreal situation. The Chairperson should commence the proceedings by outlining to the candidate how the interview will be undertaken and that the candidate will be asked questions by the interviewers after which the candidate will be given the opportunity to ask questions of the interviewers. The interview should be kept as informal as possible in such an unreal situation and everything should be done to assist the candidate to bring out the best in himself/herself in as succinct a manner as possible. The Chairperson should be skilled in his/her ability to draw information from the candidate. There is always a tendency for an unskilled interviewer to talk more than the candidate being interviewed and this must be avoided at all costs. The point of the exercise is to allow the candidate to explain or tell the interview board why he/she is the appropriate person for the job. It is up to the Chairperson to ensure fairness and that the same opportunities are given to all candidates. Initial questioning can be based on the candidate's application and questions should be asked which are of a non-controversial nature. These are intended to put the candidate at ease and allow him/her to relax. Careful watch should be kept of the time given to each candidate in order that the programme of interviewing is not compromised by an overrun causing less attention to be paid to one of the later candidates being interviewed. The timetable should be kept under control and a short gap between each interview arranged for the panel to privately (this is most important) write any relevant notes about the candidate previously interviewed. I strongly recommend that a discussion about the candidate's interview is not undertaken between interviews and that the assessment of a candidate's performance is written down independently on the rating sheet after the interview, but no general discussion takes place until the end of the whole session. This is to provide fairness, for if an interviewer has a strong opinion about a candidate he/she could communicate this to one of the other interviewers in advance of all of the candidates having been seen. This could have a detrimental affect on the rest of the interviewing and could provide an imbalance in the impartiality between the interviews.

Drawing the interview to a close

It is the Chairperson's job to monitor the progress of the interview and, particularly, the time involved. Even if the interview is a struggle and it is obvious to all concerned that the person being interviewed is not a candidate for the job they should be given every opportunity over the predetermined period of time to promote themselves to the interviewers. Interviews should not be cut short (unless it is unavoidable) because a person is patently not a suitable candidate for the job; persevere regardless, to ensure impartiality and fairness. When he/she has determined that there are only ten minutes or so left of the interview session, the Chairperson should decisively yet courteously draw the interview to a close by telling the candidate that the interviewers have asked a great number of questions and has the candidate anything to ask of them? Following this element of the interview the Chairperson should close the interview by informing the candidate of the procedure which will be used to inform all those who have been interviewed of the results. In practice, all candidates should be told that the museum will write to them with their answer within a specific time-scale. I recommend that this should be done within a week of the interview. The Chairperson should gather details from the candidate as to the period of notice he/she will require to give to their current employer and any other details such as annual leave which is already booked. Finally he/she should confirm, once again, the salary and conditions which are being offered and ask the candidate whether he/she would accept the job if it were offered. When all this has been done the candidate should be thanked and shown the door.

Judgement

It is only after all the interviews have taken place that the interviewers should consider the candidates as a group. During each session the individual interviewers should complete the rating sheet as an aide mémoire to them for their consideration when the judgement takes place. It is often very difficult to remember the details of an interview undertaken by a candidate in the morning when you have been interviewing for a whole day and are tired at the end. Therefore, the notes taken during each interview are particularly important before the selection can actually take place. I therefore recommend that a rating sheet such as that in Fig. 7 is used.[3]

As can be seen from Fig. 7, the rating sheet is relatively brief but gives sufficient space to the interviewer in order that he/she can remember various points of the interview which occurred to him/her at the time. The pen picture is particularly important and the initial recommendation as to whether the person is qualified (or not qualified) for the job is extremely important. The fact that you have said that a person is not qualified at the time that they are interviewed is quite crucial some six or seven hours later when you are assessing that person as a member of a panel. From your assessment, as it appears on the rating sheet, you will be able to remember other elements of the candidate's performance and discuss those with your colleagues and come to a decision regarding the appointment. It is possible for candidates, in certain circumstances, to appeal or complain following an interview if they are not given the job. Proper records and an adherence to fair procedures is important in this respect.

Candidate's Name (Mr/Mrs/Miss/Ms) _____ Age _____

Date of interview _____ for appointment as _____

Please tick the appropriate boxes:

	X applies	Tendency to X	Average	Tendency to Y	Y applies	
1. Neat and tidy in appearance						Has not bothered about appearance
2. Good powers of expression						Fails to make meaning clear
3. Quick on the uptake						Slow to grasp the point
4. Follows discussion easily						Has difficulty in understanding
5. Has made the most of opportunities						Inclined to drift along
6. Has well developed interests						Interest shallow or superficial

PEN PICTURE

Please note below aspects of performance or personality not covered above, e.g.: persistence, ability to get on with people, maturity, willingness to work, motivation for seeking employment/promotion. Mention any special qualifications or experience and comment, if necessary, on the candidate's suitability for particular departments or types of work. If the candidate is considered unsuitable for a particular type of work please give reasons. Where a candidate is marked 'NQ' the Chairman should indicate the candidate's strong and weak points and, the reasons why he/she is considered less suitable than those recommended for appointment. It may be necessary to refer to these comments later, in the event of an appeal or complaint.

Member's Initial
Recommendation
(Please tick box)

Agreed Board Mark

WQ = Well Qualified ☐
Q+ = Qualified plus ☐
Q = Qualified ☐
NQ = Not yet Qualified ☐

Signature _____
Name _____
Date _____

Figure 7 Example of a rating sheet

The Chairperson should control the discussion and ensure that the agreed consensus of the interview board is transmitted into an offer of appointment. If there is more than one person considered to be qualified to undertake the job it may be necessary to score the successful candidates in order of preference. Be sure to do this, and to contact the preferred candidate as soon as possible to ascertain whether they will accept the job if it is offered. Do not write to the other shortlisted candidates telling them that the job has been filled until you have a letter of confirmation from the successful candidate that he/she will take the job.

POINTS TO CONSIDER IN INTERVIEWING

It is a normal human trait to make judgements about other human beings based on how they appear to you and your initial reaction to them when first meeting them. Research has shown that many people are chosen for a job the moment they walk in the door of the interview room regardless of what they actually say or do at the interview. You must guard against this for it is hardly a scientific way of choosing your team. Conversely, you should not allow your superficial attitude to the way a person looks or acts to cloud your judgement and preclude you from making a fair assessment of that person based on their answers to questions during the interview itself. Always ask yourself whether you have done this, for it may well be that you chose a person more for their looks, their attitude or their personality, than you did for their qualifications, experience or ability to perform at interview.

It is also, unfortunately, the case that some people perform well at interview and others do not. Bear in mind that the person who interviews well may not be the best person for the job and the person who interviews badly may be ideal. You are not testing people on their interview technique, you are trying to determine whether they will be the best person for the job you have available.

As has previously been mentioned, if possible, ask candidates to turn up for interview an hour or so before the designated time in order that they can look at the place where they are to work if they are successful in their application, and to meet some of the people with whom they will be working. You should not ignore the context and environment within which your team are working. In order to do this you should assign one of the people in your department the task of showing the candidates around. Before making their final decision, the interview board can then speak to that member of your staff to determine his/her opinion of the candidates. You will be surprised to find that in most cases the interview panel's decision regarding the appointment (and it is their decision, not your staff's) will be very similar.

Always remember that interviews should never be confrontational. The object of the exercise is to draw out from the candidate as much information as you can to determine whether he/she is the best person for the job. Do not assume

67

that because the person has many attributes which are valuable you can change those which are patently and obviously negative. It is very difficult to change people and this will be your only opportunity to ensure that the right person is selected. You should not tell yourself that it doesn't really matter if you get it wrong because the person will be on probation for some months and you can always get rid of them afterwards. This is totally wrong, very expensive and not fair. In difficult cases where you feel that you are almost sure of a candidate, but wish to explore even more deeply, do not hesitate to call the person back for a second interview prior to making the appointment. Time spent carefully selecting candidates to join your team is time well spent for you, as an effective manager, are only as good as the people who work for you.

NOTES

1 Systematic job analysis from *Managing Human Resources* by A. G. Cowling and C. J. B. Mailer (1981).
2 The Seven Point Plan was devised by Prof. Alec Rodger (1952) and published by the National Institute of Industrial Psychology.
3 Reproduced with permission of the Royal Air Force Museum, Hendon.

5

Developing staff

An effective manager is only as good as his/her team and the performance of the team materially affects the performance of the manager. It is therefore in the interests of the manager to ensure that his/her team is developed to its full potential. We should therefore be aware of the importance and intentions of staff appraisal. Lip-service is often paid to this area of management and the normal view of members of the team is that staff appraisal is little more than a continuation of the end of term reports inflicted on children at school. The effective manager needs to communicate to his/her team that staff appraisal is valuable and important and will improve not only the manager's effectiveness but also the career and aspirations of the individual appraisee. The intentions of an appraisal scheme should be to evaluate the job being done and the person doing it. It should be a method of auditing what is going on within the organisation and within the individual jobs that make up the organisation's structure.

The appraisal scheme should also enable managers to construct succession plans. Succession plans are sadly lacking within the museum and gallery world and there is no clear appreciation amongst museum professionals of the need to ensure that successors are groomed for eventual promotion. Within your own organisation you should be able to identify those people with the potential for promotion (through the appraisal scheme) and then ensure they are prepared appropriately. This will be done (and the appraisal scheme will identify it) by discovering the training needs of individuals. With the recent creation of the Museum Training Institute and the consequential review of museum training throughout the profession (at all levels), the opportunities for training are more widespread than in the past. Effective managers will take advantage of this and ensure people subordinate to them (and they themselves where necessary) are provided with the training that is necessary not only to carry out their immediate function but also to be a more cohesive part of the museum profession as a whole. The Museums and Galleries Commission has recommended that a sum of money equal to 2 per cent of the salary budget should be set aside by each museum every year for training of staff. If we could but aspire to half this amount we would be doing a lot better than we are at present. Training your team is essential and does not mean, as is so often considered to be the case, that you will be improving your staff to such a degree that you will lose them. This may well be the case as they progress through their career in the museum profession but the attitude of not allowing them to be trained in order that they stay in your organisation is not only old-fashioned but wholly inequitable. Your attitude should be that you must develop staff to their full potential and if you lose them the museum profession as a whole benefits and you may, in the future, receive them back at a higher position in your organisation but more highly experienced and trained.

Appraisal schemes also provide an important motivating influence on members of staff. The appraisal interview is one of the few occasions when you are talking (one to one) with a member of your staff about him/her personally rather than about the job or the organisation generally. It is your opportunity to delve more deeply into what motivates that person to work, their goals and aspirations and what, to them, is the real world. As a result of the appraisal scheme you will therefore not only be able to motivate staff, but also develop them as individuals. Your function as a manager is to manage your resources effectively and this can only be done by having highly developed individuals working for you. An appraisal scheme will also allow you to check the effectiveness of your personnel procedures and practices. It will allow you to monitor those line managers beneath you, and your own performance. You should be aware that it is an occasion for the worker to be critical of management as well as management to be critical of the worker. By criticism I mean positive and negative constructive criticism about a variety of work-related and non-work related areas. Most appraisal schemes in museums consist of an annual appraisal review which takes place between the manager and the subordinate. This is merely reinforcing the 'school report' thinking. Appraisals should mean that managers and subordinates meet regularly for discussion of the subordinate's job, job changes, successes and difficulties. It should also include the aspirations of the individual and his/her needs and concerns in relation to work. The precise subject-matter must be established by both parties, not imposed by the senior person. The discussion that then ensues will probably take as its basic theme: What can we do to discover what has happened in the last year (month, week etc.) to discover why these things have happened and what can be done to resolve difficulties or to build on strengths?

The focus, in short, is on two people attempting to resolve problems, both contributing to the discussion and the solution. The aim should be to make the subordinate's job more effective and more satisfactory, and to allow both parties to air their views and their feelings. From this will follow the opportunity to raise productivity and ensure more effective work flowing from the individual which will, in turn, increase the effectiveness of the manager. Every appraisal interview should be conducted with a view to developing staff and building on their strengths by discovering their weaknesses and helping them to resolve problems. This starts from the first moment a member of staff joins your team.

INDUCTION

Induction of a new employee (or new member of the team who might not, necessarily, be new to the organisation) should be a high priority from the first day. As an effective manager, whatever your level, you should make a point of meeting every new person who joins your organisation or your group. This is the start of a relationship which will be built up over the whole of your working life with the person and should include an attempt on your part to find out what makes that person different from everyone else. The belief that everybody is working to the same goals, we have already learned, is misconceived. If you understand more about the person who works for you than just the work that they carry out, you will be at an advantage in your ability to develop them to their true potential. There is also a requirement to introduce a member of staff to the procedures of your organisation or group and a legal requirement to ensure that they are aware of any health and safety regulations and other details which apply. Procedural matters need to be dealt with and you should have a well documented induction system in place. In 1983 the Advisory, Conciliation, and Arbitration Service (ACAS) produced an interesting booklet, *Induction of New Employees*, which can be helpful in this area.

DEVELOPMENT

There are various methods of development which should be considered. The new employee may well be 'thrown in at the deep end' or assigned to an experienced member of staff in order that they can initially learn 'on the job'. This is rarely sufficient for all groups of staff, particularly the professional or curatorial areas. You may well wish to introduce guided practice in certain areas or lay on demonstrations for inexperienced staff members to discover how other elements of work within the museum are carried out. To assist in this you might wish to set up discussion groups or organised question and answer sessions, supplemented by guided reading. These approaches can only, in most cases, be tentative and a more proactive response is needed from effective managers. Further methods should be considered.

Work rotation

To fully develop members of staff you should understand that it is inappropriate to assign a young or inexperienced person to a single job which does not give him/her the opportunity to assimilate the workings of the organisation or group as a whole. By rotating inexperienced members of staff throughout the group or organisation you will enable them to gain a better appreciation of the overall working rather than the narrow confines of their own specific function. You can rotate work within a group in order that all members of the group carry out different elements of the job to provide departmental or group results. This will have a number of benefits. It will give the person a wider range of experience within the work group and a greater knowledge of the abilities, constraints and mechanics of the work done by others within the group. It will also ensure that you identify the strengths and weaknesses of the individual and take appropriate measures to even them out.

Job rotation

Job rotation is different to work rotation in that it often means the person is taken out of the work group and assigned to other areas which do not just include a different method of work but also a different function (i.e. job). This is useful for the same reasons that work rotation is useful but it also enables the effective manager to concentrate resources on priorities. For example, you may have an exhibition project which demands considerable staff time in order that it can be carried out in an abbreviated time-scale. The elements of the task include skills from various work groups which must be combined into a 'task force' specifically charged with this single project. In the case of an exhibition this may well be design, research, curatorial, conservation, security and marketing. By bringing together workers from all these groups, and giving them the specific job of completing a project within a time-scale, adds a new dimension to their everyday work. It has its problems, which I will come to later when we talk about matrix structures within organisations but, in many cases, the benefits of developing the people who form the task force greatly outweigh the possible problems which can arise.

Planned work programmes

If necessary, to develop a person who is not realising their full potential and who has problems, it may be necessary to introduce planned work programmes. These will provide a structure (including targets) which can be regularly appraised and discussed with the subordinate. This is a way of structuring the work of an individual who has shown that he/she has found it difficult to cope.

Secondments

If your organisation does not have the resources or the opportunities to develop individuals in the way in which you, as an effective manager, believe they should be developed you may consider arranging for individuals to be seconded to another group or organisation which can fulfil the areas which you perceive are missing within your group. These secondments may be from institution to institution, from department to department or from work group to work group.

Special assignments/projects

If you have identified that an individual could be developed more appropriately by tailoring an assignment or project specifically for him/her you should ensure that the project has a relevance to the organisation and to the work which is going on within the work group from which the individual comes.

COACHING

Part of the development of staff is to ensure that there is constant coaching by management (at whatever level). Coaching is important but can never be systematic because it consists essentially of spotting opportunities as they arise. Regrettably, coaching is usually carried out as a result of something going wrong but, in fact, should be part of everyday management. The skilled and experienced manager knows that coaching is part of his/her everyday interface with subordinates. It should, in most cases, be extremely subtle and should not take the form of the manager saying 'this is how you do this job – watch me'. A manager's function is to constantly ask questions and to query actions. This should be done in a sensitive manner in order that the person being questioned believes there is value to the process and that he/she will be better enabled to carry out the job more effectively as a result. Good managers know that they are coaching their staff nearly all the time in one way or another. Staff will only respond to such coaching if they know that the manager is capable of doing the job to a high standard and has a track record which proves that he/she knows what they are talking about. The old adage of 'do as I say not as I do', does not work in management. Managers are not respected for their ability to find fault but for their ability to accept that faults will occur and that they have a sympathetic and unerring patience with people they know are doing their best.

Coaching is also an important motivator in the sense that it can be used as a reward system. If we accept that it should not only be carried out when something goes wrong but should be a part of everyday management, we must also accept that we should be coaching when things go right. When things do go right, our acknowledgement (i.e. the reward) that we know things have been done well can be supplemented by coaching to develop the subject and give the worker motivation to do well in equal measure next time. It may also be the case that something goes right even though the job has not been particularly well done. In these circumstances coaching takes the form of congratulations on the work being done well but is supplemented by subtle and sympathetic guidance as to how, in future, the job could be equally well done but in a slightly different way. Managers should understand that they cannot criticise people for doing work differently if they themselves have not ensured that the person doing the job is equipped (i.e. properly trained) or coached in the first place.

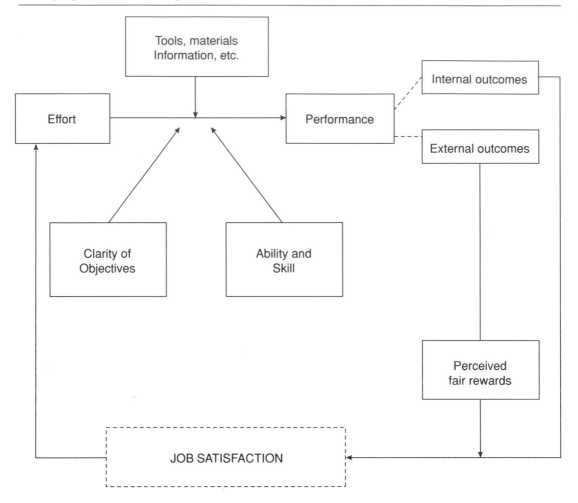

Figure 8 Factors affecting motivation

Before leaving the subject of managing people I would like to re-emphasise the relationship between factors effecting motivation. There are similarities between this relationship and the complex control loop (Fig. 5) that we discussed in the previous chapter. The control loop has standards, a way of measuring output, a way of comparing this with the standards and a way of taking action to reduce any discrepancy. When we look at the relationship between the factors affecting motivation as seen in Fig. 8 we can see that the standard can be termed as 'perceived fair rewards' and an implied comparison, generating job satisfaction and a feedback loop to 'effort' allowing it to be modified so as to reduce discrepancy. This is a control loop serving the goals of an individual and therefore is ultimately flexible and can be affected by our skill and experience in management. The links between outcomes, rewards, satisfaction and effort are all circular and the resulting performance producing the required output or (if poor performance), a lack of output, can be materially altered with careful management. By careful management I mean the understanding of why the individual works, what the goals of the individual are, what the real world is to the individual and the way in which the individual carries out his/her duties. In the most simplified format the old adage of 'treating people as you would be treated yourself' is fundamental to my argument that the effective manager is the person who sees an individual for what he/she is; a person with needs and aspirations and who will respond if those needs and aspirations are understood and in some way satisfied.

Your job, as an effective manager of people, is to ensure that you are aware of all the factors which will bear on a person's perception of fair rewards, their dissatisfaction with their job, the amount of effort they put in and their performance. This can only be achieved by careful selection of candidates, induction of people when they join the organisation (or your working group), appraisal of their performance on an ongoing and dynamic basis, and the development of them as individuals. This is not something which you should put aside and do as a chore on an annual basis. It should be something which you are aware of each day of your working life and something you practise constantly in your interface with the people who work for you. Managing people is merely ensuring that humanity is retained in the workplace.

6

Communication

It is important for managers to convey ideas and feelings in the clearest possible terms and, thus, communication is essential for effective management. Communication should have no unexpected surprises in interpretation and is formed with or without the use of words – words can only have a meaning with a context. By whatever method – verbal, written, electronic or non-verbal – a message is communicated. The basis of communication is a dialogue transmitted from a 'sender' to a 'receiver' and returned from the receiver to the sender. Thus, in its simplest terms, communication is a constantly rotating medium in which messages are transmitted and received, and where the receiver is the transmitter and vice versa. Managers need to manage the whole communication process across all levels and barriers. You need to be able to communicate to:

1   Your supervisor, manager, governing body or Board of Trustees.

2   Your colleagues, seeking advice, information or co-operation.

3   Your team, where the manager controls the flow of information between himself/herself and the team; between team members; controlling their perceptions of the team, the job, each other, and their leader. The leader also controls the flow of information into and out of the team.

4   Managers. You need to relate to other individuals, groups etc. These may be your suppliers, your customers/visitors, your professional colleagues or other organisations; to trade unions, to adults and children, to the understanding and those who cannot understand.

There are various ways of communicating. Managers and staff at all levels communicate to tell, to ask and to advise. You do this to influence how others understand an aspect of work. You may do it to control staff attitudes towards their work and thus the behavioral aspects of their performance. At all levels, the manager needs to check that the message sent is the same as the message received, also that it is appropriate and equivalent to the message which he/she meant to send in the first place.

Communication can be used as a motivator to clearly establish at the outset goals, targets and performance. This performance will be monitored and the manager can maintain a watching brief of staff achievement and thus appraise, appreciate or criticise performance, attitudes, and achievements on an immediate basis rather than the more usual piecemeal or irregular basis.

We can therefore see that the four main types of communication are to inform; instruct or advise; motivate and encourage; seek information. Let us have a look at these in detail for they are extremely important to your ability to manage effectively.

1 To inform is to give facts and information at varying levels of detail.

2 To instruct or to advise is a more specific mode. You are looking to change people's behaviour, to control and influence specific actions or areas of their action. You must delegate within clear limits which will define succinctly to your subordinates exactly what their task, responsibility and ability should be, and from which you will be able to appraise their work effectively.

3 Motivation, if correctly driven, will change the attitudes of the people who work for you towards better performance, to gain a positive change of behaviour to do (or to cease to do) something.

4 Seeking information is a vital role in any manager's ability to communicate and is so often disregarded. Managers should ask questions, they should seek information, and the good manager should be in control of the depth and area of information sought. Without limiting the vital information flow, managers should also listen, show non-verbal signs of receptivity, and wait. Often an initial response is glib, but will be followed by more in depth, probing and realistic opinion.

Each mode of communication has a different combination of needs and responses. Instruction can also motivate, and seeking information shows receptivity. A manager must know why the communication process is initiated, for what purposes it is being used and what response (without unduly blinkering that response) is needed.

It is important to understand that managers do not always initiate the communication process but as communication is a two-way dialogue, and the manager is often at the receiving end, he/she should use it to his/her advantage. In this way he/she can be informed of what is going on within his/her group or organisation, use that information to instruct, counsel, encourage, and turn what often seems essentially a one-way form of communication (through his/her own ability to feedback) into proper communication which is always two-way. However, as the receiver of communication from subordinates and superiors, the effective manager must be aware of the hidden agenda behind the others' communication, as he/she should (and surely must) be aware of his/her own hidden agenda in any communication which he/she initiates. It is essential, and I emphasise this again, that the manager is aware always of the true purpose of his/her communication.

Your staff will communicate with you to influence your decision-making. This means that they will try to distort facts and may not reveal the true picture. They may promote themselves with their communication and make you aware of all those things you should use to praise them but none of the things which would ensure a critical response from you. Depending on your leadership qualities (a subject we will deal with in Chapter 7) your staff may communicate with you to embarrass you, or even to bolster your own self-esteem. Communication can also be used as a method of drawing you away from an anxiety about their work or even a method of reverse delegation wherein they pass work back to you – beware the player manager syndrome (see Chapter 2).

You should not take communication from your staff at just the base level. You should look at the context as well as the content, and the stated and the hidden agenda. Communication of all types of information, instruction and motivation (or information seeking) should be via clear, observable, measurable means and media. Communicating with silence is also a powerful tool. Non-verbal communication and the knowledge of it in people with whom you are communicating is an essential skill of management.

Before we attack the detail let us understand that, when we communicate we are conveying ideas and feelings. Such communication is essential to teamwork and unless a group of people are able to share these ideas and feelings with each other, they will be unable to operate, except as individuals. Each could only pursue his/her own purpose in his/her own way without influence or advice from others. So, in an area which is predominantly about communication (museums and galleries), part of our job will be to manage the communication process. You will need to communicate effectively with your team and you will need to be aware of, and influence where necessary, the flow of communication between your team members. For instance, what are they saying about the organisation, the job, one another and you?

Apart from subordinates you will also be communicating with your boss, with fellow managers (and with their subordinates on occasions) and, perhaps, with visitors/customers, suppliers, trade union officials and many others. It is interesting to think of just how many different types of people we communicate with each day. So, let us break down this important subject in even greater detail.

WHAT IS COMMUNICATION?

We have already seen that communication is the conveying of ideas and feelings. Communication in its simplest form is a telephone conversation or a fire-side chat. It can be a 'telling' process where you actually 'tell' someone something. 'Telling' can be done in writing, on the telephone (where tone of the voice may be part of the message), or face to face (where not only tone of voice but also gestures and facial expressions play their part).

However, communication is not just telling people things. Telling is a one-way process. You can tell somebody something, but they may not be listening. Even if they are listening, they may not understand you. Even if they understand you, they may not reply or give any indication that they have understood. In such cases you will have 'told' but not 'communicated'. The prefix 'co' in communication implies 'together', but if you get no response to what you are trying to convey, there is no togetherness about it. You do something to the other person but you have no idea whether it has had any effect. We can see the difference between telling and communicating with some simple diagrams.

Fig. 9 illustrates telling. It shows one person, the Sender (S) transmitting a message to another, the Target (T).

S ———————————— MESSAGE ————————————→ T

Figure 9 Simple one-way communication

We could depict the T as an R for (Receiver) but this assumes that our message has been received. You should always remember that even though you are talking to somebody and they are looking at you, they may not have noticed, understood or listened to you. Target is a better description until you actually make contact. You must always endeavour to turn your Target into a Receiver. To do this you will use what you know of the Target and his/her circumstances to put your messages in a form which is more likely to be received. For instance, if he/she is illiterate, you won't write him/her a note. If he/she speaks only French you won't speak to him/her in English. But if you want to know whether, and how well, your message has been received, you will need feedback. Your Target will have to do something. His/her feedback may be merely a nod or a wink, or a laugh or a scowl. If your Target repeats your message or makes some comment on it either in speech or in writing you will know he/she has received the message. Feedback is important. It enables us to redraw our simple diagram (see Fig. 10) and, at this stage, we are justified in replacing the T for Target with R for Receiver.

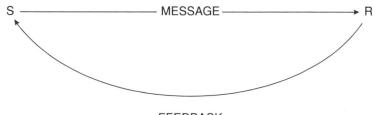

Figure 10 Partial communication

This is still only partial communication, we can see that some fuller form is possible. You have conveyed your ideas or feelings to the Receiver and he/she has acknowledged them. He/she may have asked you to clarify a point, or tell him/her more. This feedback enables you to reword or expand the message. But you are the chief communicator here; all your Receiver communicates, is information about the quality of *your* communication.

In many situations, this partial communication is sufficient. You give one of your team members an instruction and all you need is for him/her to say 'OK'. In another situation, however, this will not seem enough, either to you, your receiver or both of you. Very often, the feedback to your initial message will go beyond simply acknowledging it. It will contain so many of the Receiver's ideas and feelings that it becomes a message in its own right. The Receiver becomes a Sender and you have become the Target and, provided you are paying attention, Receiver as well (see Fig. 11).

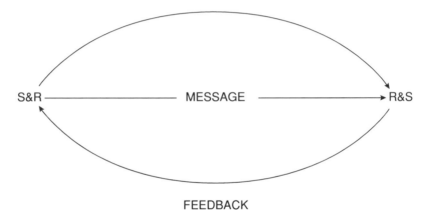

Figure 11 Full communication

In such *full* communication, you and the person are communicating with alternate roles. As soon as you have sent a message, you are ready to receive and, having received the message, it is your turn to send again. Neither party is only acknowledging the other's ideas or feelings but is also using them as a cue for expressing thoughts and feelings of his/her own. So, rather than simply asking, as you might do as a Sender 'has he/she understood?', you will also need to ask 'what does he/she mean, how does he/she feel?' Full communication is typical in conversations amongst friends and colleagues, and may also be expected in interviews and meetings. It can also occur in writing, albeit more slowly, with letters or memos going backwards and forwards.

So, activities that are normally lumped together under the name 'communication' really cover a wide range. Sometimes telling is where you express some idea or feeling but get no feedback that might signify whether or to what extent your message has been received. Then, with partial communication, you will get some feedback but only sufficient to allow you to check how accurately your message has been conveyed. Finally, with full communication, you not only get feedback about your own message, but you also receive messages from the other person.

I am not saying that telling is bad and that we should always strive for full communication. To do so would often be impractical and unnecessary. What I believe is that the difference is well worth noting, because many of the difficulties people experience with communication arise because they are operating in an inappropriate part of the range, for example, telling when they should be communicating fully. Usually this happens because they have not considered what kind of feedback is appropriate to their situation. Too much can be as bad as too little, and it is always possible to settle on the wrong kind of communication.

HOW WE COMMUNICATE

Because communication is the means we use to convey ideas and feelings to other people, it is useful to understand all the different ways by which we do this and in what context each is most appropriate. We have already said that communication is about words, even though gestures can often be equally eloquent but, we can also communicate without intending to or being aware of what it is that we are saying. We should also know that people may understand things from our words or actions (or lack of them) which we may not have in mind and have no intention of communicating to them. If we had them in mind we probably would not have wanted to communicate them to the other person anyway and thus a communication is taking place of which we have no knowledge. So, as effective managers, we must understand not only the process of communication but also the mechanics.

The spoken word

Speaking to one another is the most direct form of communication and there are a variety of ways of doing it, from the simple face-to-face conversation through to complex tele-conferencing techniques which are available these days.

The spoken word has its advantages and disadvantages and as an experienced manager you will learn to know when it is best to have a face-to-face conversation (rather than one, say, on the telephone) in order that you can see the precise effect of your words on the person you are talking to and amend them accordingly. On the other hand, if you want to avoid giving too much away you may prefer to use the telephone. You may even wish to communicate indirectly, on occasions, by doing so through your secretary or a person who works for you. Whatever method you use the amount of communication may well be the same, but the way in which it passes from sender to receiver could be quite different. Therefore you must ask yourself a few questions before you elect to choose one method over another in using the spoken word.

1   Which of the variety of methods of using the spoken word that are available to me will allow me to exert influence on the other people involved?

2   Which method of communication will allow me to acquire the type and amount (you may not want any) of feedback I desire?

3   By using which method am I most likely to obtain the information that I require from this form of communication?

Communicating using the spoken word can often seem more natural and less official than the written word, and it tends to encourage people to think that they have been personally asked for their opinion. It also enables you and those with whom you are communicating to read one another's non-verbal communication through gestures and facial expressions, and in so doing you will be able to share and compare one another's ideas and feelings. The spoken word also allows you to express your feelings more comprehensively than could ever be possible on paper and, at the same time, allows you to tailor your remarks to the responses of those with whom you are communicating and therefore put your message across more effectively.

The written word

There are also a wide variety of ways of communicating in writing, from notices on noticeboards, through memos and letters, to reports and articles, in-house journals or newsletters etc. With some of these the manager is more likely to be the receiver than the sender. Indeed, you may find yourself actually wondering what other people mean in their messages. With some types of written communication you may be both Sender and Receiver at different times, and you may have to exercise considerable ingenuity to discover the ideas and feelings of others who write to you. The written word has a tendency towards being used more for telling rather than full communication with feedback. The reason for this is that the sender cannot obtain immediate feedback from the target and he/she may not even know that the target has received the message. People often ignore written messages (especially if they are long, use jargon or are difficult to understand) or they read them hurriedly and either fail to see the main point or misunderstand it.

There are, however, a number of advantages to be had from communicating in writing. It enables you to be careful over how you phrase your words and gives you the ability to reshape your thoughts until you are quite satisfied with them and how they read on paper. It enables you to express your views, thoughts or feelings without the social pressure of having to cope with a response – either interruptive or immediate – from the people with whom you are communicating. It, most importantly, provides you with physical evidence of what you have said, how you have imparted information or instructions, advice or opinions to a particular person on a particular date. It provides an exact way of checking what was said to the person. This is especially important when you are determining whether your instructions have been carried out at some later date. It also allows you to circulate a number of people more cost-effectively than gathering them together for a meeting.

Non-verbal communication

Words are not the only way of sending messages. We all know that it is often not what we say, it is the way that we say it and the tone of voice can mean one thing when the words mean something totally different. We need to be aware of non-verbal communication and behaviour, for most people find it difficult to control the things they do not say. As effective managers we can determine whether what they say is really what they mean by the way their non-verbal behaviour is transmitted in addition to their actual words. We should also be aware that regional accents can affect the way messages are received. It is a sad fact that a regional accent outside of its indigenous area often prevents an immature or inexperienced manager from taking the speaker seriously. We know this is ridiculous but, unfortunately, regional accents which are out of context can make us believe a person is not as intelligent as we would otherwise believe had their accent been similar to our own. A similar example is the person who, when confronted with a foreigner who does not speak his/her language, does not modify his/her process of communication at all, except perhaps to shout louder, and somehow believes that this will (possibly by volume alone) assist the unfortunate receiver to understand the incomprehensible language which is being transmitted to him/her.

The pitch of a person's voice may affect your perception of them; a high pitched voice will tend to command less respect than a low pitch. The words may be the same but a low pitched voice will carry more conviction than that of a high pitched or youthful voice. This is also true in dealings with people of the opposite sex. A man may consider his female colleague a lightweight merely because of the high pitch of her voice and conversely a woman may feel that the low pitched voice of a man carries more conviction. You may remember that, upon becoming leader of the Conservative Party, Mrs Thatcher was very quickly coached to lower the pitch of her voice. Tone, accent and pitch are factors we must consider when we communicate using the telephone, as is the use of silence. Where, when, and for how long there is a period of silence in a conversation is important, and we should be able to analyse such silences to determine exactly what message is being sent. In face-to-face communication the tone of voice and the use of silence are just two ways among many of communicating non-verbally but, as we all know, body language also plays a part.

We can learn a great deal about other people, their feelings and their sincerity from their facial expressions, the way they sit, stand or move around, their gestures and the way they look at us or, in some cases, the way they do not look at us. Understanding non-verbal communication is essential for the effective manager because it is a form of communication which people are using unconsciously and therefore it is (if we understand it) an advantage to us if we are able to read the hidden agenda in the communication being offered to us. The danger, if we are not aware of it, is that we may respond to it at an emotional level thus affecting our own communication. What is actually happening is that there is an unknown element of non-verbal feedback circulating between us which affects the primary object of our communication. For example, we may be alienated by a weak handshake, by someone who will not look us in the eyes or conversely, seems intent on staring at us. We may come to loath the speaker who waves his/her arms about like a windmill during a lecture and thereby totally disregard the good information he/she is trying to impart. We may have negative feelings towards a person who slouches in his/her seat or turns away from us, we may think he/she is bored with the conversation. If a person folds his/her arms and rolls his/her eyes we may consider that he/she is resistant to what we are going to say. If he/she fidgets or scratches himself/herself we may guess that the person is under some kind of stress. If the person comes too close to us and stays there (taking our space) we may suspect that he/she is trying to dominate and influence us by the power of his/her personality.

As a result of all this we must understand that the person's body language may lead us to guess not just what he/she is thinking or feeling but also the sort of person that he/she is. We may see him/her as a dominating or authoritarian person, a show-off or enthusiast, a weakling or a bully. Unfortunately, we may be wrong but this should not stop us reading the meanings of people's non-verbal communication because they may be doing it to us at the same time. We must ask ourselves not only 'what am I saying verbally?', but also 'what is my body saying?' at the same time.

There are more ways of conveying ideas and feelings without using words. We have so far talked about tone of voice, pitch, body language etc., but consider for a moment that we can also determine a great deal about a person from their habitual behaviour and the choices they make in cars, friends, the clothes they wear, and even the furniture they use in their offices. These are all liable to communicate something to us about other people. We should consider this when people are consistently late for meetings or keep us waiting when we have a firm appointment with them. Are they trying to tell us that their time is more valuable than ours, that they are more important than we are, etc.? Would you think it strange if a person who has habitually come to work in a suit and tie suddenly starts turning up in a sweater and jeans, or vice versa? These are areas where we should ask questions and, because they affect human behaviour, we must ask the same questions of ourselves. What kind of image are we presenting to others and what kind of image are they attempting to present to us? We should also understand that there are barriers to the communication process.

BARRIERS TO COMMUNICATION

The message may be imprecise, unspecific or we simply cannot decide what to say, perhaps because we don't know what effect we want to have on the person with whom we are communicating or because we are not sure what that person needs to be told in order to achieve our desired effect. We may not want to tell him/her everything or, we may wish to make the decisions about the way in which we communicate as we go along. Once we start talking, the receiver will give us feedback which will enable us to expand on certain areas and, perhaps, choose the amount of information we give to him/her. This is why we often jot down main points of what we want to say before we start speaking (particularly in public presentations or telephone calls). This is also an appropriate way of preparing to conduct meetings. We may also want to rehearse in our minds by jotting down notes of exactly what we are going to say.

When we write down messages we can choose our words and polish the text as much as we like but, without feedback, the barrier is there. We are unable to reword our messages as we go along. To enable this barrier to be minimised it is good practice to have in mind your Targets when writing to them. Imagine that they are sitting with you, listening to you as you write, and reading your words aloud. What might their responses be? If you can imagine this feed-back you can, perhaps, respond to it in your prepared message. I am sure we have all asked friends or colleagues to read and comment on drafts of text before they are finalised. This is good practice and should be used before documents are issued. Conversely, we may wish to actually send the receivers a first draft to obtain from them their comments (feedback) before the final document is prepared. Whichever way we choose, the written message should, where possible, be held back for a short time (which could be from hours to days) in order that we can look at it again with a fresh eye prior to it being transmitted.

The presentation of our communication must be appropriate; the right medium for the right message or recipient. We may choose the right medium but the presentation is poor (e.g., the typeface may be too small, the print may be too crowded, our public speaking may be too fast or our meetings may be insufficiently structured). Written messages must be instructive and structured, and verbal communications must be relevant and organised – and carefully timed.

The capacity of the recipient should be considered, their intellectual level, approach to the task, their willingness to receive the message – all should be considered for we tend to respond selectively to messages. We tend to screen out aspects of the message that threaten us or don't fit with our prejudices. We should consider whether the limited capacity of our audience could be overcome by training (e.g., improve their reading skills, teach them how to interpret technical drawings or diagrams etc.). Any attempt at communication involving statistics or figures and calculations is highly likely to run into this sort of problem unless the sender is very thoughtful about the target's ability to receive the message clearly and to gather the same understanding from it that is intended when it is transmitted.

You should be aware of unstated assumptions or different perceptions. Words may mean different things to different people and can cause catastrophic misunderstandings. Trouble arises not because we think we have failed to understand a message but because, unbeknown to us, we *have* misunderstood it.

We have already talked about the 'real world' and this is a factor in our thinking with regard to barriers to communication. People may fail to communicate because they see the world differently to each other. Examples of this can be seen in everyday life. We have world conflicts between cultures and nations with different values and aspirations. It is rare that people with such conflicting views can resolve their differences just by talking. Their values and aspirations are so different that they are almost direct opposites; shared understanding might well be impossible. There may be nothing you, as a manager, can do about this but having an awareness of why it may be happening could lead you to provide a solution which benefits the individuals or organisation concerned.

You may find that people with whom you communicate have decided that it is not in their best interests to tell you what you wish to know. They will therefore refrain from communication or else they will communicate ambiguously making statements that they know will be misinterpreted. This type of deception is quite common and at worst will mean that people will lie to you, hoping that they will never be found out or, if they are, that you will be powerless to do anything about it. The communication of lies or 'misinformation' is an everyday occurrence both by managers and their subordinates. You may be trying to get your subordinates to do something or tolerate something that they would refuse to do if they knew the real state of affairs. Your subordinates may be trying to make you feel more benevolent to them by giving you answers that you want to hear. Even though this sort of communication is (on the surface) open, it is in fact failing. It is non-productive and will result, if allowed to become widespread, in low morale and poor motivation. The productivity of the organisation is also likely to diminish, as is the quality of working life for those involved. Effective and mature managers learn to understand and recognise where deception is taking place and to correct it decisively.

Even good communication is sometimes disrupted. We are often unable to concentrate properly, we may have other things on our minds, there may be noise in the background, the telephone line may have static upon it, and the written word can sometimes be disjointed through interference. Environmental factors may have an effect on our ability to communicate effectively. It is difficult to retain effective communication skills in an uncomfortable environment when an office is too hot or too cold, where there is inadequate light, or noise from machinery or other sources. Our health also affects the way in which we communicate and may cause a message to be misread or misheard. Remember the symptoms of stress (see Chapter 2)?

There are usually channels through which we communicate in any organisation. As an effective manager, you should ensure that these channels exist, for if they do not, communication can be difficult. If you suspect that other people in your organisation possess information you need, yet you do not know who they are, you may have a problem with ineffective information channels. There may be people to whom you would like to have given advice or instruction, or encouragement, but there does not seem to be an effective way of doing so. You must, as the manager, create these channels and communicate the fact that they exist to your subordinates and your peers, and in so doing you will know what your subordinates, superiors and colleagues are communicating or not telling you.

You will never break down all the barriers to communication for they are often cumulative and lead to a generally distorted element of internal communication or, worse still, degenerate into 'corporate gossip'. The longer the chain of people through which the message passes, the more distorted it will be by the time it reaches the other end. You should always be aware of the accuracy of the messages you receive and respond accordingly.

7

Leadership

By accepting promotion, and thus making the transition from player to manager, you also accept that you must provide leadership, for everything we have discussed thus far demands it. We read and hear quite a bit about leadership – what is it? Can we distinguish between management and leadership?

Whilst we can probably think of plenty of leaders who are not managers, it is probably hard to think of a manager who is not also a leader. There are a number of questions surrounding this subject:

- Are leaders born or made?

- Can anyone become a leader?

- Is there a particular trick to it?

- Is there a particular style which we should adopt?

- Can we learn from the examples of great men or women?

- Do we have to be popular to be a good leader?

- Do we have to sacrifice popularity to get things done?

I shall answer these questions by looking at the theories of leadership and then going on to develop techniques to improve your leadership skills.

LEADERSHIP THEORIES

Leadership has been distinguished from management by separating the former as being to do with people and the latter as being about resources (money and materials). This view illustrates one of the problems of leadership training. Most people believe that they have an innate ability to get on with others. As a result training is often recognised in management subjects, but matters of leadership are not considered necessary. There are many myths surrounding leadership, so, in order to develop the subject and give you help in refining your own leadership techniques we will start by discussing the four principal theories which have been proposed over the years:

1 *Trait theory*: The idea that leaders have certain inherited and acquired characteristics, i.e., are born not made.

2 *Style theory*: The hypothesis that certain ways of behaving in leadership situations are more effective than others.

3 *Contingency theory*: More complicated views which maintain that the style can change, and should change, to fit different situations.

4 *Type theory*: The combination of the first three which suggests that there are different types of leaders who flourish in different contexts.

We will look at these theories in brief detail, but they are only theories, simplistic and, in some cases, out of date. There are no easy and simple answers to the question, 'How do I become an effective leader?' However, by discussing the four theories and then developing them further we can discover more appropriate ways in which to act as a manager and a leader.

Trait theory

Trait theory proposes that individual personality and talent are the key factors. You are either a good leader or you are not and there is little that you can do to make any changes to this. Trait theorists believe that good leaders have above average intelligence but hardly to genius level. They have a capacity to perceive the need for action, or initiative, and then do something about it. This characteristic appears to be closely related to energy and, in many cases, declines as people get older. These leaders are also confident and self-assured, and they normally believe in what they are doing. This is also related to people's perceptions of their place in society, and to their own aspirations. However, their self-assurance does not necessarily mean that they are aggressive; they can, in some instances be self-effacing in manner.

Trait theorists also believe in the ability of the leader to rise above a particular situation, like a hovering helicopter, and see the situation in its broadest context and then descend to attend to the details – we should all strive to do this. There is no stereotype of a great leader in terms of any physical appearance for, as we all know, Napoleon was short and De Gaulle was very tall, Churchill was quite fat and Ghandi very thin. It is interesting to discuss the trait theorists' view but they are no longer taken very seriously. I prefer to think that anyone can be an effective leader if he/she is committed to the job and thinks hard enough about his/her behaviour.

Style theory

Leadership 'style' became a topic for discussion following research undertaken in the late 1930s. At that time three different styles were exposed:

1 *Autocratic*: The leader decides what will be done and how.

2 *Democratic*: Decisions are made after discussion.

3 *Laissez-faire*: Group members work on their own and the leader is much the same as other group members.

From this research was found that the most productive group was under autocratic leadership but the leader had to be present all the time. Democratic leadership was the most popular and the most consistent in both quality and productivity. Laissez-faire leadership rated poorly in all aspects.

The general thrust of this theory is that the more democratic your style the more productive you and your team will be in the long run because involvement generates more commitment and energy from the group.

However, the preceding two theories do not supply us with believable answers to all our questions. Whilst it would be wrong for us to decide on a definitive theory, a mix of those which we have already discussed, plus our empirical knowledge that there is more to leadership than this simplistic approach, leads us on to the next and probably most significant theory, which bears greater scrutiny for it has elements which can actually help us to become a more effective leader.

Contingency theory

Contingency theory comes closer to common experience and to common sense than the theories already outlined. Theorists have suggested that, in each situation, there are four variables that have to be taken into account when analysing leadership:

1 *The Leader*: His/her personality and preferred style.

2 *The Led*: The needs, attitudes, and skills of subordinates or colleagues.

3 *The Task*: The requirements and goals of the job to be done.

4 *The Context*: The organisation, its values and prejudices.

It has been further established that leadership falls, generally, between a directive style and a consultative style. Some situations require one or the other and some any degree in between. In an attempt to make the theory more precise it is considered that a directive style works best when the situation is favourable to the leader, and a supportive or democratic (consultative) style

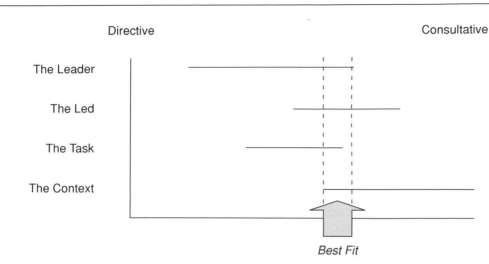

Figure 12 A 'best fit' in the middle range

when unfavourable. To make situations favourable to the leader the following must apply:

- The leader must be liked and trusted by the group.

- The task to be done must be clear and well defined.

- The power of the leader *vis á vis* the rest of the group is high and is respected.

Under these circumstances, directive leadership is the straightforward way to do the job but this should not imply autocracy. However, although the consultative approach is best when things are unfavourable it is imperative that the direct (and even autocratic) approach is used when situations are *very* unfavourable.

In order to use the contingency approach it is necessary to fit the variables mentioned above to a style of leadership. An easy way of illustrating how such a 'fit' might be accomplished is by following the diagram in Fig. 12. Each of the variables in Fig. 12 will tolerate a small range of styles. The 'best fit option' is where the overlap occurs. In this hypothetical situation the organisation (the context) has a dislike of very directive behaviour but otherwise has few requirements. The group does not want to be told everything but does not want to be left too much to its own devices. The task can be totally structured or turned into a 'how to?' problem, and the leader is by inclination a director rather than a democrat. It is clear that the only point where all the requirements overlap is at the consultative end of the leader's range. If the leader is more directive than consultative he/she will get the job done but he/she may upset the group and perhaps the organisation, storing up problems for the future.

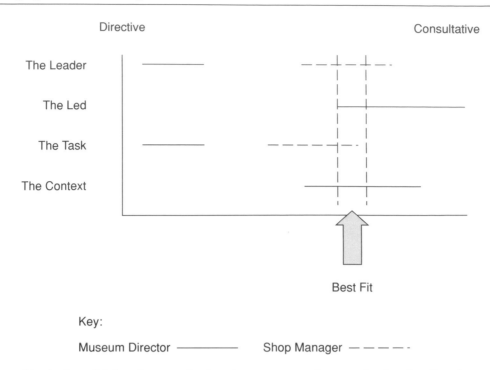

Figure 13 A 'best fit' for the consultative shop manager, but 'no fit' for the directive museum director

Using the contingency approach to a situation, and the method of analysis summarised above, we can look at a situation within museums or galleries. The scenario is of a museum director wishing to change the working practices of staff in a museum shop and introduce the wearing of a uniform to project a new corporate image. Previously the staff had worn their own clothes and the shop had been run as counter-service operation. A redesign of the shop into a larger self-service outlet was considered the appropriate time for the introduction of uniforms, a reduction in staff and a change in job descriptions of the remaining staff.

The 'best fit' option for a style of leadership under Contingency Theory in this case can be ascertained by drawing a diagram as before, and adjusting the style to that which is most appropriate for the situation (see Fig. 13).

In this situation the Director has an autocratic style and the shop manager has a more consultative approach. The group of shop employees see the proposed changes as affecting them so closely that they should be consulted as much as possible, particularly regarding the wearing of uniform and the possibility of redundancy. The task is clearly defined by the Director and is only negotiable in detail, giving little scope for consultation. The museum itself has always prided itself in its consultative process; all senior staff are educated and qualified professional people resulting in a democratic approach to change.

As can be seen in the diagram, a more consultative approach by the leader is needed unless he wishes to risk problems with his policy.

Just a glimpse at Fig. 13 shows that a continued directive (bordering on autocratic) approach to the situation will not 'fit'. It is unlikely that the variables of the group or organisation (i.e., the context) can be changed and the task is imperative for the future of the museum shop and, indeed, the museum itself. The Director's autocratic approach is the only variable that may result in a 'best fit' situation. In this case it might be more worth while for the Director to delegate the task to his shop manager who not only has a more democratic approach but is also in a more favourable position with the group. As we can see, there are various options open to the Director of which I will select three:

1 Change his approach – be more democratic, consult with the group and put himself in a more favourable position.

2 Continue without change – he has the authority to carry out his plan but will the goodwill and morale of staff be affected so much that success in the new shop is more difficult?

3 Delegate the work to his shop manager – this will provide a 'best fit' by virtue of the manager's different approach and will not involve the Director having to change himself. This will only work if he can properly delegate to his manager.

It is therefore obvious that the Director should be more consultative in his approach or, failing that, he may delegate the task to his subordinate (the shop manager) giving him clear instructions, defining the task, the degree of discretion, and the forms of control. If this was done, Fig. 14 shows the style required from the Director if he chooses to change, or that which is appropriate for the shop manager should he have the task delegated to him.

The following points should always be borne in mind:

1 It is easier for you, the leader, to change your own style than to change the other three areas.

2 It is rarely possible to change the group's (the led) attitude unless they particularly respect you. It is even more difficult to change the composition of the group or to remove people from it.

3 It is possible to change the task because, after all, you set it in the first place. However, many tasks are set by others and you may be unable to make changes to their tasks.

4 It is possible to change the context but usually only in the long term.

Contingency theory therefore tends to focus on the leader working with a group of individuals on a task, and has been called 'action-centred leadership'.

93

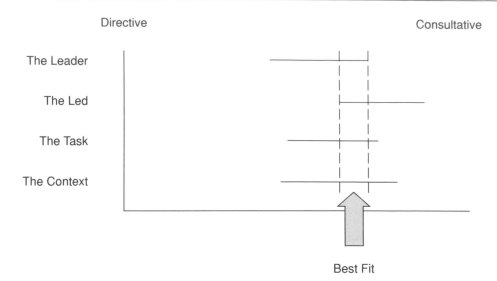

Figure 14 A 'best fit' in the consultative range

For most of us action-centred leadership is what is important because this is where we can change things and can therefore improve our effectiveness as managers.

Type theory

However, some recent studies into leadership concentrate more on the 'context' and take an almost anthropological view of the leader in the organisation. Looking at the organisation as a culture or tribe is the basis behind this theory, which results in trying to describe the behaviour and the types of personalities which are effective within the group. Research in this field has found four character types of successful leaders. Few individuals were pure examples of one type; most were mixtures with one type dominant. No type is superior to another – they all have their value in the right place – and there are good and bad examples of each. The four types are:

1 *The craftsman/woman*
   The most traditional character, motivated to building products of high quality, interested in the process of making something. Self-contained and exacting, this type of leader can also become uncooperative and inflexible if he/she feels that others are trying to push him/her around. As a leader, the craftsperson is the master builder and the parent-figure of apprentices. His/her characteristic weakness is self-contained perfectionism. He/she builds teams and leads by ordering subordinates to apply what he/she decides is the one best solution.

2 *The jungle fighter*
   This type of leader needs power. Although he/she may see himself/herself as leading the righteous, he/she spends his/her life at work as a contest for survival in which winners destroy losers. At his/her best as a leader, this leader is a lion, calm and protective to his/her family, and ruthless to his/her competitors. However, this dominating attitude drives away independent and creative subordinates, and can create enemies in his/her immediate circle, or alternatively fawning 'yes men or women'.

3 *The company man/woman*
   Orientated to service and to institution-building, concerned with the human side of the company, committed to maintaining corporate integrity and controlling reckless subordinates. At his/her worst, he/she is a sentimental careerist whose sense of identity is based mainly on being part of a powerful and protective organisation. As a leader, he/she can sometimes sustain an atmosphere of co-operation and a sense of service, but under pressure may become too fearful and conservative. He/she lacks the daring and the sense of adventure to lead highly competitive and innovative organisations.

4 *The gamesman/woman*
   This type likes to take calculated risks, is fascinated by techniques and new methods and thrives on competition. The contest pushes up his/her adrenalin and, at his/her best, he/she communicates enthusiasm, energising peers and subordinates like a captain on a football pitch. He/she is fair and a team player. Unlike the jungle fighter, the gamesman/woman competes not to build an empire or to build up riches, but often to gain fame, glory and the exhilaration of victory. His/her weaknesses are the opposites of his/her strengths: rashness, the tendency to create a fantasy world, to lie and manipulate, and a gamelike devilment that cuts him/her off from emotional reality.

It is suggested that the gamesman/woman became the ideal of American leadership when every corporation expected to grow and problems were only challenges to be overcome. During the recession it became obvious that the gamesman/woman style is, in many cases, inappropriate. This is because in such circumstances the bad side of the character comes out and, faced with the need to compromise and sacrifice, without shared ideas and trust, each person plays for himself/herself – at the expense of others.[1]

So, at first sight leadership may have seemed a relatively simple concept. We all think we know what it is: 'Getting the best out of people' or 'Getting the job done'. As we try to identify what this actually means the whole subject becomes more complicated. All the theories we have looked at either leave something out or ask you to juggle with many variables.

Using just some of the theories to explain leadership is imprecise. In fact trying to explain it in this way makes it unduly complex; I have done so to get to grips with those areas that are inherent in all leaders, but not necessarily to advocate a particular style. A leader has to be directive at one time and consultative at another. However, we can learn something from these theories. The main message is that there are things we can do to become effective leaders. There are some general principles and there are particular styles and attitudes we can develop, but there are no magic ingredients. There are, in leadership, particular styles suitable to particular situations. You must also be capable of changing your style to suit the situation and to be aware of the predominant style you would normally use in order that you can change your normal style if it is inappropriate for a given situation. There is no one 'right way' of managing or leading.

DEVELOPING LEADERSHIP SKILLS

If we assume you can improve your leadership skills – how do *you* do it? We shall look at two different, but related, ways to improve these skills: management of the situation and the functional approach.

The first develops the 'best fit' Contingency Theory analysis which we have just discussed and looks at all the possible options and considerations which have to be balanced if you are to put yourself in the best position to be effective. The second method focuses on the specific things that any leader needs to do in any situation: the practical things like planning, controlling and evaluating. To do the first without the second would be pointless. To do the second without the first might be directing efforts and energies to an impossible situation. You need to understand and then to act.

Managing the situation

We already know that anyone in a leadership situation has four variables to consider: the leader; the led; the task; the context. We also know that we will not have complete freedom to change all four variables to suit our preferences. Examination of each of the variables will show that there is often more room to manoeuvre than may have seemed possible at first sight. It is tempting for the inexperienced or immature manager to rush straight into new situations, trusting to instinct and experience. Wise leaders spend time analysing the possibilities.

If management is the art of the possible, leadership is the means of turning the possible into the practical. Let us look at each variable in turn to see what flexibility there is.

The leader

We are seldom capable of changing our behaviour across the whole range from directive to consultative. The extent of the range of styles we can tolerate is influenced by at least five factors:

96

1 *Our personal system of values and experience*
We each have our own sense of the proper way to behave. Many feel that a leader has to assume responsibility and should not share it with subordinates. Such an attitude would necessarily drive you towards the directive end of the scale. Others may feel exactly the opposite, believing that the leader is the voice of the group and should always consult them. Such people are at the consultative end of the scale. Some enjoy telling others what to do, others hate it. None of these attitudes is wrong (or right), but they can restrict your range, or possibilities. It is wise to be honest about, and deal with, your instinctive preference. There is no point in pretending to yourself. Personal self-confidence comes across as consistency – something that people value in a leader.

2 *Our confidence in our subordinates or colleagues*
No one gives responsibility to idiots. A more participative style requires people who can handle responsibility. Parents tend to move from the directive to the consultative approach as their children grow up and earn more confidence. When parents are too permissive too soon children may become insecure with the burden of the decisions they are expected to take. If parents are too directive for too long then their children are likely to rebel. It is the same with adults, and with leaders and groups. Immature, untrained groups need directive leadership until they grow more mature and more confident.

3 *Our need for certainty*
An open style of leadership involves handing over some control to others. There is a positive gain but also a risk when you relinquish such control. If you, as an individual, have a low tolerance for uncertainty, you do not like risks, or you do not think that the situation justifies risk, then you will prefer the directive end of the leadership range.

4 *Our personal contribution*
Our need for certainty is affected by our estimate of what we can contribute. If we believe that we know what is the right thing to do, we would not want to treat the problem as an open one and would tend to want to tell the group what to do rather than consult with them. As far as we are concerned the problem is simple and so is the solution. Curators who have done every job in their department (a very common occurrence in museums and galleries) tend to be directive. This is natural even if, on occasion, it is inappropriate.

5 *Stress*
Stress usually pushes people to one end or other of the scale. People either become very directive, in an attempt to reassert control over the situation, or they abandon control all together and become apathetic rather than consultative.

The led

Colleagues and subordinates will have their own preferences for a restrictive or an open response to situations. These preferences will be influenced by at least four further factors:

1 *Their expectations*

It is usually evident whether people expect to be told or asked. Their expectations may be brought about by your customary leadership style. We all have a style which we would commonly use but we must understand that it is not necessarily the appropriate style for all purposes. Our style can, therefore, be altered; but not easily or quickly because people who work for us will immediately question why a style with which they have become familiar, has suddenly been changed. Subordinates may become resentful if they are suddenly put in control when they have been used to a directive approach or vice versa.

2 *Their interest in the problem or situation*

If the situation is trivial, routine, or uninteresting, the subordinate group will not wish to devote much of their time or energy to a participative approach. They will not need to be asked to do something they have done a hundred times before and are familiar with. They will prefer a structured approach and a directive leader. Similarly, if they feel that they can have little influence on the outcome of the decision they will not want to be involved in a consultation process over what sort of decision you, as the manager, will take. Consultative styles are not welcomed for simple problems.

3 *Their tolerance of ambiguity*

Like the leader, subordinates will have a certain tolerance for risk or uncertainty, and the responsibility that goes with that. The more insecure or uncertain they are, the more they will want to be directed and to act under orders. Your confidence will influence them to do the job properly and well, but it is unlikely that your lack of confidence will motivate them to assist you in making the decision in the first place. A wise parent educates a family gradually and so does a wise leader with a work group.

4 *The past experience of the group*

Our expectations are shaped by our experience. If previous experience of an open approach to a situation has been successful, we are likely to be more amenable to be involved in the next open discussion towards a decision using an open approach. If the group has not worked together the members need to have respect for each other's competence as well. New groups, or inexperienced people, need more structure and initially are more comfortable under a directive approach. You, particularly with new groups which you have formed, must recognise this and prepare yourself to be directive in your approach in the initial stages but to change gradually and subtly as time goes on, as your group becomes more comfortable and more confident in its ability to be consulted.

It is important to see that both parties in a leadership situation have realistic expectations of each other. There seems to be an unwritten contract between the leader and the led which is often unconsciously broken. You, and the persons working for you, should be clear on such points as:

- Who takes responsibility?

- Who gets the benefits?

- Does the group, or individual, have the right to refuse or question?

- Does participation mean that the group makes suggestions or makes decisions?

The task

The task often seems to be the one thing that is fixed; a problem, a job that needs to be done. In practice, however, the leader often has more opportunity to change the detail of the task than of any other variables. It is important, therefore, to understand how the definition of the task or the job alters the choice of leadership style.

1 *The nature of the task*

Is the task *making decisions* or *carrying them out*? Is it routine or problem-solving? Are the answers to the problem known, so that it is only a matter of carrying them out (as is the case with most routine or standardised work) or are the problems new ones? Open-ended problems require a more open approach. The leader, however, does have some choice in defining the nature of the task. Even in straightforward operational tasks he/she can prescribe exactly how the work has to be done (a directive approach) or he/she can define the goals to be achieved and leave the operator to work out how to do it (more towards the consultative approach).

2 *The time-scale*

Participation (i.e., consultation) takes time if several people are involved. In emergencies, or under pressure of time, the leader is forced towards the directive end of the scale. If, therefore, you want to encourage a more open approach it is essential to stretch out the time available; you will need to make time if you want to consult with colleagues and occasionally there will be no time in which to do this. In these cases, and when you believe a consultative approach is the most appropriate, you should explain to those people who work for you why you have elected to go for a directive approach.

3 *The complexity*

The more difficult and complicated the problem, the more you will need to consult as many people as possible. On the other hand, complexity can be confusing as more and more people get involved. This is a vicious circle you should try to avoid. It may therefore be necessary for the leader to conceal some of the true complexity by tidying up the problem before handing it to the group. The normal way you should do this is by giving different groups or sub-groups different parts of the problem. Complexity is managed by you, the leader. You will retain the overall knowledge about the complexity of the problem but pass details of part(s) of it to the group in order that, for them, it is more simple.

4   *Room for error*
In a problem-solving situation there will usually be fewer mistakes the more people that are consulted. A directive approach can be more risky although, ironically, a cautious leader is temperamentally more likely to adopt a fixed or a directive style. On the other hand, in an operational situation, it may be necessary to keep control in the hands of the leader in order to prevent serious errors. A good example of this is in the aerospace industry (which cannot afford even the smallest error), where manufacturing processes undertaken by skilled professionals go by rigid rules even though the design and problem-solving side of that industry is well known for its open, consultative mode of operation.

The leader's freedom to define the task is an important element in leadership. He/she can, in many cases, define the task as an operation to 'do this', or as a problem, 'How can you achieve this result?' For example, he/she can vary the time-scale, by asking for a project to be done 'today', to create more pressure for a directive style than by saying 'next week' and allowing consultation to take place. Autocratic managers seldom like formal plans, they often do not need them because they prefer to work to shorter time-scales in most situations; they do not want formal plans because these limit their room to manoeuvre. Finally, the leader can break the problem up into parts or delegate the whole problem. In this way you are managing the complexity to fit the style you think is appropriate to the group and to the general situation. There is much more flexibility in adjusting the task than you might think.

The context

No one, not even a manager at the most senior level, is a completely free agent in adjusting the requirements of the leader, the led and the task. It is all done in the context of the organisation for which you work, with its structure, its technology, its control systems and its own way of doing things – by this I mean its 'culture'. We will look at organisational culture in more detail later but suffice it to say that the context of the organisation is extremely important and, of course, the environment within which the organisation itself is positioned has a part to play. All of these factors have their implications for the kind of leadership that can be used, so let us look at each of them in turn.

The structure You will know, from your own experience, that some structures leave plenty of room for individual discretion and some leave none at all. Some organisations have organisational structures which are tall and built like pyramids with authority and responsibility spread over many layers. This tends to mean that individuals are closely supervised, with one boss to six or seven subordinates (or more). A tall thin structure therefore gives the leader a smaller group and a superior who knows him/her and his/her work well. The room for manoeuvre will depend on the relationship between the leader and his/her superior.

100

A more decentralised structure, built around product or project groups, profit centres or autonomous businesses (the Science Museum and its various out-stations for example) would usually mean that individuals have more freedom in the way they do things. There is no absolute right or wrong in this matter of structural form, it depends very much on the kind of work being carried out within your museum and gallery; often called the 'technology' of the institution.

The technology Some work allows each unit to be different. Schools, for instance are encouraged (within broad limits) to do things their own way and, within schools, teachers are independent in their own classrooms. No teacher needs to be a carbon copy of any other teacher. Banks, however, have to be like one another. The branches of chain stores, post offices, outstations of museums and galleries, libraries; these all have to conform to standard practices because they are part of a facsimile process. If each were not like the others the system would not work.

Other organisations are tied into an interlocking process. One job locks on to another, for example, acquisition, cataloguing, restoration, display, conservation. Much administrative or office work is part of an interlocking process with each form contributing to another form, each report linking with another report.

The point is that a leader who finds himself/herself in a facsimile or an interlocking process will not have much freedom to define the task, or the roles of the members of the group. These things will probably be laid down in a manual or procedures file, or by a leader in 'head office'. Only in a unit process, where each unit can choose to be different, is the leader able to move more freely in the ways which have been described. This is normal within a museum departmental system. However, you must decide what sort of process you are in; there is often room for manoeuvre within museums and galleries.

The control system Organisations work with two different principles of control: before-the-event and after-the-event. In the first case you ask permission before you act, proposals are approved, estimates and plans are accepted and passed, details are checked. In the second case, results are monitored; these are compared with budgets and estimates and are found acceptable or not.

Before-the-event control systems are essential in many forms of work because they avoid costly errors. However, they are not always as essential as they seem. In some offices all letters have to be signed by the leader before being dispatched. What would happen if individuals were to sign their own routine letters? There may be occasional mistakes, but the risk has to be outweighed against the expense of such close control.

After-the-event is riskier but allows more discretion to adjust leadership patterns, particularly with groups of people who are confident, well qualified and experienced. As you move into management you may want to grasp control directly and use before-the-event systems, but bear in mind that if you want to adopt a consultative management style you must move slowly towards after-the-event control systems in order to give responsibility to your subordinates.

The culture Organisations themselves have their own style of management, which is closely linked to the kind of work they do. There is an accepted way of doing things in one organisation which may be different from the ways of others. A good example is the difference between hospitals and department stores or between leisure centres and museums. Different cultures allow different degrees of discretion to individual leaders and it is difficult, and usually unprofitable, to go against the prevailing trend within the organisation. Bureaucracies, for instance, prefer everything to be predictable and standardised. Project groups, on the other hand, must be allowed flexibility.

The context of the organisation, therefore, is often one of the constraints limiting your choices in arranging a leadership pattern. Constraints, however, are not always fixed and forever. They can be bent, negotiated or removed. Your superior is the chief representative of the organisation for you. It is with his/her approval that you can change or ignore the context. If you need to make some important adjustments to your leadership pattern, you cannot take these suggestions to your leader unless you are confident and aware of the patterns that you must choose. Hence, the need to discuss these matters and be aware of how leadership style can change.

The functional approach

Our last look at areas to assist you in developing your leadership ability is the Functional Approach which was formulated by Professor John Adair as 'Action-centred leadership', and has been widely used in British industry for some years. Adair's theory is not so much a way of developing leadership skills but is based on the assumption that the work of the leader is to bring together the needs of the individuals, the group and the task, into a production whole. Adair sees it as a 'three circles model' (see Fig. 15), and sees the leader's job as giving direction.[2]

There are eight elements to John Adair's approach and these are useful for you to use as a checklist as you look at your role as a leader following your transition into management, and thereafter:

1 *Defining the task*
   Everyone knows we must have a purpose and an aim in what we do, but the job of the manager (or leader) is to put the generalities of those aims and objectives into specific (manageable) areas of work. It is all very well having, for example, an aim to increase admission numbers, but this is not a task until the detail is broken down into its constituent parts in order

102

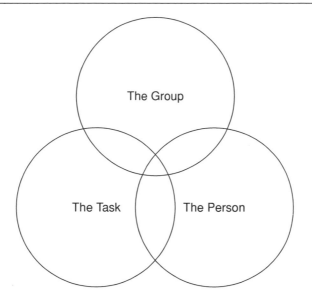

Figure 15 Adair's three circles model

that individuals in the team are aware of their role in the whole scheme
to achieve the aim.

2   *Planning*
    In an ever-changing environment where competition within the museum
    and gallery sector is growing we must be creative in our planning by
    thinking laterally and using the ideas of others in the group. You will find
    that there are always more options open to you than at first you realised
    but this will rarely be evident unless you consult with others. Once the
    options have been discussed they can be consolidated into a working plan;
    your task is often to turn what might seem to be a negative situation into
    a positive one by virtue of your ability to plan creatively.

3   *Briefing*
    Once you have determined your options and your planning is complete,
    communication is essential. We dealt with communication in Chapter 6
    and you should now know that it is a vital contributing element to your
    success as a leader. You should never rely on one form of communication
    and you should be skilled at preparing presentations and bringing life to
    the subject by simplifying and clarifying it. Good preparation is essential
    if you are to be successful in communicating to the group the way in which
    you require a task to be done effectively.

4   *Controlling*
    Here we go back to our first principle of management, the fact that having
    set standards (i.e., explained the options and planned the task), you should
    identify those areas which need monitoring in order that you can see that

your plan is working and that the standards you have set are either being reached or exceeded. John Adair makes the point that it is useless trying to control others if you cannot control yourself (remember time management etc.).

5 *Evaluating*

A necessary partner to the controlling of the task is the ability to assess the consequences of the efforts of your team. Progress reports or debriefings are essential, the people as well as the task need to be evaluated and your techniques of appraisal will become essential. You cannot expect people to work hard if they cannot see what they are achieving.

6 *Motivating*

We have already looked at motivation. Your job, as manager, is to motivate your team and one of the simplest ways of doing this is by recognising their efforts and commending them. Success tends to motivate individuals to do even better and therefore if you set achievable targets, carry out frequent monitoring, ensure praise is given where praise is due, and give careful counselling when people fall below the standard you expect, you will find a new sense of energy and urgency in the group you lead. Control should never outweigh motivation and your enthusiasm should be equal in both.

7 *Organising*

There is little point in setting your group the tasks to fulfil a planned objective without also supplying them with the resources with which to carry out their work. It is your function to ensure that the organisation is up to the task and that the materials, finance, information etc. required by your group is available to them. You will probably not have to do this personally but you should ensure that you delegate it to people who can do it for you. It will be management that is blamed if the resources necessary to carry out the task are not available on time and in the right place.

8 *Setting an example*

The people who work for you will be inclined to work even better if they know that you are a hard worker and work to the same high standards you are setting them. People take more notice of what you are and what you do, than what you say. This does not mean that, as a manager, you must do all the tasks you would have done as an operator, but you need the integrity which illustrates to those who work for you that you believe in what you do, and what those who work for you do on your behalf.

Whatever style or pattern of leadership you choose, you should always remember that your success as a manager will depend on your ability to adapt your style to suit the circumstances. Have a consistent approach, using the points derived from John Adair's work, to ensure that the style you use is consistent. Bear in mind Adair's eight-point checklist for it will be of use to you at whatever level of management you attain and whatever the complexity of the tasks you are required to carry out.

POWER, INFLUENCE AND AUTHORITY

In order to be a good manager and leader you must be able to distinguish between power, influence and authority. Power is the ability to influence. Influence is the process where you try to get someone else to do something, or think something, which they would not otherwise do. Your authority is your right to use your power, for example by delegating. It is important that you should understand these differences as they will give you a better understanding of your position in the organisation and your role as a leader. We will deal with them separately and explore how we can use power as a source of influence which will then become authority. We shall also see that this will depend on the type of power you have and how you have obtained it.

Power

There are generally thought to be four types of power within organisations:

1   *Resource power*
    Obviously, if you have the resources that someone else wants you must have power over him/her. This could be, at its simplest level, just physical strength but it is more likely to be the ability to control financial and other resources within an institution. However, you must be able to use the resources you have at your disposal and if the person over whom you wish to have power does not need those resources you will not be able to use them against him/her. The person must want, or not want, the resources you have. Bear in mind that you can give away or neutralise resource power. For example you may allow people to earn incremental increases in their salary by being with the organisation a pre-determined number of years. In this sense you will be giving away the resources. Alternatively, you could make increments dependent on achieving a level of performance. You can decide whether you wish to control your resources vigorously or give them away. Neither is appropriate or inappropriate to every situation, but you need to know what is best in order that you can judge how to use your resource power effectively.

2   *Position power*
    When you are promoted into a management job you take up a position which has, in itself, an element of power. Because you hold a title and position within the organisation you are entitled to give instructions to people in lesser positions, call meetings, authorise expenditure, annual leave etc. Your position is backed up by the resources of the organisation and everyone knows exactly what your position is. Regrettably, many managers rely wholly for their power on the position they hold in the organisation. It therefore becomes the main source of authority. Inexperienced and immature managers soon find that, in today's world, subordinates do not accept authority as they may have done in years past. Individuals are no longer so impressed with the authority that comes with position power; they prefer

to be asked rather than told. You should not think that acquiring a management position will allow you automatically to be either directive or authoritative in your style. Your position tends to give you authority more over situations than over people and you must have more power than this if you are to be successful.

3 *Personal power*
This is the one that will make you successful. This is a form of power that you cannot take for yourself for it is given to you by other people. It will depend on your personality, your way of doing things, how people feel about you, your charisma. It does not mean that you have to be 'soft' or that everybody must like you. However, if those who work for and with you recognise your personal power the authority that you need will flow from it. Good leaders usually have a great deal of personal power.

4 *Expert power*
You will find it a lot easier to be an effective leader if you are well qualified at what you are doing and respected by those who work for you as being an expert in some area of skill appropriate to the job. This does not mean merely paper qualifications, for if they are inappropriate to the job you are trying to do, expert power will not flow from them. Like personal power, expert power cannot be personally awarded. You may claim to be the world's expert in your field but if others do not believe it you will not be given the power which comes from being an expert. Remember also that your expertise as an operator (which may be very high) will not be sufficient for you to be given expert power by those who now work for you when you become a manager. Expert power at technical subjects may not necessarily carry over into the authority you require as a leader.

The more expert and personal power you have the more readily the people who work for you will follow your leadership and obey your instructions. You will already have been given the position power upon your promotion into management and you may also have resource power as a result of the resources put at your disposal, but these will only partly assist you until you acquire the confidence of those who work for you and they give you either personal or expert power. Once given you can then turn this into authority and exercise that authority legitimately in your organisation. Never forget that, as personal and expert power can be awarded to you, they can also be taken away if you lose the confidence of your subordinates. It is also possible for you to bring expert and personal power with you to a job if your reputation was good in a previous post. You should not assume that this will automatically happen and you should prepare yourself with the assumption that it will not.

Influence

We now know those various elements of power which we have to understand to be a good leader and we are aware that from power we will derive authority;

particularly by virtue of the power that is given to us by our subordinates (i.e., expert and personal power). Influence is what you do with that power. If your power is both legitimate and accepted by those who work for you, your influence should follow almost automatically. Influence is therefore essential to understanding those areas where you have a power but your authority is not great. These are usually areas in your relationships with people at the same level as you, in informal situations, or when you are trying to persuade somebody above you to do something.

Influence works across organisations whereas authority tends to come from higher up. Your influence over your superiors has a profound effect on your authority and power with your subordinates. If the people who work for you are aware that you have influence over your superiors they will be more inclined to accept your authority for they will have confidence in your ability to influence the organisation and its strategy.

Inexperienced or new managers often worry that people they tell to do something may not do it. They seek some cast-iron way in which, having told someone to do something, they can guarantee that it will automatically and unfailingly be done. You can never really rely on this happening but you will have a better chance of being successful if you rely on those areas of your power which are given to you by the people who work for you. You will have earned your expert or personal power and they are the types of power you will use most. You may have the power of your position and the resources that you control but these types of power will probably not always be highly esteemed by those who work for you; they will acknowledge that you have these types of power but this alone will not make them work better for you. You will always have to check that the work you have asked to be done is done properly and to the time-scales and standards you have set. The more expert or personal power the more likely your instructions are going to be self-enforcing and will need less control, because the people who work for you will be more committed to carrying them out. This is the reason why I advocate a more open or consultative style of leadership – because it is self-enforcing. If you rely solely on your position and you have a directive or authoritative style (which is common in museums and galleries) then you will be constantly monitoring the progress of the work you have set to determine whether your subordinates are carrying out your instructions correctly. This will be time-consuming and it is possible that your subordinates will eventually resent the fact that you are constantly checking on them. If you are unlucky enough to have to rely solely on your position and resource power you will invariably also have to resort to a directive style of leadership.

The other thing you may find yourself doing with position and resource power alone is operating in a negative manner by stopping things being done rather than actually initiating them. In fact many positions within museums and galleries seem to encourage managers to see their main task as being to process work which needs no real initiative; the process is an end in itself. The attitude then is that the only function of the job is to ensure that things do not go wrong. Anyone with a boring or regular set of duties can sometimes be tempted to exploit their negative power; they know, in some instances, they could stop the whole organisation carrying out its work if they exercise this abuse of authority. You should ensure that you are aware of the position power of those below you. There is often a temptation to concentrate on your own ability to get things done (or to stop things being done) without realising that your subordinates have power too. They can undoubtedly make things difficult if their morale is low or they are resentful of you or the organisation. This is particularly apparent where a directive style leads to subordinates feeling their views or aspirations are neglected.

As I have already said, there is a contract between you and the people who work for you. This contract is unwritten and unspoken and different people will have different views on what it contains. Usually this unwritten contract is a number of assumptions about what you as a leader can demand or ask of your group and, in turn, what they can expect of you. This contract is unlikely to incorporate pay or hours of work, for they are usually covered in the written contract everyone has with the organisation. However, the unwritten contract between you and your subordinates covers such things as the standards expected of you, your behaviour, and the style which is preferred by your subordinates. It will depend on whether your subordinates accept your perception of your authority and whether they have acknowledged your expert or personal power. They will expect a level of discretion to be left to them and their input into your decisions will be part of that expectation. Subordinates will also expect you to be regarded credibly by the rest of the organisation and to have some authority, on their behalf, with your superiors. Whatever is in this unwritten contract you should not expect it ever to be articulated to you. It may be acted out by people and they may read your version of the contract from your own behaviour. However, you should be aware of it and react accordingly.

Delegation

There are two common misconceptions about delegation. Some people think that it will be easy to tell others to do things when they become a manager and others believe that the purpose of delegation is to get things done by others which you do not wish to do yourself. Delegation is an essential part of management but should not be taken lightly and, in the initial stages following transition into management, can be extremely difficult. The reason for this is that delegation encapsulates all the skills of leadership and it is unlikely that you will evolve into a good leader quickly. You should expect your first faltering steps at delegation to be difficult but do not succumb to the temptation to do everything yourself. Part of your function is to manage your's and other people's time.

There are four distinct factors which will affect your decisions about delegation. You will be concerned about the results, the ability of the individual, your relationship with the individual and how much time each of you has. The more consultative you are the more participation you will have in the process of dealing with the individual rather than the task. If you tend towards the directive you will be more task-orientated than person-orientated. You will find it hard to delegate tasks to people (particularly if you think they are incompetent) if time is pressing, but you will have to do this or your own time will become difficult to manage. This is the reason why all managers should be constantly trying to improve the people who work for them. As the skill quality of the people rises, then the ability of the manager to delegate becomes less difficult. You should be able to define tasks in such a way that you can delegate them to others with greater ease, and by better planning make more time for yourself and your subordinates. You should be constantly striving to improve your relationships with the people who work for you by coaching and counselling them, by acting as teacher or consultant. This is a continuing process and not something that can be done occasionally and then set aside. Like everything else in management, consistency is important and people who work for you should know that you are consistent and systematic in your delegation.

You should look for ways in which you can quickly develop skills of delegation following your transition to management. In the short term delegation can be regulated by careful attention to the following:

1 *Definition of the task*
   As we have discussed before, the task should be broken down into manageable parts and each of these delegated to individuals in order that the whole task can be carried out but no part of it is too difficult or too complex. Your job as manager is to oversee the task as a whole and you should decide who in your organisation should carry out those elements which are most suited to them.

2 *Degree of discretion*
   You may wish to give your subordinates total freedom to carry out the task but, there again, you may wish to ensure that certain parameters are delineated at the start. You may want the person to report back to you at regular intervals in order to ensure that the standards you have set are being maintained. Conversely, you may ask a person just to go ahead and carry out a task and ask them to report back to you when the task is completed.

3 *Form of control*
   Controls can be implemented before or after the event. That is to say, you can tell the person to whom you are delegating that you wish to know of any problems as and when they happen or you can request a report at regular intervals. On some occasions you may not wish to know about the progress of a task until certain milestones are passed or budget limits are exceeded. You must determine how much discretion you wish to give to an individual for this will determine whether the task is controlled by

ends rather than by means. Either method can motivate or demotivate so you must be careful to choose that which is most appropriate to the person chosen and to the task itself.

You can reward and motivate staff by the way in which you delegate. As a person's competence becomes more developed you can shift the way in which you control tasks from regular before-the-event control, more progressively towards control by results. This will allow the person's job to be enriched. However, you should never merely tell a person to get on with the job without defining the task, the degree of discretion, the form of control and, most importantly, ensuring that the person to whom you are delegating the task understands fully what you asking him/her to do.

SUMMARY OF LEADERSHIP

We have talked a great deal about this word 'leadership' and how it determines whether you will be a successful manager. Your attitude and style are fundamental to the possibility of success as a manager. By success I do not mean your success in terms of promotion and the ability to command a higher salary. I mean your abilities to get things done through others, manage the resources of your institution, enrich and develop the people who work for and with you and contribute to the life of the organisation you work for. This is what sound management and good leadership are all about: your ability to acknowledge your strengths and weaknesses and those of the people who work for you; your knowledge of yourself and your subordinates as well as your awareness and influence over your superiors. Management demands responsibilities and these should never be taken lightly. You will have power to significantly affect the lives of the people who work for you. You should understand that power and be ready to use it when necessary, but always in a fair and human way. You should understand that the reasons why you, and those who work for you, come to work may be extremely different. The fact that you receive satisfaction from your job does not mean that other people in your organisation have similar feelings towards their work. The fact that you know exactly how to carry out a task does not mean that the person to whom you are delegating that task has a similar understanding.

Your leadership style should not be rigid and you should be prepared to look at yourself as well as those who work for you if you believe there are difficulties in managing a task. It may be your attitude which is making life difficult and not theirs; you should be prepared to make changes within yourself where necessary rather than use your power and influence to change other people. Be constantly on the look out to help those who work for you to better themselves, whether mentally, financially or physically. You should be mindful of working conditions, salaries and service conditions, education and training, social facilities and welfare. An awareness of what is going on around you is essential; a knowledge of the feelings and aspirations of the people who work for you, coupled with a sympathy for them as human beings, individuals and valued employees. However, you should not be perceived as weak and neither should you seek to be everyone's 'best friend'. Fairness is imperative but weakness will help neither the people who work for you nor yourself. When necessary you should be prepared to be hard and firm – but always fair. You should be prepared to enforce the rules of society and your organisation, but also to turn a blind eye to them when necessary. Management requires a maturity which is not necessarily derived by age but more by training and experience.

NOTES

1   A full description of Type Theory may be found in *Understanding Organizations* by C. B. Handy (1976).
2   *Effective Leadership* by J. Adair (1983).

8

Strategic planning and the management of resources

You can only control an organisation effectively if you have constant and up-to-date knowledge of how its resources are performing. You have two primary areas of resource: people and money. In previous chapters we have talked at length about people, in this chapter we will talk about money. Nothing in management happens in a vacuum. Much the same as Newton's Law, everything is subject to an action which stimulates or prompts a reaction. If you cut an exhibition budget you should expect a reduction in output from the exhibition department; this may well be followed by a lowering in staff morale in your workshops which, in turn will be noticed by the visitors who will complain to the attendants. If you are lucky, the attendants may tell you they are receiving complaints – if not you may never know until you find the finances still do not balance as visitor numbers fall off. A downwards spiral is difficult to control and your intelligence system is essential to prevent this.

Proper management of resources is imperative, your job as manager is to monitor the general situation. You should have systems in place to give you up-to-the-minute feedback on the financial position of your organisation and an intelligence network which gives you early warning of discontent, poor performance, ineffective performance, inefficiency and, most of all, a divergence from the aims and goals you have set.

FINANCIAL CONTROL

This is the area where many museum managers fall below acceptable standards but is, in fact, one of the easiest areas to control. Provided that appropriate systems are implemented control will always be possible. Administrators and accountants will develop the most complicated and difficult systems imaginable to monitor the financial situation of an organisation. They will present page after page of computer generated garbage which may mean a great deal to them but is of no use whatsoever to the busy manager. You do not need to show your expert knowledge of local authority, government or corporate fiscal planning. The worst possible managers in the museum and galleries

112

sector, that I can think of, are would-be chartered accountants. They have a tendency to know the price of everything and the value of nothing. However, a curator with a finely tuned sense of financial awareness can train himself/ herself to maintain control over financial resources. There is a place for the chartered accountant in museums, but not in charge of anything more than the accounts department.

The first thing you should do is to formulate a budget for the coming financial year. Usually this is constructed using a base line from the preceding year, adjusted for such things as:

- inflation
- salary awards
- known changes
- contingencies
- redevelopment

Inflation

Inflation is always difficult to estimate and the method of adjusting for it will vary depending how your organisation is funded. In the case of government institutions (national or local) a figure will be calculated for you. Invariably this will be an estimate and will probably be on the disadvantageous side. Beware, you may well have to find extra money from already depleted budgets to cover for this underestimate. The experienced manager knows this and will have over-estimated other variable headings in a, usually vain, attempt to counter the reduction in real funding that these bureaucratic calculations inflict on us. It is impossible to counter the whole error but that is why careful financial control is so important in subsequent months.

In privately funded museums it is often easier to be more accurate with inflation predictions but, let's face it, if we were such good fortune-tellers we would all be starring at the London Palladium or working in the Cabinet, there is little difference! A best guess, based on current rates and predictions, will suffice and should also give an indication of what you should be charging for admission, shop sales and other services. Do not overlook this aspect of the budget.

Salary awards

In some cases, particularly in government funded and/or union monitored institutions, the manager does not have much say in salary negotiations. They are often agreed centrally and we must cope with them as best we can. Even in the independent sector we are negotiating against a background of the pay round generally. In both these cases it is regrettable that the museum and galleries sector is so small that our particular institution usually has little importance when weighed against wage negotiations which have taken place industry-wide by our trades union or other representatives on behalf of people who work in a different sector but to whom our salary conditions are allied. However, we should ensure we are paying the 'going rate' or we will lose the good people we need most. This is a balancing act which will be familiar to anyone who has managed even the smallest organisation. However, our budget needs to have built within it a factor that will cover any prudent settlement which may be agreed. Some years you will get it right, other years you may under- or over-estimate. Once again, accurate in-year management accounts (we will come to these) will allow you to adjust accordingly.

Known changes

It may seem obvious but some managers are caught out each year by costs or projects which could and should have been foreseen but are not included in their budgets. You should consult your department managers or people who work for you who have responsibility for spending money in your organisation (i.e. budget holders). Ask them, in good time before you draft the budget, exactly what they believe should be included. By asking direct questions such as these you will be able to say, later, that they cannot have the money they are seeking because they did not ask for it. Conversely, when they come to you, you will be prepared because you have included it in the budget. Other known changes will be the inevitable fluctuations in service charges. It is quite easy to obtain estimates for increases (there never seem to be decreases) in utilities and other services which are provided to your organisation on a regular basis. These are fixed costs and therefore, when you are looking for savings during the financial year, they are areas where it is highly unlikely you will be able to reduce expenditure. The fixed costs in your budget should be as accurate as possible and any known changes should be identified and inserted.

Contingencies

It is hardly ever possible to plan for the unexpected but you will rarely have a financial year where the unexpected does not occur in good measure. In national and local authority museums it is unlikely that you will be allowed to plan for contingencies within your budgets, but it would be a foolish official who did not build into his/her own departmental budgets the possibility that you, in your museum, may suddenly come to him/her for extra cash to cover an emergency. In the independent sector you should plan for such contingencies and build a modest figure into your budgets to take into account the unexpected.

114

Redevelopment

A museum or gallery which does not move forward is, in actuality, retreating. Museums are dynamic entities, always collecting and, hopefully, improving. Very few are profit-making and therefore surpluses of income over expenditure should be channelled back into redevelopment. The size of budgets allocated to redevelopment will differ from institution to institution and depend to a great extent on the size of projects which are scheduled for any particular year. However, in the public sector, there is some resistance on the part of funding bodies to allow managers in museums to budget for redevelopment during difficult economic times. This is a false economy as a lack of redevelopment for longer than three years will result in regression which may take more than twice that time to rectify.

The budget will therefore be compiled from estimates produced by the departments within the museum and you, depending on your position within the management structure, will either be required to have input to those estimates or to receive them from your subordinates. The estimates are a best guess from each department as to their costs for the coming year but they can only be guesses for, in some cases, we are calculating the cost of something more than eighteen months ahead of when we actually spend the money. Nevertheless, the estimate process leading to the budget is an essential part of effective resource management.

The estimate process should start no more than six months and not less than three months before the beginning of the financial year in question. You, as the manager, should call for estimates from all those people who work for you and have any responsibility for money. The job of collating those estimates into a departmental estimate is yours if you are a department head, and so it continues up the ladder. The Director's job is to collate the estimate submissions and to compile, in consultation with department heads (particularly the head of finance), the museum's total budget.

BUDGETS

The final budget should not be set in concrete, but you should be quite specific as to who can vary the budget within your organisation. Once the budget is produced the departments can then be allocated resources accordingly and there should be clear rules as to the delegation of responsibility for spending that money within the museum. These rules should not be hearsay but should be written down and everyone with a responsibility for spending money should understand the limits of their delegated powers and when they should come to a superior to seek permission to spend more.[1] Income is treated in much the same way. The only difference here is that I would not expect anyone to need permission to make more money than the budget forecasts! However, the targets for income generation need to be monitored as closely as the budget for expenditure. Income targets are powerful tools for motivating staff and may be used as performance indicators for appraising staff.

Your whole organisation (and its individual departments) will perform against the budget which is set prior to the start of the financial year so this is an important document and careful preparation should be undertaken before it is finally approved. I would expect that the governing body of a museum and gallery would be the final approval mechanism for annual budgets although, in national and local authority museums the funding department may also have input to this decision-making process. Obviously, the final budget should be communicated (i.e. circulated) to those in the museum with responsibility for its implementation.

FORECAST OUT-TURNS (MANAGEMENT ACCOUNTS)

Once the budget is set you have the task of managing that budget throughout the financial year. This is the area where most museum managers have difficulty and where most problems occur. It is essential that you have at your finger-tips regularly updated management accounts which will enable you to make adjustments to the budget, cash flow and rate of spend, in order to stay within the budget at year end. I suspect that most museums and galleries are looking towards a year end break-even figure or perhaps a modest surplus of income over expenditure – 'profit' in commerce and industry.

In order to manage the budget throughout the year you are interested in five specific figures:

1 Current financial position.

2 Spend to date.

3 Committed spend to date.

4 Forecast of
   (a) income
   (b) expenditure.

5 Out-turn.

These figures together comprise the 'Forecast out-turn' document which should be produced a few days after the end of each calender month. An example of such a document is shown in Fig. 16.

On the left-hand side of the document you will put the account headings for all areas of expenditure and income within your museum or gallery. These should be broken up into manageable sub-sections in order that you can determine the cost/benefit of specific areas of operation within the museum. Everything within the document is based on the previous year's actual performance followed by the budget which has been set during the year. From these you will be able to see trends and determine the performance of the museum against the previous year on a month by month basis.

When each out-turn is compiled (at the end of each month) a spend-to-date amount can be calculated but it is also most important that budget holders admit to the amount of money they have *committed* to spend at that date as well. Even though money has not yet been spent you, as the manager, need to know if your staff have committed money within their budgets in advance. This is often the case, particularly with expenditure on exhibitions or advance orders for conservation work. If you know your actual spend to date and your committed spend to date, you have a performance indicator for the period up to the most recent forecast out-turn document. You will therefore be able to detect any trends and determine whether your cash flow is in line with that for the previous year or that which was estimated before the financial year began (i.e. against budget).

The document also looks to the future and forecasts the amount of income and expenditure you will expect by the end of your financial year. There is always an element of guesswork in this (particularly during the early months of the financial year) but, by the tenth month you should have accurate figures to judge precisely what the out-turn for year end will be. By using this relatively simple method you can produce a forward estimate of your out-turn up to eleven months before the end of a financial year; in other words, after one month of the new financial year you should be in a position to know your end-of-year financial position. As a result of this forecasting you are always aware of your financial position in relation to how your balance sheet will close at the year end. However, it is all very well trying to estimate what the out-turn will be, but what do you actually do with that information as it comes in?

The key factor is to be aware, on at least a monthly basis, of your financial position. This will enable you to take steps to adjust the finances of your institution if things start to go wrong or to devote more resources to important areas if they go particularly well. Museums and galleries are quite different to commercial companies with regard to the ways in which they disperse surpluses of income. We have no shareholders and we do not pay dividends on profits. However, we do have to stay within national or local government accounting procedures and these may mean that we can only plan (financially) on an annual or, at most, a triennial basis. We may not be allowed to carry money over from one financial year to another. This is financial madness in the extreme and no commercial company would survive under these strictures. However, it is the lot of museum managers to have to operate commercially in a most uncommercial environment. This means that we must be even more aware of our financial position for if we make a loss there are usually few reserves to cover it, and if we make a surplus we may not be able to carry over the money to the next year.

It is not a bad practice to allocate budgets to departments but only delegate a proportion of the allocation up to a particular period during the financial

Forecast Out-Turn Year End [date]	*ACTUAL SPEND PREVIOUS YEAR* £	*BUDGET SET FOR THIS YEAR* £	*SPEND TO DATE THIS YEAR* £	*OUT-TURN AT YEAR END* £	*UNDER OR OVER SPEND AT YEAR END* £
EXPENDITURE					
PERSONNEL COSTS					
Salaries/Wages					
Superannuation					
Recruitment Costs					
Staff Medical Fees					
Staff Welfare Fees					
Staff Training Costs					
Uniforms/Special Clothing					
Staff Travel					
Sub-Total					
CURATORIAL OPERATIONS					
Exhibit-Design Dept					
Visual Arts					
Temporary Exhibitions					
Microfilm					
Still Photography					
Sub-Total					
MARKETING/PR/ADVERTISING					
Mktg/PR/Advertising (Site 1)					
Consultancy Services					
Education Services (Site 1)					
Sub-Total					
UTILITIES					
Business Rates					
Water Charges					
Gas Charges					
Electricity Charges					
Furnace Fuel Oil					
Sub-Total					

Figure 16 Example of a forecast out-turn

GENERAL ADMINISTRATION					
Subs to Societies					
Stationery					
Printing					
Postage					
Telephones					
Cleaning of Premises					
Insurances					
Audit/Accounting Fees					
Consultancy/Legal Fees					
Fixtures/Fittings					
Office Machinery/Computers					
Routine Building Maintenance					
Sub-Total					
SPECIAL ITEMS					
Redevelopment Costs					
Museum Purchase Grant					
Maintenance of Premises (Special)					
Sub-Total					
TOTAL MUSEUM EXPENDITURE					
INCOME					
Balances brought forward					
Admission Charges					
Donations/Collections					
Archives Photocopy					
Library Photocopy					
Public Telephones					
Friends of the Museum					
Catering Concession Fee					
Mktg/Conference Space Hire					
Audio Tours					
Trading Co Covenant					
Sponsorship Income					
Value Added Tax (Output Tax)					
GRANTS					
NET SURPLUS/(DEFICIT)					

year. This allows you, the manager, greater flexibility in adjusting allocations to meet the actual performance of the museum part way through the year. I have heard captains of industry who are trustees of national museums express surprise at the accuracy of the out-turn forecast against the final balance sheet for, in some museums with multimillion turnovers, the forecast some months before the end of the financial year can be measured in hundreds. When the balance sheet actually confirms this at the end of the year everyone, except the good manager, is surprised! But this is the key to managing non-profit financial resources effectively. You should never be surprised by an unexpected change in financial circumstances. If you are, your estimates and your budget were wrong or you did not build in contingencies to take into account the unexpected. You should always be aware of exactly where your institution is financially from one month to the next. If a situation deteriorates you may wish to have management accounts produced weekly and you should have an infrastructure set up which will achieve this without undue disruption or alarm. All budget holders should be consulted and should be made aware not only of their position within the organisation but also the situation with regard to their colleagues and the other budgets. This overall knowledge on the part of managers of what they and their colleagues are doing (financially) makes for greater understanding between departments and therefore even tighter budgetary control.

I cannot emphasise enough the importance of this area of management. You may be the finest leader and most effective manager of personnel there has ever been but, if you cannot manage those parts of your institution which provide the funding to allow those people to carry out their jobs, you are a failure.

MANAGEMENT KNOWLEDGE

The specialist curator turned manager cannot absolve himself/herself of the responsibility for being financially aware within his/her organisation. He/she should not just be aware of the financial performance of the museum in relation to forecast out-turns and budgets as we have already discussed. He/she should also have an awareness of the detail surrounding how that money is spent and earned. The following is a list of areas to which you should be able to give an immediate answer to the question 'How much does it cost . . .':

1 Salary costs and the percentage of salaries against overall expenditure.

2 The cost of the following areas of the museum's operation:
   (a) Curatorial operations.
   (b) Marketing/public relations.
   (c) Education services.
   (d) Administration costs.
   (e) Redevelopment costs.
   (f) Temporary and permanent exhibitions.

120

3 On income you should be aware of:
  (a) How much you receive from admission charges each year coupled with how much is the average spend on admission per visitor.
  (b) The annual turnover of your trading company or shop.
  (c) The profit covenanted from your trading company or shop to your museum annually.
  (d) The spend per visitor in your museum shop.
  (f) The amount of money earned by your museum in trading through non-shop related activities.
  (g) Your total grants from government, local authority, trusts etc.

All these may seem simple but time and time again I have spoken to museum managers who do not have answers to these questions to hand. You may think that this is unnecessary, but if a manager does not have these figures almost permanently available in his/her subconscious, he/she cannot be aware of the performance of his/her institution at any given time. More importantly, the manager will not know whether the organisation is doing well or doing badly until it is too late.

One of your jobs is to manage information as well as to manage finances and people. As the leader you must have the ability to hover over the whole institution if you are Director, or over your own department/section if you are a budget holder, in order to home-in on areas of poor performance and rectify the problems. Likewise you should be able to identify areas of high performance and commend those involved.

NOTE

1 An example Code of Financial Practice may be found in the Appendix to this book.

9

Managing organisations

Before we start to learn how to manage organisations we must look at how to organise and describe, or categorise, the different types of organisation. Here we will look at the structure, function and performance of organisations, and the behaviour of groups and individuals within them. Organisation theory has rarely been applied to museums, so I hope to demonstrate how the historic and contemporary thoughts of organisation theorists can be applied to museums and galleries. Thus far we have concentrated predominantly on the application of techniques of management to individuals or groups and the financial aspects of running museums. Whilst there are considerable similarities, and genuine overlaps between management and organisation theory, in this book I have separated them in the hope that the reader will gain a greater understanding of the differences.

The study of organisation theory has evolved in one or other of the supporting disciplines of anthropology, sociology, psychology or social psychology; inevitably the theoretical perspectives of academics in these non-management areas, and their overall research training, has coloured approaches to the problems of organisations. In this chapter we will explore management and organisation theory in order to discover generalisations applicable to museums and galleries. Every act of a manager rests on assumptions about what has happened and conjectures about what will happen; the totality of the manager's action tends to rest on theory. Theory and practice are inseparable; there is a necessity continually to examine, criticise and update thinking about the organisation and how it functions; museums and galleries are organisations so if we wish to be effective managers we must learn and develop the theories appropriate to them.

The concept of organisational behaviour is important when examining organisation theory generally. The task of management can be assisted by the organisation of the individual's behaviour in relation to the physical means and resources to achieve the desired goals. The most basic problem is to determine how much organisation and control of behaviour is necessary for efficient and effective functioning. Two schools of thought are involved in solving this problem. On the one hand, there are those who may be called the 'organisers' who maintain that more and better control is necessary for better efficiency.

They point to the advantage of specialisation and clear job definitions, standard routines and clear lines of authority. This is typical within museums. On the other hand, there are those who may be called 'behaviourists' who maintain that the continuing attempt to increase control over behaviour is self-defeating, leading inevitably to rigidity and apathy in performance. Counter-control through informal relationships means that increased inefficiency does not necessarily occur with increased control. These are continuing dilemmas, and organisation theory has been built around them. It is not possible to opt for one view to the exclusion of the other; an eminent author, in the introduction to his book *Organization Theory, Selected Readings* writes:

> It is one of the basic tasks of management to determine the optimum degree of control necessary to operate efficiently . . . It is through a study of the constraints in relation to the objectives that most efficient organisational control systems are established.

(Pugh, 1971)

We shall therefore deal with three main themes here and in Chapters 11, 12 and 13; these themes dominate organisation theory and focus on problems within organisations generally, and museums in particular. The themes can be categorised under the following headings:

1 Structure: problems arising from the way roles and relationships are structured within the organisation; this includes problems for the organisation and problems for the individual.

2 Relationships: problems arising from relationships between individuals and groups, in particular, culture and conflict in organisations.

3 Change: problems arising from change in the organisation's affairs.

STRUCTURE

The importance of organisational structure is rarely understood but this structure is continually changing in the museum world. This is a result of the realisation in the mid to late 1980s of the inappropriateness of the organisational structure of many museums and galleries. Between 1984 and 1988 over two-thirds of the director's posts in UK national museums and galleries were vacated and new appointments made. It was the end of an era encompassing the academic figurehead of the great national institution. With increasing pressure on resources, and central government policy pointing towards greater income generation from within, trustees were obliged to look for directors who had shown expertise in the areas of management and entrepreneurship. The problem facing the employer was to find a suitably qualified person in the academic sense, but with a record of leadership ability and commercial flair. This phenomenon saw a drawing together of key senior members of the museum profession into the new vacated posts. In three cases new directors of national museums were drawn from within the museum framework but from outside the national sector; something which had hardly ever happened before. When the post of Director of the Science Museum was advertised it was the first time that a national museum had made it clear that candidates with managerial experience, but not necessarily museum experience, would be considered. The traditional system of internal trawling for senior management posts also started to fade and more posts began to be filled as a result of open competition.

With a freshness of new talent being introduced these individuals have taken a close look at the organisational structures of the institutions they are now required to direct. They have found that the traditional approach is inappropriate as a result of the changes that have taken place in museums over the past decade. This new approach enables us to discuss the individual (the behaviourist approach); the organisation and its form (the organiser's approach); and the systems and interaction within the organisation. We can draw analogies from the benchmarks drawn as a result of the changes which have taken place in many of our largest museums and galleries.

RELATIONSHIPS

Organisations are collections of individuals and political systems. Individuals have separate personalities, needs, intellects, aspirations and ways of adapting to rules. Political systems usually have quite well-defined boundaries, which include an element of administration, quite complex goals and values, and a hierarchy which disseminates power. These two features (individuals and political systems) which make up organisations can be joined together and then we have a force which includes power and influence. However, if these features drift apart inevitable problems ensue. Nevertheless this creates a useful (though artificial) sequence to describe the study of organisations – people, power and politics. The link with many of the elements already described earlier in this book is intentional for the overlaps between management and organisation theory are such that they become one. However, discussing museums and galleries as organisations involves looking laterally at many other disciplines associated with management theory, but equally important is the environment in which the organisation operates and the culture of the organisation.

The environment within which museums operate is constantly changing, but these changes have been particularly noticeable over the past decade. Museums, like other organisations, function by combining resources. There are fundamental principles that come into play when resources are combined. In recent years the organisational structures of museums have been forced to react to three important principles.

The law of diminishing returns

The law of diminishing returns will apply frequently when output depends on several inputs (e.g. labour, machines, materials) and when some of the inputs are constant then, beyond a certain limit, increases in other inputs result in smaller related increases in output.

A simple example would be a museum with fixed costs rising as a result of a variable demand by visitors. It is perfectly conceivable for the variable demand to grow to such an extent that the fixed costs cannot cope with the upsurge. Whilst this theory may have seemed far removed from the practical world of running museums and galleries a few years ago, it is nevertheless a symptom of the current environment. If more variable units (visitors, archive collections, exhibits etc.) are added to the fixed factors (a museum with limited resources in staff, space and finance) the output (public satisfaction, catalogued collections, exhibit displays etc.) may increase or improve rapidly at first, but will eventually slow down and inevitably decline. This is occurring in some of the national and many of the larger local authority museums, and has certainly been seen to a greater extent in the university sector. These museums are seeing their Grant-in-Aid reducing in real terms and their only hope of maintaining standards is to increase their ability to make commercial income in addition to grants. Inevitably, as they earn their own income there are two sides to their balance sheet – income and expenditure – whereas there was once only one (expenditure). This gives their funding body more information as to their effectiveness and therefore allows them to offset any income against their own expenditure – a recipe for continuing reductions in Grant-in-Aid. When competing priorities for the customer/visitor are added, coupled with a huge increase in leisure attractions, and the introduction of Sunday trading, the decline in income as a result of a reducing number of visitors is a distinct possibility for all museums and galleries.

The law of increasing costs

The law of diminishing returns illustrates what happens to output if one factor remains fixed. The law of increasing costs examines what happens to production, and therefore costs, as all factors of production are increased. An example would be a museum which tried to double its annual temporary exhibition programme; increases in costs would be inevitable, as would a reduction in work done elsewhere on other programmes as a result of staff resources being devoted towards these exhibitions. Increasing costs could also come about as a result of the competition for resources – very likely in the case of smaller museums and galleries where resources are limited.

When comparing costs in this way (resources or cash) there is an opportunity cost. The opportunity cost of something is whatever has to be given up in order to produce something. In the museum example above the opportunity costs would include all those programmes that were cancelled, reduced or postponed as a result of staff resources being devoted to the increased temporary exhibition programme. A simpler example would be the common problem of holding cash in a current account instead of investing it in securities (because it is thought necessary to have the money instantly

125

available); the opportunity cost in this case is the value of the interest that is forgone.

Economies of scale

The principles examined above (diminishing returns and increasing costs) seem to place limits on the ability to combine resources and produce results. However, the principle of economies of scale is that as a product is produced in larger numbers so the cost of producing each individual item becomes smaller, i.e., production is likely to become more efficient. This is a well-known and well-understood phenomenon in manufacturing industries, but there is little opportunity to exercise it in museums. Nevertheless, it is usually understood in those areas of museums concerned with publishing or retailing, particularly by believing (erroneously in some cases) that large quantities and lower unit prices are advantageous. Whilst economies of scale may take advantage of technology and divisions of labour, a time will come when they are exhausted and costs begin to rise again. This is often predictable in manufacturing industry but is less so in museums and galleries. Generally, the increase in production in museums will only result in the laws of increasing costs and diminishing returns being applied. Where economies of scale are sought there is often little justification for believing that a museum will benefit from them. However, examination of the stockrooms of many museum shops will show how purchases of large quantities of goods have been made in order to take advantage of economies of scale; closer investigation may also reveal that there is an opportunity cost because of the long period of storage needed before the real costs can be recovered, coupled with the write-off costs for soiled and damaged goods, and the cost of storage itself. Remember, your function is not only to manage a museum but all that goes on within it; this may often include trading and other commercial activities.

Legal environment

The principles above show how, on the one hand, organisations must deal with constraints which govern human behaviour, and on the other hand with the constraints placed by nature on production. In the case of all organisations, and particularly museums, there are also legal constraints. These are placed upon an organisation and the market, and reflect contemporary political, professional and social ideology and norms.

The legal environment is a framework of rules within which organisations operate. Human behaviour and the natural world both constrain and help organisations; the legal environment also does this. The law (including professional codes of practice) constrains organisations by preventing them from doing what they wish to do, or making them alter the way they do things, often with higher cost implications. It may also force them to do things they might not otherwise choose to do (e.g., health and safety regulations etc.). The law is also an enabling medium helping organisations to pursue their objectives. For example, they are able to formulate their policies and determine their responsibilities and liabilities according to known rules of law and codes of conduct, benefit from legal protection, and acquire resources and sell products and services through the mechanism of contract law.

The seeming contradiction between 'enabling' and 'constraining' does not really exist. The simple analogy of a game of football serves to illustrate this. The laws of the game prevent the players from doing certain things, but they also enable the game to actually take place. The game could neither start nor end without rules; more importantly (in a sporting and business sense) it would also be extremely difficult to ascertain who the winners were in any given match. In essence the law regulates the activities of organisations by providing a framework of rules governing their formation and dissolution, their use of resources and activities; and their responsibility and accountability to providers of finance, employees, customers and the community in general. Codes of conduct and professional rules also require that specific standards are upheld by individuals and are a medium which can be used to assess the performance of groups or individuals in the work they carry out. The law also provides a number of methods for resolving conflict. Unlike the environment generally, it would be quite wrong to see the legal environment as being in a state of constant flux; indeed, one of the characteristics of a stable society is certain legal rules. However, the forces of contextual/environmental change are always present and over a long period the process of change is clearly evident.

CHANGE

When considering change it is essential to contrast substantive change with procedural change, and organisational change with institutional change. Recent changes to employment law are examples of substantive change, and affect the way in which organisations may engage employees in work; they are changes to the rules of employment, to the substance of law. Procedural change is where the process by which rules are enforced has changed, not the rules themselves. The changes mentioned above as substantive are organic and result from the interaction of the forces which constitute the total environment: social, economic, professional and institutional change. There are also changes which are less the result of natural forces and more the result of conscious acts. An example of institutional change is the introduction of admission charges in national museums. This transformation will have significant effects on the institutions that make up the national sector and a peripheral (although different) effect on other museums. The most significant change is the transition of the 'visitor' into the 'customer' with all that this entails. The public perception of museums will therefore include a value-for-money element which was hitherto absent. We must prepare for this; it is not sufficient merely to install turnstiles and take people's money. Customer care programmes and visitor

127

service awareness, coupled with a rethink about the way we interpret our collections, are all needed before this sort of change can be made.

Returning to organisations generally, it is accepted that they have responsibilities not only to their investors, members, creditors, etc., but also to the community in general and they must be accountable to all. This is even more important in the museum context than it is in business organisation. Investors in museums are the visiting public generally and, in many cases, individual donors of artefacts or money. The membership of museums can range from a small number of university students to a world-wide population of researchers or committed lay-visitors, with an interest in a national collection. The local community or a very discrete area of interest is very important to local authority museums or museums with single themes. Museums as an educational resource also necessitate a particular responsibility to the community of young people and students.

As a consequence of all these responsibilities, the legal environment may facilitate an organisation's activities but it can also, paradoxically, impose constraints and obligations. Without this control it would be possible to pursue activities and employ methods which are socially, economically and politically unacceptable. The law restrains the minority to assist the majority and is a major factor within the environment in which any organisation operates.

A changing environment has produced a profound effect on museums and galleries, resulting in different approaches to management becoming ever more necessary in the latter part of this century. The environment includes other, less profound, but equally important factors that have come together in the last few years to produce a catalyst for change. Factors to do with the economy and politics are affecting the lives of people on an international scale. Social change in recent years has included a move from the traditional structure of the extended family to the more typical unit consisting of parents and children – the nuclear family. The family exists separately and is not supported by other family members. The rise in the nuclear family is associated with greater social and geographical mobility, changing social values fundamentally from those which were traditional. The shape of the family in the United Kingdom affects the audience for museums. The nuclear family has modified its shape still further as divorce has become almost endemic. There has also been a tremendous change in the role of women in society. The single parent family is becoming a significant minority.

The spread of state education brought about great changes resulting in the Education Act of 1944. The general raising of educational standards affected the way in which museums were used by, and communicated with, visitors. Teachers' disputes in the late 1980s in state education had a profoundly adverse affect on the number of visitors to museums.

The growth of ethnic minorities began with immigration from the West Indies in the 1950s which was encouraged to deal with the labour problems of full employment in the UK. The multiracial society that has resulted has changed the environment radically in those areas (particularly inner cities) populated by these ethnic minorities. Museums, generally, have yet to make conscious attempts to cater for this change. In this respect the UK lags behind many other countries. Sadly, it must be admitted that the attitude of many people to ethnic minorities is simply one of prejudice and museums have yet to address this, both in the way in which they design exhibitions and the composition of the museum profession itself. In the USA the black minority has existed for over a century and has thus had time to make specific contributions to that country of a nature not yet possible in say, the UK or France where wide-scale settlement is more recent.

For most people the quality of life has improved over the last twenty or thirty years and people have more leisure time and consume more goods and services. In 1964, 46 per cent of the population lived in homes which they owned; in 1984, this figure had risen to 61 per cent. As an example of the consumer revolution, it is acknowledged that the UK has one of the highest percentage per capita of ownership of video recorders and home computers in the world. This, in part, explains the particular effect that education, technology and leisure time have had on museums. The visitor is better educated, capable of understanding relatively complex technology, and increasingly available as a customer (by virtue of increased leisure time and disposable income). The quality of life has not necessarily been enhanced by these changes. Life is more stressful, more frenetic, and there has been a dramatic increase in crime. The implications for museums are those that take advantage of one (by making museums respond to the positive trends) and guard against the other (by ensuring that security is capable of reacting to the adverse trends).

Generally, museums have recognised the differences in the community between the rich and the poor better than many other organisations. Unemployment in the 1980s increased the gulf between our 'two nations' because of the distinct geographical bias where the south of the country was mainly prosperous, while deprivation was concentrated in more northern areas. This distinct differential has disappeared in recent years, but museums and other organisations must realise that serious inequalities still exist and that there are fundamental disagreements about how to cope with the problem. On the one hand there are those who see the regeneration of the economy as the first priority in order that welfare services may be more affordable. Then there are those who believe that the inequalities must be reduced before it is possible to make progress on economic issues. The effect of this on museums in northern parts of the country may be more pronounced than in the south and museum managers must alter their perspectives to suit local conditions.

Demographic changes are a significant influence on how museums attract an audience. If organisations do not understand or adjust to changes in their environment they cannot hope to provide for themselves, their investors, members or community. Lack of understanding of the environment will compound a false impression of the economy and society itself. For example, when studying the population it is necessary to establish how size and compositions change or evolve. Similarly, with politics it is change that is of most concern. For organisations to believe that they are their own world is often as fatal a mistake as it is for individuals. Their products and services must constantly evolve as a result of internal influence and the macro-world of the environment in which they operate. It is particularly important that senior managers understand the complexities of environmental influence on organisations, for it is often counter-productive to their work; a correct appreciation is vital, for empirical resolution to organisational problems that are discussed here and subsequently are often inappropriate. In most cases the study of organisations is better than opinion, and analysis better than supposition.

I do not intend to delve into organisation theory in such depth as to provide a definitive study of the subject, this is to be done elsewhere. The purpose of this part of the book has been to add to those management theories described earlier and to develop them, where appropriate, into the management of institutions – this is organisation theory.

Organisational theory is achieved by looking briefly at the historic perspective, including an element of defending some of the early theories. The specific problems of museums operating in an interdisciplinary sense and the problems of structure are all fundamental to organisations, and these are included, as are those relevant to the divisions of work within museums. Co-ordination of activities, like division of work, is an area of research that requires greater emphasis in museums and the experience and findings of organisation theorists – applied to museums – results in a better appreciation of the role of managers in organisations generally, and museums and galleries in particular. They give an appreciation of the need for management to ensure the linking together of museum departments to achieve a goal; the temporary exhibition is a good example for it often requires the input of a wide variety of co-ordinated departments to ensure success.

The two final elements are interrelated and concern the culture of organisations and the resolution or identification of conflict. Culture, like the environment, is often changing and an appreciation of the manager's ability to bring about change is an important area that we should look at. The identification and resolution of conflict is becoming ever more important as change is being brought about within our museums and galleries. We shall therefore look at this in some detail.

ORGANISATION THEORY

Organisation theory comprises such topics as structure, authority, power, formal organisation, informal organisation, bureaucratisation, professionalisation, democratisation and the impact of changes in size, technology, task, uncertainty and public accountability – quite a long list but many of these will have a ring of familiarity to museum professionals. The study of organisation theory is particularly appropriate to museums as a greater emphasis is applied to the problems of coping with uncertainty and the information processing required. It is the purpose of this book to broaden the meaning and to progress it onward from the psychological concepts in information processing capacities through decision-making and directly into those areas of relevance to the peculiar requirements of museums. In looking briefly at the historic perspective it is necessary not only to recall the research of theorists, but also to realise that the subject does have an empirical arm. This area of study should not be purely theoretical, nor should the emphasis on theory put the reader off for we shall delve into important topics which are of relevance to the aspiring manager.

The organisation is a mixture of functions directed towards a common goal. Organisations are not, in themselves, purposeful systems. Most commonly they are corporations, schools, universities, armies, hospitals, museums and other formal organisations. But they could also be football teams arranging a competition, or a criminal gang undertaking a robbery, or a band of guerrillas set on revolution. While organisations of the former type usually have a legal existence, formal organisation and formal boundaries, these characteristics are not necessary for the social system to be an organisation.

Whilst a number of approaches have already been discussed as management theories in previous chapters (particularly classical and Contingency Theory), it is necessary for us to be aware of additional schools of thought where the theories are applicable to organisations in general. The Classical School has already been examined and is one of the fundamental principles, not only of management theory, but also of organisation theory.

Traditionally, the majority of museums have followed the Classical Approach, and the present structures are still characterised by hierarchy, a division between line management and staff, and a series of precisely defined jobs and relationships. The upshot of this application is that museums, generally, are being managed in an inappropriate way in the light of some behaviourists' findings. Behaviourists' theories accept hierarchical form but believe it can be much improved by less narrow specialisation, by permitting more participation in decision-making on the part of the lower ranks and by a more democratic attitude on the part of managers at all levels. These features are not impossible to achieve with classical principles, but in the case of museums they are often used too rigidly; more emphasis on human resources may lead to greater motivation and a greater use of the entire resources available within museums.

One suggested organisation structure based on behavioural theories is the 'Organic Organisation' – a structure in which there is a minimum of division of duties. Theoretically each person in the organisation contributes to the best of his/her ability to the solution of any problems that arise, and so far as the regular work is concerned there is more or less general agreement about who should do what, since each person is known to possess certain skills and to lack others. This approach is certainly appropriate to small museums and galleries where there are few staff. There are many museums where people

131

have job titles which indicate that they are expected to do a certain type of work, but the boundaries of their jobs are not set formally or precisely; they often carry out work which is ordinarily not expected of a person with a similar title – work demanding either a higher or a lower skill than they ordinarily exercise. This also takes place with some small groups within larger museums that are essentially organic in nature. It is often practical to divide work to be undertaken by implementing temporary task forces in which membership will shift as needs and problems change. An example of this application might be the development of a temporary exhibition programme within a museum, where groups of multi-disciplinary individuals are brought together for the temporary task of putting together specific displays.

It may be possible to have several different types of groups, not necessarily temporary, within the same organisation. The work of these groups will be, (a) largely repetitive and routine, (b) work that requires solutions to non-repetitive problems, (c) work which may be unique but repetitive, and (d) work that would be unique and non-repetitive. The first type of group would be largely organised along classical lines, but feedback on results should be to members of the group as well as to the administrative system; members of the group would be expected to present suggestions and improvements. The second type of group would negotiate with the administrative group on resources and output, and specialists within the group would largely determine the processes to be used. The third type of group, which would be made up of quasi-independent craftsmen or professionals, would have still greater autonomy while the fourth type would have a high degree of autonomy with major responsibility for both planning and control of its work. This 'organic-adaptive' structure on a semi-permanent basis presents a sound justification for its use in museums. Nevertheless, fundamental changes would be needed to the classical principles (which are, in museums, so often allied to Taylorism) and by individual managers with regard to their duties as described earlier.

The equilibrium, or survival opportunities and possibilities, of an organisation depend to a very large extent on its ability to induce co-operation, particularly in discussing decisions. The hierarchy of decision-making has been expanded into a method of actually structuring an organisation, the suggestion being that the structure is designed through an examination of the points at which decisions must be made and the persons from whom information must be acquired if decisions are to be satisfactory. The theory has been termed 'the decision-making approach' an element of this approach has been called 'functional teamwork' which ensures that decisions regarding various areas are made by those most expert in them. This logical sequence of decisions can be illustrated by part of a typical organisation for a medium-sized museum (see Fig. 17).

An organisation has many properties in common with a living organism. Like any living creature the organisation develops by growing, reaching a peak, then often (or usually) a decline, and finally death. The organisation also, like a living being, reacts to its environment. Like any biological organism, organ-

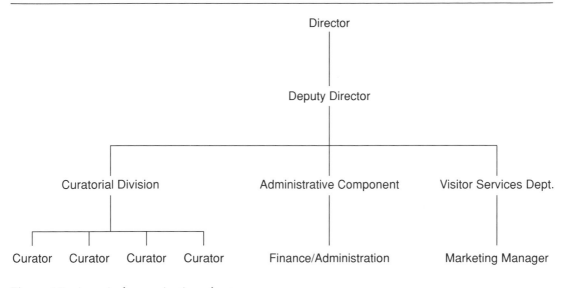

Figure 17 A typical organisation chart

isations comprise many parts that interact with each other in varying and complex ways. This has led some theorists to conclude that an organisation, like an organism, cannot grow and still function unless the balance between its various parts is maintained in an exact ratio, an example of which could be the ratios in geometry; i.e., the relationship between the radius of a circle and its circumference remains the same no matter how large or small the circle is. One theorist (Haire, 1966) has actually developed what he calls the 'square-cube' theory which explains this phenomenon. He states that as the mass of an object is cubed, its surfaces are only squared. This could happen within organisations, for example, we all know that once the staff costs of an organisation go beyond approximately 60 per cent of the total annual revenue expenditure there is likely to be insufficient resource left for those people to carry out their duties properly. This is a serious problem for many national museums which currently face stagnation (in real terms) as a result of reductions in Grant-in-Aid by government, which is forcing them to seek alternative funding. In the 1983–86 report of the Board of the Trustees of the Victoria and Albert Museum (V&A), the Chairman admitted that the V&A spent 82 per cent of its total grant on wages and salaries. He said: 'If the present system continues, a forward projection into the 1990s brings that amount up to 90 % or over, leaving us with far too little money to run the museum, let alone improve it' (Voak, 1986, p. 5). This is a recipe for disaster which has been acknowledged by those in the museum and gallery profession but has yet to be resolved by those who provide Grant-in-Aid.

The future requires that all museums and galleries become more business-like in earning their own income to offset the inevitable decline in subsidy from traditional public sources. There is strong evidence to assume that the organic inevitability of stagnation, decline and eventual death, is being reversed in many cases by innovative management of many museums. However, I predict (with some sadness) that many of the new museums created in the 1980s will not last, particularly those which were founded as a knee-jerk reaction to the closure of industrial plants, or even whole industries in particular areas.

10

Organisation structure

The structure of an organisation comprises all the arrangements by which its various activities are divided between its members, and their efforts co-ordinated. Indeed, without such structure, the people involved would simply be a group of individuals or at best a collection of cliques, and not an organisation at all. To be an organisation, whether a multinational, a multicorporation, a workers co-operative, a museum or gallery, implies some kind of structure. The most fundamental problem that can arise is when the structure is inappropriate to the function of the organisation.

Structure is normally associated with formal responsibilities, the typical organisation chart is an example of this (see p. 133). However, it also covers the linking mechanisms between the roles and the co-ordinating structures of the organisation, if any are needed. The environment in which the organisation operates and the culture of the organisation itself all have a bearing on an appropriate structure. Whether the structure is appropriate or not would be determined by a variety of forces: technology, market, size of the organisation, and its people.

Clearly, there are many different ways of deciding how an organisation's work is to be divided up and co-ordinated. Different decisions would give rise to different structures. To be as efficient as possible an organisation needs an appropriate structure. What may be best for one organisation might not be best for another. What may be good for one museum may not be good for another. In addition, what may be perfectly correct for an organisation during one period of time may not be appropriate during a different period of time, or if the environment or culture changes. Museums tend to have particularly traditional structures many of which have remained intact or unchanged for some years. Recognising that structural design and organisation structure generally should be reviewed (and if necessary altered) regularly to take account of external and internal changes, is a fundamental part of a manager's ability to properly manage his/her organisation. It is not difficult to assume that if an inappropriate structure is either chosen or perpetuated after it ceases to be relevant, structural problems will ensue.

Many of the current organisational problems within museums and galleries are a direct consequence of inappropriate structures. This is usually as a result of a lack of recognition of external and internal problems by managers. Any organisation may encounter problems concerned with finance, output, marketing, technical developments, the law, its association with its staff and public, and so on. However, these do not necessarily bear greatly on the problems arising out of the way the organisation is structured. Paradoxically the structure exists in order that the organisation's work may be accomplished, yet that structure can itself create problems in accomplishing the work. Whether it actually does so or not depends on how appropriate the structure is to the individual organisation and how well that organisation implements its own structural design.

It is not always apparent that structural problems exist. Indeed, such problems may often appear to be due to individuals' inadequacies rather than overall inappropriateness of the main structure. We must be aware of the symptoms which will manifest themselves if our organisation has structural problems:

- low motivation
- morale problems
- late or inappropriate decisions being made
- conflict
- lack of co-ordination between departments
- rising costs
- inadequate response to change
- an inevitable decline.

Practically every organisation will display a few of these symptoms, but museums and galleries often have a high proportion. This is particularly applicable during times of change; recent years have produced changing circumstances for museums and galleries throughout the world. Most organisations are not designed, they develop. Indeed, we have already discussed the biological analogy that describes this organisational phenomena, but not all organisations adapt equally well to the environment in which they grow. Many, like the dinosaur of great size but little brain, remain unchanged in a changing world. This need for continual growth and development is paramount, particularly in museums which are already thrust into a radically changing environment. Many museums, particularly those in the national sector, have been in existence for many years. They have grown and developed from small private collections to large bureaucracies. During their existence the environment in which they operate has changed frequently; elemental changes regarding funding, employment law, visitor services etc. have all produced an effect in recent years which has demanded a review of the appropriateness of their structures. In many cases such a review has not been carried out. The upshot of this is that there are a number of traditional museums which have inappropriate structures whereas the relatively new, admittedly smaller, independent sector museums have opened with some thought being given to the appropriateness of their structural design.

To illustrate the contrasting approaches to structure and the fact that different basic designs give rise to organisations with very different characteristics, it is interesting to look at the two extreme ends of organisational structure. At one end is the kind of organisation which is best described as a bureaucracy; bureaucracies normally have a rigid hierarchical structure at their heart. At the other extreme is the rather loose organisation of an 'adhocracy'. This type of structure is often built on a temporary, loose and informal basis. Between the two extremes, some organisations remain bureaucratic and others will be largely adhocratic. Both will probably have some tendencies towards the other. Any of the possible mixtures could be appropriate to the organisation's circumstances at the time so we shall look at both types in detail.

BUREAUCRACY

We have already discovered that museums, generally, observe scientific and classical principles of management. These approaches tend to produce an organisation that is essentially bureaucratic, a term that was defined by sociologist Max Weber (Gerth and Wright Mills, 1958) as an organisation in which:

1 The regular activities are distributed in a fixed way as official duties.

2 Jobs are arranged in a hierarchy with each job holder's authority to command and to apply various means of coercion strictly defined.

3 There are written documents to govern the general conduct of the organisation.

As a form of organisation bureaucracy has been with us for thousands of years. It is the dominant type of organisation in most kinds of activity, whether industrial, commercial, military, public service, or museums. It is accepted as such all around the world and is probably, in general, the most efficient and the most fair way of structuring organisations of almost any size. To many people the word 'bureaucracy' denotes an organisation that is inefficient and frustrating to work for, or to deal with. The extent, however, to which an enterprise organised on classical lines exhibits these faults depends less on the organisational structure itself than on how rigid the rules are, and how much leeway is permitted to the job holders at various levels. Weber thought of a bureaucracy as the most efficient form of organisation in that it would substitute a rule of law for a rule based on the whims of those who happened to be in charge at any particular time. In the latter case, he said, superiors were apt to be moved by 'personal sympathy and favour, by grace and gratitude' (Gerth and Wright Mills, 1958, pp. 196–239). Some of the complaints that can be made against bureaucracies are as follows:

- rigid rule following
- over staffing
- empire building
- paper shuffling
- impersonality
- stifling of initiative
- slowness etc.

Weber, from his observation of existing organisations, set out to describe the 'ideal model' of a rational, efficient organisation. Any organisation would be appraised as more or less bureaucratic in terms of how closely it fitted the features picked out by Weber following his outline of the 'ideal model' of bureaucracy. Weber's (1938) model of bureaucracy included:

1 Specialisation: the work of individuals and departments is broken down into distinct, routine and well-defined tasks.

2 Formalisation: formal rules and procedures are followed to standardise and control the actions of the organisation's members.

3 Clear hierarchy: a multilevel 'pyramid of authority' clearly defines how each job holder at any level is under the control of a job holder at a higher level.

4 Promotion by merit: the selection or promotion of staff based on public criteria (e.g. qualifications, examinations and proven competence) rather than on the unexplained preferences of superiors.

5 Impersonal rewards and sanctions: rewards (e.g. bonuses) and disciplinary sanctions are applied impersonally by standardised procedures, so that justice is seen to be done.

6 Career tenure: job holders are assured of a career structure and a job for life, in the expectation that they will commit themselves to the organisation.

7 Separation of careers and private lives: people are expected to arrange their personal or family life so as not to interfere with the activities of the organisation.

This model is obviously of an ideal organisation, but it is not difficult to apply the outline to many (particularly the larger) museums and galleries. However, that should not be taken to mean that museums and galleries have an ideal structure, for the wholly bureaucratic model may no longer be appropriate for the circumstances or environment in which we operate. It is also highly unlikely that any organisation can be made to run as a totally fair and efficient, impersonal machine. Many of the features of bureaucracy can on the one hand be beneficial, yet on the other hand reflect badly on the organisation. A compromise must be sought.

The ideal bureaucracy excludes irrelevant or secret criteria for choosing, promoting, rewarding or punishing employees and establishing rules and procedures. Employees are to be assured of job security even if they lose their original skills or their skills eventually become outmoded. Each employee knows the rules and procedures that delineate his/her own area of responsibility. At the same time, the vertical hierarchy establishes clear lines of authority so that each employee knows who his/her boss is. The private lives of employees are to be kept separate from their lives in the organisation.

The desire to separate private lives from the day-to-day life of the organisation may well have been appropriate in Weber's day but it is now recognised that the effect problems at home can have on an employee's work are often significant and cannot be disregarded. The caring organisation has a duty to support the employee, and the manager who wishes to build a loyal hard-working team needs to understand this. However, the open criteria to protect employees against unfair treatment from prejudiced superiors was a precursor to employment protection legislation which is now the norm in most developed countries. The separation of private lives and organisational lives may also protect employees from having their efficiency or job satisfaction threatened by how well, or how poorly they or their colleagues are getting on with their spouse, children and others outside the workplace. The promise of job security encourages employees' commitment to the organisation and increases their willingness to master new skills that might be of limited marketability outside the organisation. This is particularly appropriate to the museum context because of the very specialised nature of many of the tasks undertaken by museum professionals.

Employees may well appreciate the fact that their jobs are clearly defined, so that they know the limits of their responsibilities without fear of reprimand for overstepping the mark. Employees also appreciate the vertical hierarchy that indicates from whom to seek a decision and to take problems.

There are, nevertheless, potential problems. There is no doubt that, in some cases, job security may make employees complacent and/or lazy. Rules and procedures for reward may leave it unclear as to how to deal fairly with any achievements and malpractices that are at all out of the ordinary. In museums this is particularly relevant if some employees feel alienated by the degree to which their highly specialised jobs are defined for them, leaving them little room in which to be individuals rather than replaceable 'cogs in the machine'; such alienation can be increased by what may seem to be the uncaring impersonality of an organisation that fails to take account of the personal lives of its members.

There is an increasing dissatisfaction in museums and galleries with the lack of contact between subordinates and senior management, particularly in the large local authority and national sector museums. This also produces an effect in the university sector where senior management of a university museum may well be vested in academic professorial staff with very little day-to-day contact with the workers in the museum. These situations may result in power becoming unhealthily concentrated towards the top of the hierarchy, leading to, and supported by, a disinclination to take responsibility followed by apathy much further down the structure.

These are potential structural problems. Whether or not they actually develop within a particular bureaucracy depends, among other things, on the sensitivity and skills of individual managers in applying management techniques to organisational problems.

The same mixed picture of benefits and potential problems will appear when a bureaucracy's rules, routines and standardised procedures are examined. In fact, standardisation is the very essence of an ideal bureaucracy. It is meant to provide organisational control by ensuring that members behave in predictable ways. Standardising those parts of the organisation's affairs that can be predicted means that people do not waste time reinventing the wheel. Nor are different people inside or outside the organisation dealt with unfairly, or with very different degrees of effectiveness, merely because the organisation's members they deal with happen to differ from one another in values, preferences or approaches. The code of conduct for museum professionals is an attempt to standardise professional conduct from sector to sector and in so doing has reinforced the bureaucratic benefit of a defined structure for professional tasks in museums. Nevertheless, this beneficial bureaucratic approach poses several potential problems for management. Many organisations become so preoccupied with rules, regulations and routines that they cease to act in the best interest of employees, clients or customers. The rules become the masters rather than the servants. The staff begin to act as though the organisation's prime purpose is to maintain its own procedures.

The chief problem, however, emerges if the affairs of the organisation become less predictable. In this case, the benefits of standardisation seem to weaken. If the organisation is changing, growing, and entering new fields (or if things are changing around it), then its rules and procedures may be the cause of it being stifled and eventually brought down. They may also prevent it from changing fast enough to cope with the changes in its environment and culture. New types of decision and action may be required by the new circumstances but, since these are not governed by existing rules or routines, they may be too difficult for members to contemplate, let alone change. Instead, people may go on applying (or misapplying) rules that no longer properly relate to the situation being dealt with. The result will be unfair treatment and frustration for the organisation, its employees, its clients and customers.

It may well be that changing the rules and routines of a bureaucracy is, by its very definition, nobody's business. Someone may eventually recognise that 'the market is being lost to our competitors' or that 'all our best specialists are being enticed to another museum', but it will then be too late to do anything about it. By the time a properly constituted working party is commissioned, has received and considered a confidential report from some specially authorised research group, and reported back to a board or committee, the organisation may well be in a particularly parlous circumstance.

In his book *Administrative Behaviour*, Herbert A. Simon discusses the unity of command, a particular feature of bureaucracies, and concludes that it is often incompatible with the principles of specialisation:

> One of the most important new systems which authorities put in an organisation is to bring about the specialisation in the work of making decisions, so that each decision is made at the point in the organisation where it can be made most expertly. If an accountant in a school department is subordinate to an educator, then the finance department cannot issue direct orders to him regarding the technical, accounting aspects of his work . . .

> The principle of the unity of command is perhaps more defensible if narrowed down to the following: In case two authoritative commands conflict there should be a single determinate person whom the subordinate is expected to obey; and the sanctions of authority should be applied against the subordinate only to enforce his obedience to that one person. Even this narrower concept of unity of command conflicts with the principle of specialisation, for whenever disagreement does occur and the organisation members revert to formal lines of authority, then only those types of specialisation which are represented in the hierarchy of authority can impress themselves on a decision.
>
> (Simon, 1957, pp. 23–6)

Simon could be describing the current situation in many museums and galleries where senior management (particularly at the keeper/director level) are subject-specialists in their own right. The possibility of decisions being made with a bias towards their specialisation (or at least closely allied to it) are more than likely. This conclusion, therefore, advocates the fundamental change in the current system of appointing subject-specialists to senior hierarchical positions within museums and galleries. Obviously, there is a need for academic excellence to be correctly supervised and high academic achievement is a precursor to acceptance in the museum and gallery profession at the higher level. However, there is every reason to believe that senior posts in museums should be occupied by subject-specialists with considerably more management experience and training than is currently the case.

Bureaucracy generally works best when the organisation is large, when its sphere of operation and its activities are stable and predictable, and when work can sensibly be standardised. These conditions seem to apply in the vast majority of organisations employing more than a handful of staff, but where an organisation faces changes and uncertainty, standardisation may no longer be so helpful. If it is to survive and prosper, the organisation must then be free of its established procedures and respond afresh to this changed situation. Clearly this can be done or many of our most successful institutions that are still organised according to bureaucratic principles would not be in existence. There is every reason for believing that the principles of bureaucracy are valid within museums, but there is a need for a parallel structure that can be invoked when changes are perceived to be necessary, and there is a requirement for building in some form of structure which will allow museums to manage their way out of potential structural problems at a time when certain aspects of bureaucracy have become inappropriate. It is obvious to me that the beneficial features of bureaucratic structure should be maintained within museums but there is a definite move (particularly in recent years) for something else to provide those benefits without allowing the disadvantages to take hold in such a way that the organisation becomes inefficient and declines.

As luck would have it there is a description for the alternative view, the Latin term 'ad hoc' is now used in this sense to build the word that best describes this alternative structural form – adhocracy. This is at the opposite end of the scale to bureaucracies and is wholly inappropriate to any type of museum or gallery if used on its own. However, there are elements of it which may alleviate problems caused by the traditional bureaucratic system.

Adhocracy

An adhocracy is an organisational structure which is constructed to deal with some special issue, probably for a limited period of time. It is not like other structures (e.g., hierarchies) set up to deal with issues for the foreseeable future. Adhocratic structures may be set up fast, in response to a sudden need, and usually have a very short life. They will be as well planned and effective as the people involved make them. They are temporary task forces in which membership will shift as needs and problems change. These task forces, apart from being temporary, will probably be created to adapt to changing circumstances and will be organised around the problem that needs to be solved at the time. They may be made up of relative strangers from different departments and with different skills, but they will always need co-ordinating people who can link together the forces within the group to produce an effective result. These groups will probably evolve in an organic rather than a mechanical way, as they emerge and adapt to problems. Those that join the group will find that their rank or role will not be as important as in a normal work situation; rather their skills, experience and training will be the deciding factor as to their status within the group.

Task forces, working within an adhocratic framework, are a positive advantage in museums and galleries who normally operate a bureaucratic structure. In order to bring life to a project, and ensure it is completed on time and to budget, setting up such task forces is a positive managerial solution to the negative problems of bureaucracy. Obviously, there is no such thing as a 'pure' adhocracy. Like bureaucracy, adhocracy is a model, an ideal, a standard of comparison. An organisation will be more or less adhocratic, or will have more or fewer adhocratic systems within it.

The quintessential adhocracy contains a variety of specialists and there is little status difference between the members. The authority to be exerted by anyone would depend upon how his/her expertise is received by the group rather than on his/her position. It is difficult for the museum structure to equate with a system where few rules and standardised procedures exist. Particularly if such limited procedures or rules are unwritten or open to negotiation. Since adhocracy is expected to be flexible, adaptive and responsive to new situations, standardisation and formalisation tend to be avoided. In addition, decision-making will be decentralised. Teams of mixed specialists will be assigned to temporary work groups and given a problem to solve, a project to launch or a task to accomplish. As one team is forming, others are dissolving, having completed their assignments.

One of the first tasks within a new team will be to decide what each member's responsibilities are to be. Members of the team will participate actively and democratically in the decision-making. This is the approach where specialists are formed and disbanded on the completion of their mission. The emphasis is on creativity and adaptable response to unforeseeable eventualities. Roles within the team are largely interchangeable and usually cannot be specified in advance. Status differences are often irrelevant. Such task forces are still used, even within organisations that are essentially bureaucratic, when some out-of-the-ordinary problem or opportunity calls for an adaptive, creative response that can most probably be provided through the temporary coming together of diverse specialists. This approach is used significantly in museums where exhibition planning, design and creation is carried out by groups of specialists working in very close-knit groups with a particular aim in view, after which they are disbanded or moved on to different teams to carry out work of a different nature. I have also used the technique myself and found it to be particularly appropriate when the project is only likely to be undertaken successfully if people of varied experience are brought together for a short term period.

At the heart of the adhocracy is the matrix structure. Fig. 18 shows a simple example.

Here, two project teams are superimposed on a functional structure. Each project team includes one or more staff from each of the three specialist departments. In this example 'Team A' might be set up to create a new exhibition and 'Team B' to plan a new publishing enterprise. The talents drawn from each department are therefore proportioned accordingly.

There is one feature which clearly distinguishes the matrix from a purely hierarchical structure. It is obvious from Fig. 18 that the lines of reporting are not as restrictive as in a hierarchical structure and, thus, the matrix has a tendency to break the unity of command principle that is essential to a purely bureaucratic hierarchy. Each person in the team has two bosses. His/her project manager will be responsible for his/her contribution to the project while his/her departmental manager will be responsible for his/her career development, pay, promotion prospects and, necessarily for any contributions he/she may be able to make to the work of the department as a whole during gaps in his/her

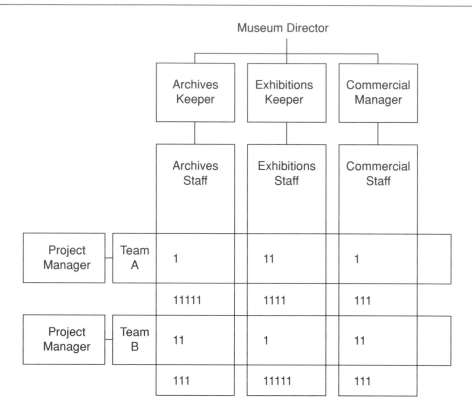

Figure 18 The matrix structure

project team duties. Matrix structures are not used a great deal in museums to date but there are many examples of how their use could be beneficial. The matrix is often temporary and only part of an organisation is so arranged. Sometimes it can be permanent, and some organisations (or at least main divisions within them) have 'matrixed' their whole operation.

Whilst the contents of the teams change, the principle of matrix structure can be permanent. The matrix is thought to offer several benefits, for example:

1 It avoids the multiplication of specialists, task by task, which is often impossible for smaller organisations.

2 It allows flexibility in situations where neither are purely functional nor a purely product structure is advisable.

3 It may enable staff to regroup quickly in response to new demands.

4 It may, through its multiple reporting relationships, encourage more open, and potentially creative, communication between different parts of the organisation.

5 It may reduce the decision-making load on management.

There are also potential problems which should be guarded against in managing any matrix structure:

1   The main problem is that of conflicting loyalties. Since the matrix structure flouts the 'unity of command' concept, a person may have two (or more) bosses who may be making conflicting demands.

2   The bosses (functional and project) may have conflicting objectives and want to put their joint resources (especially people) to different uses. This can, in some circumstances, lead to a continuous debilitating power struggle. There may be complaints of lack of co-operation versus unreasonable demand. The functional departments may be complaining about the lazy elements within the project teams who think they are entitled to the best of everything, while the project teams are complaining about the staid attitude of functional departments who are too set in their ways to give proper co-operation.

3   If conflicts like these arise, the decision-making load on management may increase rather than diminish.

4   Some well-regarded members of a functional department may find themselves overloaded with demands from too many project teams, all wanting their services at once.

5   People whose membership of project teams is temporary may worry that they will lose their places in their department's seniority while they are so engaged. They may also be concerned that they might have difficulties in resuming work in their original department, particularly if they believe it to be relatively humdrum as a result of their experience during the project.

So, as with bureaucracy, an adhocratic structure coupled with task groups, may bring benefits if used appropriately. This is usually in cases where the organisation is faced with a situation too dynamic or challenging for the solid virtues of bureaucracy to respond suitably. But, if used inappropriately or mismanaged, adhocracy will run into problems as severe as, though different from, those of mismanaged bureaucracies; in particular, the routine predictability of life in a bureaucracy may be replaced by role conflict, power struggles, confusion, insecurity and anxiety. The key to ensuring that a system works is the quality of its management. It is therefore inevitable that an inappropriate structure gives rise to structural problems, but the advantages and disadvantages of the bureaucratic and adhocratic systems may settle dilemmas according to the needs of the organisation. Many structural problems will require different types of solution as these may be applied to some degree as a matter of choice or design. The important fact is that no two organisations can, or ever will, be alike. This is the difficulty for theorists for, in the quest for basic laws, many social scientists stress the similarity of organisations, seeking ever more general (and even more unenlightening) statements about such matters as leadership, morale and the nature of organisations. There is therefore the pragmatic view that each organisation is unique in its own way and must be dealt with accordingly, rather than the academic theory that determines generalities for all.

It is therefore essential for managers in museums to understand that organisations have basic similarities but senior members of the museum profession need to know more than these simple similarities. They need to understand the principles behind producing change within an organisation; they must be able to organise and control their institutions within a changing environment. The inappropriateness or otherwise of the structure as a symptom of failure, whether by design or default, is paramount. Many contingencies can affect the structure an organisation adopts, for instance:

1 Policy decisions: the strategy adopted by senior management to achieve what they see as the organisation structure.

2 Personal preferences: the workforce (including management) may have strong feelings about the kind of structure under which it would or would not be willing to operate.

3 Type of product of service: national museums will be likely to need a different structure from local or single theme museums.

4 Technology: the type of equipment and technical processes involved, and the degree to which they are used, can affect the roles and relationships required in the workforce (e.g., computerised archives versus traditional card-based indexing systems).

5 Diversification: an organisation that expands in a variety of distinct fields needs a different structure from one that has a single product or market.

6 Size: the bigger the organisation, the more complex the business of dividing up and co-ordinating its activities.

Many of the above elements interact and the larger the organisation for example, the more likely it is to be diversified and to use complex technology. Similarly the larger the organisation, the more likely it is to be bureaucratic. Adhocracy is common in small organisations in the early stages when innovation and flexibility are of the essence but, if such bodies are to grow, survival usually depends on the introduction of bureaucratic structures to ensure the standardisation of those aspects of the work that can safely be standardised. Paradoxically, however, especially if the organisation is to be in a position to change with the times, adhocratic structures may need to be grafted on to the bureaucracy to keep it alive. Museums are essentially object-orientated organisations, rather than product-orientated. They have to work very hard to be market-orientated. They do not manufacture in the true sense of the word, although the function of carrying out their public service could be called 'production'. Museums have an academic, interpretive, administrative, curatorial, advisory and commercial framework within which to operate. The complexities involved in such diverse operations require bureaucratic procedures in part and an adhocratic preparedness – with an essential watch on the environment, culture and competition.

146

Co-ordination of work within complex organisations is paramount. As human knowledge broadens, it becomes more and more difficult for any one person to know everything in a given field. Museums, by their very nature, are already filled with subject-specialists, but management specialists are often few and far between. This leads to a narrow specialisation in curatorial/academic subjects and an almost total lack of specialisation in management. This will not affect the operation of the smaller museum in the same way as it does the medium or large. It is perfectly possible for a single curator running a local museum to acquire enough knowledge for the day-to-day management of his/her institution. In a larger organisation, with more complex problems, many more staff etc., these problems would take up the full time of several people. The problems can be compounded when departments and functions are widely separated geographically. Inevitably, as organisations grow they become more bureaucratic, but this should not lead to an inappropriate structure if the bureaucratic nature of the organisation is designed efficiently and combined with adhocratic elements by a manager who understands the benefits and pitfalls of both 'ideal' models.

11

Structural patterns and the division of work

It is often easier for managers to think more about personalities than about the job carried out by individuals. Whilst it is important to think of personalities, the prime aim should be consideration of both the nature of the work to be done and how the work can best be allocated and carried out. This requires a decision as to what kind of jobs need to be created and for what reason. It is also necessary to review whether existing jobs are suited to the organisation's current needs and to those of the individual job holders. Having achieved an appropriate structure, members of the organisation will be aware of how the organisation is configured, especially with reference to the relationships which its planners believe ought to exist. In a more specific sense, structure is a map of how organisational activities and processes are arranged and linked to one another. This is characterised by the organisation chart itself. In museums, organisational structures have been designed through tradition; nevertheless they are slowly responding to environmental opportunities and threats.

Organisational structure can be viewed as a map which reflects the organisation's linking relationships as they have been perceived and identified by management. It is obvious from this definition that structure involves a division of work. This division can occur in three dimensions. First there is the issue of allocating an organisational work role. This is often considered to be a horizontal differentiation or division of work. Horizontal usually means that work is allocated to units that are at equivalent hierarchical levels; in museums, for example, research, restoration and conservation. The second dimension is the vertical differentiation, or the division of administrative functions. It is possible to perceive that such vertical differentiation is keyed to the first, or horizontal, differentiation. The horizontal differentiation identifies operative work that is involved in mainstream transformations of the organisation's product or service and vertical differentiation identifies managerial and co-ordinated work. The third dimension exists to distinguish the organisation from its environment. The determination of the organisational boundaries is, perhaps, the most nebulous of these three dimensions of differentiation. However, the horizontal and vertical differentiation aspects of structure are in need of additional development. This can be accomplished by reviewing various aspects of structural configuration and efforts to measure it perceptually and objectively. In addition there is a distinct requirement to judge the best method for dividing work within organisations, deciding which individual should carry out which tasks, and what kind of tasks are allocated to them.

CONFIGURATION OF STRUCTURE

The general problems of configuration centre on what is an appropriate balance between achieving a reasonably small span of control while avoiding an unduly long vertical chain of command. Traditionally it was thought that generally the span of control of senior managers called for an upper limit of approximately eight people and about thirty for lower-level supervisors. However, recently it has been considered more important to expand the span of control in order to reduce the number of levels in a vertical hierarchy. This gives rise to controversial argument between the 'tall' and 'flat' structure of an organisation. The results of research in this area has determined that there is little difference in performance between the two types of structure when considering the time required to complete a decision but there were favourable results for the tall organisational structure when measures of profits and the rate of return on sales were considered. However, this obscures the basic premise that, in the museum context, the structure usually evolves according to changing circumstances.

We can look at other investigations which have improved the understanding of organisational structures and which were centred on perceptual and objective measurement techniques. As implied by the name, perceptual techniques gather information regarding organisation structure via the use of surveys which are completed by individuals in the organisation. As with any such system this approach is limited by the richness of the questionnaire, as well as the abilities of individuals to assess and report their perceptions.

The objective approach to measurement technique designs a structural attribute directly, without human perceptual transformations as an intervening link. An individual may still be the source of information, but the intent of the approach is to have the individual serve as an informant who reports objectively valid data. Thus an individual acting under properly controlled circumstances, should be able to report the actual number of levels in the hierarchy. In the simplest of terms the research that has been done into this area of organisational theory has found that organisations having more professionally trained employees also have less observation of rules and more participative decision-making, organisations with more individual involvement in decision-making tended to be less bureaucratic.

OBJECTIVE MEASURES OF STRUCTURE

The ambiguities and frustrations regarding the configuration and centralisation approaches to structure have encouraged further research. The most widely cited findings regarding dimensions of structure were created by a group led by D. S. Pugh and known as the Aston Studies (Pugh et al., 1968). This group began their research on the basis of a survey of literature from which they were able to find six dimensions of organisational structure; specialisation, standardisation, formalisation, centralisation, configuration and flexibility. The first five of these dimensions were then split into 64 component scales which identified specific descriptive data and related documentary evidence that were to be collected in 46 subject organisations. The investigators avoided the use of perceptual data and also omitted any items which did not apply to the full sample of the 46 organisations. The factors were then analysed and manipulated to reveal four mutually independent factors:

1 *Supporting activities*
   This dimension is composed primarily of such variables as standardisation, specialisation, formalisation and vertical span of control. The researchers observed that the advantage of concepted structuring is that it is generally applicable to all parts of any organisation, whereas a concept such as bureaucracy has more debatable applications. As an example, it is possible to use the structuring concept equally well to analyse the structure of positions of administration hierarchy, clerical jobs or jobs in a manufacturing shop. Further, since the scales are made operational in a variety of organisational types, it is expected that they will improve a manager's ability to compare structures between organisations relative to what is possible with an abstract concept such as the ideal bureaucracy.

2 *Concentration of authority*
   This aspect of structure encompasses such variables as centralisation, organisational autonomy, and standardisation of selection procedures, and is, perhaps, similar to the centralisation/decentralisation concept already discussed. Concentration of authority refers to the extent to which decision-making authority is limited to the upper levels of the hierarchy. At the centralisation end of the scale, managers would expect to find decisions made at the highest level, more workflow supervision in the hierarchy, and more standardised selection procedures. At the decentralisation end of the scale they would expect to find more specialisation and a dispersion of decision-making to lower levels; museums would seem to be candidates at this end of the scale, in spite of the fact that, currently, in most cases decision-making takes place mainly at the higher levels.

3 *Line control of workflow*
   As implied by the label, this structural dimension represents the degree to which line personnel can personally control workflow as opposed to having it controlled by other impersonal means. Researchers in museums' archives, or skilled conservationists working on rare artefacts, are examples of line personnel in museums who have personal control of their workflow. In contrast museum attendants and some administrative grades have little or no control of the workflow; rather, they are regulated by the system.

150

4 *Size of supportive component*

This dimension is composed primarily of scales relating to percentage of clerks, vertical span of control, and percentage of non-workflow personnel. As suggested by its name this dimension is focused on organisational activities other than those that are part of its mainstream operation. Some examples of supportive components in museums are catering, general cleaning and building maintenance.

THE EFFECTS OF SIZE

It is also important, when discussing the objective methods of structural dimensions to take note of the effects of size. An organisation's size is positively related to specialisation, standardisation, formalisation and vertical span but negatively related to centralisation. It seems that the size of an organisation is closely related to the overall size of its administrative component. Since we usually think of administrative costs as overheads, there is always a tendency to minimise them as far as possible. Indeed, the administration departments of museums are, in many cases the single 'poor relation' of the other departments. However, the size and efficiency of the organisation in general is usually linked very firmly to the performance and size of its administrative component.

The link between a knowledge of structural patterns, and the ability to properly divide the work in museums, centres on departmentation or the aspects of organising which consist of specifying those parts of the organisation which are to be autonomous work groups. Following this type of process, groups of individual jobs can be co-ordinated to provide a tight-knit unit of responsibility that can be assigned to individual managers. Such decisions are, at least partially, determinants of the structure that we have already discussed. For example, in making departmentation decisions, senior managers must allocate the work of the organisation, tell members what is expected of them, tell people who is in charge and provide any needed support. These are basic principles, but nevertheless important and often forgotten. The objective measures of structure (structuring of activities, concentration of authority, line control of work flow, and size of the supportive component), simply reflect the cumulative effects of these practical management decisions. In this sense it is necessary to identify some of the guidelines or bases which can be commonly used by managers in museums who are required to make decisions with regard to the creation of departments when they are considering the structure most appropriate to their organisation.

COMMON BASES FOR DEPARTMENTATION

The bases for departmentation are the criteria or guidelines used by the manager to determine an appropriate grouping of jobs. It should be obvious, already, that with limits to span of control, and the problems along hierarchical structures, the departmentation decisions can critically limit an organisation's effectiveness. Managers have tended to use nine criteria in the making of departmentation decisions:

1 Departmentation by numbers of workers.

2 Departmentation by time of duty.

3 Departmentation by function.

4 Departmentation by process or equipment.

5 Departmentation by location or territory.

6 Departmentation by product.

7 Departmentation by customer.

8 Departmentation by market or distribution channel.

9 Departmentation of services.

The following are descriptions of each of these and, where possible, examples that can be attributed to the context of museums and galleries.

Departmentation by numbers of workers

This is the simplest approach to implement since it requires only that the manager be aware of his/her total workforce requirements and have some idea of appropriate work-group size or number of supervisors available. The approach assumes that the effective workers are not differentiated with respect to skills or other qualities. An example of departmentation by numbers is the military infantry squad, which is usually composed of a specific number of individuals, including the squad leader and his/her deputy.

Departmentation by time of duty

This method, like departmentation by numbers, is most likely to be found at the lower or operative levels of the organisation. But, unlike the numbers base, departmentation by duty time may be necessary with skilled as well as unskilled workers. Further, time-of-duty departmentation may be needed even though the workforce involved is a mixture of skills, including high-level skills. This base is still required in some modern organisations, usually for technological or economic reasons. Museums certainly depend to a large extent on time-of-duty departmentation in order that they may operate unsocial hours and maintain a high level of security on a twenty-four hour basis. As more and more museums take on new technology, particularly communications, security and computing systems, so they will be forced to add more members of staff to the system whereby the type of work done is allied very closely to the times of duty.

Departmentation by function

Functional departmentation is one of the most widely used grouping methods and is used to some degree (or at some level) in almost every organisation. As suggested by the label, this approach groups together jobs which share a common function. At many levels of the organisation the positions grouped together may be identical. Thus, for example, all museum attendants are assigned to a leading attendant. At higher levels, one may find that the functional grouping pattern combines many different jobs, but they all focus on some primary function of the organisation. Thus, the Museum Administrator may be responsible for many functions relating to administration including clerical, financial, perhaps even building maintenance, security and maybe others. Somewhere in this grouping will be the museum's attendants and their leading attendant. Commonly used main functions in museums are departments concerned with specific collections, display and design, library, archives and conservation. These may be as high as the primary level of the organisation, which is usually taken to mean the first level below the chief executive. It is worth noting that the terms 'production', 'sales', 'finance', are used in the generic sense when discussing museums. Museums, hospitals and universities obviously do not have manufacturing in the ordinary sense, but they do have parallel mainstream services which are carried out by their equivalents in manufacturing. The methods of managing manufacturing enterprises have often been discounted by the museum profession, but there are definite links in terms of management and organisation theory. The point is that functional organisation bases can be used in many types of organisation, the absence of functions such as production or sales is not necessarily an indication that some other method should be used.

The major reason for using the functional approach to departmentation is that it focuses the attention of managers on the organisation's *main* functions and the effective use of the resources needed to accomplish them. Any senior department head in a museum is responsible for producing a high standard of work from his/her staff as efficiently as is practical. The subordinate managers, in turn, are responsible for the efficient use of the resources in their departments towards targets set by their superiors, and to the overall aims and objectives of the museum itself. Unfortunately, it is common for functional specialists to focus so directly on their specific speciality, that they tend to lose sight of other functions and the overall operation of the museum. If this can happen in the manufacturing organisation where an identifiable product (the quantity of which is measured consistently) is manufactured, there is little wonder that, in museums (where no specific product is produced), people can lose sight of the objectives.

Departmentation by process or equipment

To use this base the manager simply groups jobs together which are needed to operate a given machine or to implement a particular process. This is common in departments organised around automatic production machines or data processing equipment. As such there has, in the past, been little requirement for such design to be used in organisation structures in museums. However, the increasing introduction of information technology and its application in data processing and archive retrieval within museums makes this area of departmentation more important. This is particularly so when the technology involved represents major capital investment, especially for the smaller museum. Where this is the case, managers should seek to protect the investment by carefully planning, co-ordinating, and monitoring the implementation and use of the equipment. From an organisational standpoint, one way to do this is to assign managerial responsibility at a specific point with reference to the process and/or equipment.

Departmentation by location or territory

The point of this approach is to group all the positions and activities at a given location under the control of one manager who is responsible for the operations at that location. Many museums occupy more than one site, or have outstations some distance from the main building. However, this approach is not necessarily attributed to a distant location or a geographical separation. Territorial differences may exist within the same building. Poor communication, the need for time and action, or better co-ordination and control, are not good reasons for choosing the territorial base. Such difficulties may often indicate problems other than structural format. The best reasons for using the territorial approach involve possible economic advantages and the benefits of local participation in decision-making.

An example may be where a museum creates an outstation for its conservation department in an area that is economically more viable in terms of rent and other overheads rather than its confined central-city premises. It may be possible to employ craftsmen from a particular area associated with local history exhibits, or to acquire warehouse facilities at a more economical rate than within the city. It may also be possible that the stored collection can be opened as a regional outstation by providing public viewing facilities. The primary advantage, therefore, of this approach can be found in economy of operation and decision-making. However, one problem with the format is that it requires a larger number of generalists who can serve as managers of territories rather than specific departments, i.e. the administrative component.

Departmentation by product

The notion here is to group jobs and activities that are associated with a specific task or product. This structural form often evolves in organisations which were originally structured by function but have grown in size and number of tasks to the point where managers' spans of control have become severely strained. This is a typical reaction to the growth in recent years of independent museums (started in some cases by development corporations or local enthusiasts), which have grown as a result of public acceptance and demand. As more and more tasks and employees are added, functional lines of co-ordination and control can become stressed or overloaded. The structural remedy is to appoint task managers at a level just below the chief executive who are responsible for a given task or series of tasks. The effect is to create several smaller groupings, each focusing on a particular museum task or series of tasks. The primary advantage of this structural format is that it commits the departmental, or task, manager within a museum to concentrating on a given task to ensure that it is efficiently carried out and that efficiency is optimised and delays avoided.

The major problem with the task format is that it may not efficiently perform the main functions because of the required duplication of functional resources. Taking a large national museum as an example: the Science Museum has outstations at York (the National Railway Museum), Bradford (the National Museum of Film and Photography), and Wroughton (outstation or large store area open to public on limited days of the year). Each of these is a separate tasked division; to some extent they must therefore duplicate the functional activities of the others. For example, there is no doubt there are separate research departments at York, Bradford and South Kensington. There are also individual administrative, education and conservation departments. Duplication is not a problem provided the volume of work is sufficiently large to utilise the functional resources and, in the case of the Science Museum, is an absolute necessity. However, areas such as payroll and personnel should be handled centrally at the South Kensington site on behalf of the other sites rather than making a duplicate department in each area.

Departmentation by customer

It is also possible to group activities and positions together in a way which is compatible with the unique needs of some specific group of customers. Customers, in the museum context, should be understood as both visitors and researchers (but see also Chapter 13). The two examples within museums are the differences between our customers, who usually fall into a number of categories which can be identified as the museum visitor, the academic researcher, the museum 'friend' or volunteer, representatives of commercial companies providing sponsorship or seeking advice, users of museum facilities, purchasers in shops and catering areas, and others. It is therefore logical to establish a merchandising department to handle sales through the shop and a marketing department to market that merchandise to the public. However, it is also applicable to design a structure where marketing input is required for the museum as a whole, and not just on the merchandising and retailing side. The customers therefore differ in several ways: in the volume of purchases made or whether purchases are made at all; as regards the price they pay for the product, for they may be ordinary purchases, friends/supporters (and staff) buying special offers or privilege discounts, or trade customers buying items in quantity. Other customers hire the museum's facilities/space for conferences or evening events. These clients have special needs and expectations, and museums (as the suppliers), should find it convenient to departmentalise accordingly. On the other hand, where such structural distinctions are made it may become difficult to co-ordinate the distinctive groups created.

A special problem is caused by the somewhat unequally timed expansion and contraction within the demands of industry and consumers, to the extent that when such changes occur, one customer-orientated department may be relatively overused or under-used compared to others in the same organisation. As museums are predominantly product-orientated this type of problem may well manifest itself more as time goes on. Nevertheless, it is obvious that many museums are recognising that they do, in fact, have 'customers' rather than 'visitors', and are designing departments within their organisations accordingly. Current thinking advocates strongly that the visitor is looked upon specifically as a customer for this will, in itself, improve relations between the museum and its visitors.

Departmentation by market or distribution channel

Departments in this case are organised according to the market or distribution channels they serve. When organising according to markets it is necessary to group activities deemed necessary to reach special segments of the markets such as businesses likely to use museum facilities. Primary and secondary schools are likely to use learning aids and skills of the education department, universities are more likely to use publications and documents of the archive department etc. To organise with reference to distribution channels is not easy for museums but the museum manager should consider the specific marketing linkages to the ultimate customer. The whole area of marketing and its emphasis within museums is expanding and there is no doubt that the introduction of marketing techniques will enhance the necessity for designing structures that are organised according to the distribution channel and the market served.

Taking an education service of a museum as an example, there are two distinctive markets. On the one hand there is the primary school market where the difficulties of arranging visits by a group of children are minimised simply by the fact that a single teacher makes a decision for a group (i.e., his/her specific class) and, on the other hand, there is the secondary school where the decision to bring a group of children is made by a number of teachers as no individual member of the teaching staff has control over a single class. An obvious marketing technique to attract the more difficult segment of this market (the secondary school class) has been to introduce materials specifically designed for project work. Recent changes in examinations for secondary school pupils following the introduction of the National Curriculum has opened up a new market which was, in the past, a difficult one for many museums to attract. Museums should recognise the different (and potential) markets they attract and design distinct organisational units to deal with them or, failing this, at least make the staff involved aware of the differences in order that they can departmentalise their own work according to the anomalies defined.

The obvious drawbacks to this approach are that it may be necessary to duplicate specialities in the various marketing divisions of a museum, and confusion can occur in those areas that research and develop new markets in their attempt to serve the needs of uniquely different groups. It is, therefore, necessary to safeguard some activities and ensure that they remain under centralised control. However, an awareness of markets and distribution channels in museums is a necessary precursor to future success against competition from other museums and leisure-orientated organisations.

Departmentation of services

In most organisations it is usually necessary to group together the people and activities needed to provide special services to the rest of the enterprise. Examples of the services provided include personnel, accounting, purchasing, plant maintenance, statistical reports, electronic data processing and typing/secretarial services. Specialised service departments are designed to provide the needed services in a manner that is efficient and under control. There are three main problems that can occur in such departments – inefficiency, excessive control and a luxury service. In the case of inefficiency, one may find that data processing produces reports that are the epitome of efficiency and content but, for some reason, managers are unable to use them.

In the case of excessive control, the specialists of the service department lose sight of their service responsibilities in the zeal of their expertise. For example, those responsible for purchasing buy equipment and/or parts which are cost effective but which fail to meet the needs of the craftsmen who have to use them. This is often the case in modern data processing departments where the data processing manager understands the equipment fully and purchases it because of information he/she has received from other colleagues in the same field, yet it is not the product that those having to use the online machinery would have desired had they been given a choice. Many museums are equipped with inappropriate computer systems purchased more as a result of salesmanship than the technical specification of the equipment.

The problem of the luxury service is really a problem of determining an adequate level of service that your museum wishes to supply; deciding whether to staff a department to meet peak loads or to provide the service function as required for an average level of workload. So, it is often the case in museums that some departments have built themselves into large groups and, during slack times, they are observed by others as having little to do and the managers in charge are accused of being empire builders. Nevertheless, departmentation of services is necessary, particularly in museums where academic departments differ so radically from service departments.

Having examined organisation structure in terms of its configuration, its structural dimensions, the effects of size and the bases for departmentation, we can see that structure can be viewed as organisational configuration, which is determined by decisions regarding the structuring of activities, concentrations of authority, line control of workflow and the size of the supportive component. Furthermore, managers are likely to make grouping decisions using some of the nine bases described for departmentation. Finally, the structure which actually emerges from this process will be effected by the size of the organisation being planned.

Museums are professional bureaucracies. They are marked by a large operating core and support staff with a small strategic apex of key policy-making senior managers. This configuration is appropriate for organisations whose technology is largely implemented by a highly trained professional group who make up its operating role (the curators). Other examples of the professional bureaucracy include universities, hospitals and consulting firms. Because of its dependency on the skills of its professionals, the professional bureaucracy gives them substantial autonomy and control in implementing technical systems and providing the organisation's services to its clients. It is often the case in universities, hospitals and other organisations that the professionals have learned their skills and procedures through education and experience outside the focal organisation. However, in museums the present career structure ensures that few professionals come from outside the museum world. Museum professionals are therefore not as well equipped as their counterparts in other organisations who have learned to deal with problems using standard procedures and approaches, and thus the organisations they belong to need less of a large technical structure to plan and formalise procedures and standards. There is often little need for a large middle line in these organisations, but museums are forced to operate slightly differently and the middle area is often larger as a result. Nevertheless, it may be the case that museum professionals require less close supervision than their counterparts in other structures, but the skilled manager would have to closely watch this.

The professional bureaucracy operates best in an environment that is complex but stable and with a technical system that is not regulating or complex. The point is that the technical system should not regulate the activities of the professionals. In this sense the professionals control the pace of workflow and not vice versa. A large support staff is needed to perform routine jobs and leave the professionals free to perform their duties. All this suggests that the professional hierarchy should be decentralised while the support staff should be centralised. On balance, the professional bureaucracy will involve high standardisation, professional skills and personal specialisation, but limited formalisation and vertical hierarchy. In museums, departments are likely to be determined by function rather than market and will involve a wide span of control. The standardisation of professionals skills permits the organisation to be sufficient but restricts its adaptability and flexibility.

A large museum that operates outstations may structure its organisation as a divisionalised operation. It will function in a similar way to several small companies operating under a corporate umbrella. In the museum context, at the parent museum level, the division is seen as a single entity having well-defined standardised goals; the performance control system is designed accordingly. As a result, goals and performance standards become excessively more specific down through the divisional hierarchy (i.e., to the outstations), which encourages more bureaucracy. Further, since the parent body holds the outstation managers' responsible for achieving standards, they in turn retain tight control over their division. Overall, this means that divisional structures do not adapt well to change, even though adaptability to change is the intention of such a structural form. This inability to change is evident in a number of large museum outstations that have found it difficult to achieve the high standards of the parent body.

The 'adhocracy' emerged to meet the distinctive needs of such industries as information technology design and manufacture, software writing, think-tank consulting and film-making. These organisations must contend with environments that are both complex and dynamic, and involve very complicated technical systems. As we have already seen, adhocracy is flexible and capable of complex innovation. Nevertheless, it is probably only appropriate to the most entrepreneurial and independent of museums; except when the adhocracy is a small part of a larger structure as in the task force sense, to form temporary groups for the purpose of carrying out specific duties. Four questions must be answered in order to produce useful organisational structures:

1 Are the internal elements consistent?

2 Are the external controls functional?

3 Is there a part that does not fit?

4 Is the right structure in the wrong situation?

It is possible that some managers insist on designing structures that may seem to be merely fashionable. A basic understanding of structural design is necessary in museums, as it is in all organisations, yet it is one of the most difficult problems that museum managers face.

To summarise, configuration approaches are concerned with the shape of structure; that is, whether it is tall or flat. Research concerning organisation shape has produced mixed results, so researchers have turned their attention to more specific measures of structure. The first measurement efforts were based on the perceptions of members of an organisation's structure. Methodological problems limit the use of such measures for comparison between organisations, so researchers sought to develop more objective measures of structure. Four commonly used dimensions of structure have been outlined here: structuring of activities, concentration of authority, line control of workflow, and the size of the supportive components. We have also looked at nine commonly used bases for departmentation. It is essential to learn both the strengths and weaknesses of such criteria through practical experience and to use these strengths and weaknesses in the design of the structure for your museum or gallery. The final five basic structural configurations show how configuration, the dimension of structure, the bases of grouping, and the effects of size are all interrelated. It was noted that many design problems occur as structures are adapted, or complete structures are created, because they are in vogue rather than being appropriate for the particular organisation. The ideal is to have components which fit together, as well as match the situation. The designer of a structure has a range of structural options. These options are arranged along a scale together with notations regarding factors favouring their use. This scale must be understood by senior managers of museums in order that they can manage the evolution of their organisation and structure to meet changing needs and circumstances.

The trap is to allow structures to form themselves, or to build them with no knowledge of the likely effects of an inappropriate structure. Owing to the lack of understanding in this field, it is uncommon for museums to have structures which either suit their needs or equip them properly for the work they have to carry out.

12

Culture, conflict and change

The title of this chapter suggests that there is a link between organisation culture, conflict and change. There is little doubt that the culture of an organisation is something that every manager must understand in order to be effective in his/her role as a policy-maker as well as a resolver of conflict and initiator of change. Museums each have their own culture and it is this seemingly intangible area which marks them as entities different from other organisations, particularly businesses and industrial concerns. Furthermore, each museum's culture is different from another's, and the skilled manager needs to identify the type of culture with which he/she is dealing and adjust his/her methods accordingly. The recognition that organisational culture plays an important part in the management of organisations is fundamental and it therefore follows that an ability to deal with conflict within the culture and the organisation, for whatever reason, is a prerequisite skill of any person occupying a senior management position. We have already discussed the changing environment within which museums are operating and these changes have produced a requirement of senior museum managers to formulate new policies of change for their organisations. The previous chapter dealt with the design of organisational structures; this chapter will explore the methods of evoking change within such organisations.

ORGANISATIONAL CULTURE

The culture of an organisation is influenced by the social networks that are operating within it. Culture, in this sense, is defined as the 'total of the inherited ideas, beliefs, values and knowledge which constitute the shared basis of social action' and 'the total range of ideas and activities of a group of people with shared traditions which are transmitted by members of the group'. In his article 'On studying organizational cultures', A. M. Pettigrew defines the concept of culture and simultaneously connects it to individual jobs:

> In pursuit of our everyday tasks and objectives it is all too easy to forget the less rational and instrumental, and more expressive social tissue around us that gives those tasks meaning. Yet in order for people to

function within any given setting, they must have a continuing sense of what that reality is all about in order to be acted upon. Culture is a system of publicly and collectively accepted meanings operating for a given group at a given time. The system of terms, forms, categories, and images interprets peoples own situation to themselves.

(Pettigrew, 1979, pp. 570–81)

An understanding of culture and its elements helps to interpret how some managers and entrepreneurs are able to communicate purpose and secure energy and commitment in their organisation. Such forces can be directed towards the formation of new ventures or the redirection of an existing organisation. However, to fully comprehend the impact of culture one must understand its offshoots. Among these are symbols, language, ideology, beliefs, rituals and myths. The importance of culture to museums and galleries has only recently received the attention it deserves. The value of organisation symbolism has been overlooked in the past.

The symbolism of an organisation expresses its underlying character, ideology and values. It does this through stories, myths, ceremonials, rituals, logos, anecdotes, and even jokes. Certainly those who have served in the armed forces, or other disciplined services, are well aware that such organisations contain symbolism and, indeed, flourish as a result. The culture of the organisation should have a strong impact on the employees and it is this impact which commonly is the most difficult to cope with when moving from one organisation to another. It is necessary, if there is a wish to understand the deep structure of an organisation, that managers make a study of its symbolism and attempt to understand its social and information processing networks, or 'grapevine'. This network conveys the value of the culture to its members and where the network leads to widely shared beliefs, the organisation's culture is usually strong. Where the network fails to produce shared beliefs, the culture is weak and will have a limited impact on members. The possibility that organisation cultures can either be strong or weak is something which should be considered by managers interested in improving the performance of their museums or galleries.

There are several reasons why managers should have a good understanding of organisational culture. Where cultures are strong, people feel good about what they do. Where social information networks have generated widely shared values and beliefs about the organisation and what it does, employees come to believe that they are part of something important and they take pride in this fact. Even outsiders notice this if the institution and its culture are highly visible – like many large museums. This is particularly important within museums where it is difficult to motivate employees by giving them production targets, work schedules, bonus pay, and other easily quantifiable rewards. If employees know that they are an important part of a museum which also has a good reputation, and they believe in the value of the work they do, they will give better value and more satisfaction. They will also communicate this to outsiders such as visitors or researchers. In addition to helping the employees take pride in what they do, a strong culture informs employees as to how they are to behave. It has been estimated that a strong culture may potentially save up to two hours per day per employee by making expected behaviours clear. Managers should communicate a pride in the institution for which they work.

Managers should also understand the culture of their organisation because it is likely to influence their careers. After several years of being exposed to a culture and its values it becomes a part of them and therefore an employee attempting a move from one culture to another may encounter difficulty in making the change. In addition, an employee wishing to move from a very strong, well-respected culture to a weak organisation may not wish to make this ultimate change even though it offers career advancement. On the other hand, a strong organisation may not wish to take an employee from another organisation if it knows that organisation has a weak culture and poor standards. In his book *Understanding Organisations* Charles Handy (1976) identifies four examples of culture: power, role, task and person.

THE POWER CULTURE

The power culture is frequently found in the smaller type of organisation and is usually similar to an adhocracy, with very few bureaucratic procedures or rules. Control would be exercised from the centre largely through the selection of key individuals. These cultures, and organisations based on them, are usually proud and strong. They have the ability to move quickly and can react well to threat or danger. Everything that happens within them very much depends on the person or persons in the centre; the quality of these individuals is of paramount importance with the succession issue as the key to continued high performance. Individuals employed in power culture organisations will prosper and will be satisfied to the extent that they are power-orientated, politically minded, risk-taking, and rate security as a relatively minor element in their psychological contract.

By their very nature power cultures need to remain relatively small and these cultures can be seen in the smaller museums where a great deal of faith is put in the individual and little time is given over to committees. In the medium-size and large museums they are more likely to be seen in those organisations that are sub-units of larger parents. They would probably be the type of organisation that had a very strong Director with a reputation of being tough or abrasive; though successful they may well suffer from low morale and high turnover in the middle layers of management as individuals fail or opt out of the competitive atmosphere that may result from having a hard taskmaster at the head.

THE ROLE CULTURE

Role cultures are often stereotyped simply as bureaucracies. They are controlled by procedures, job descriptions, authority and there are rules for everything.

They are co-ordinated at the top by a narrow band of senior management and everything is planned. At first glance it would seem to be the ideal analogy with the typical museum or gallery situation. The essence of this grouping is the role, or job description; in museums this is often more important than the individuals who carry out the actual work, in the sense that individuals may be selected for satisfactory performance of a role, and the role is usually so described that a range of individuals could fill it. Additionally, performance over and above the job description is not often a requirement and, indeed, can be destructive at times. Position power is the major power source in this culture. Personal power is frowned upon and expert power tolerated only in its proper place. Rules and procedures are the main methods of influence. The efficiency of this type of culture depends on the rationality of the allocation of work and responsibility, rather than on the individual's personality.

Museums have operated with this type of culture for many years and they have been successful, but the crucial element that is necessary to provide success to the role culture is that it operates in a stable environment. When next year is the same as last year, so this year's tested rules will work consistently, then the outcome will probably be good. Where the organisation can control its environment, by monopoly, where the market is stable, predictable or controllable and where the product life is a long one (i.e., gallery displays can be kept alive for a long time), then rules, procedures and programmed work will be successful. National museums holding a monopoly, and other large local authority museums, are capable of having role cultures and continuing to be successful.

However, the changes that have taken place to the environment in which museums operate in recent years have shown the insecurities of role cultures. The influx of new management to senior positions in national museums and (in those cases where new management has replaced existing management) the introduction of expert consultants to advise the existing senior level managers, has shown the weakness of this type of culture within the museum context. Role cultures may offer security and predictability to the individual. They may also offer a predictable career progression – an essential part of the national museum promotion structure whereby a person entering that sector from university will be assured of a certain level of promotion, almost regardless of performance. They may also be frustrating for the individual who is power orientated or who wants greater control over his/her work, and who is eagerly ambitious or more interested in results than methods. Many museums have role cultures and some are changing them at present. The role-culture dominated organisation will be found where economies of scale are more important than flexibility, or where technical expertise and depth of specialisation are more important than product innovation or product costs. Museums have, in the past, been used to operating with little competition and, in many cases, with a monopoly on the type of work they were doing (i.e., there were few other major attractions of a similar nature). As a result there were few penalties for any lack of innovation in the way that they operated. Things have now changed and role culture is no longer a wholly appropriate form for museums.

THE TASK CULTURE

The task culture is job or project orientated and consists of some of the adhocratic principles we have already discussed coupled with task forces to carry out project work. This sort of culture is extremely adaptable. Groups, project teams, or task forces are formed for a specific purpose and can be reformed, abandoned or continued. All the decision-making powers required are in the task culture and individuals will find a high degree of control of their work. It is therefore popular. Judgement by results, easy working relationships within the group, with mutual respect based upon capacity rather than age or status, make it appropriate to the museum context.

As more and more museums realise that the environment within which they operate is changing and that their culture and structure needs to be changed along with it, the task culture becomes more appropriate. The task culture predominates when the product life is short and where speed of reaction is important. In the past, competition from other organisations has not been as profound as it is today and, therefore, museums have had a 'product life' which was much longer than is currently the case. It is now necessary for museums to change their exhibitions regularly in order to attract new visitors, and such task cultures may well be born within these areas. They may also include teams working to design and manufacture new exhibitions or develop fresh information technology approaches to collections management or documentation. Nevertheless, the task culture finds it hard to produce economies of scale or great depth of expertise and should not grow to any great size. It thrives where speed of reaction, integration, sensitivity and creativity are more important than depth of specialisation. Apart from those departments concerned with exhibition production, which have already been mentioned, there are also obvious pointers towards marketing and education departments taking on task cultures in museums.

Control of departments operating task cultures can be difficult. Control is normally retained by means of allocation of projects, people and resources by the top management of the museum. Vital projects are given to good people with no restrictions on time, space or material. However, little day-to-day control can be exerted over the methods of working, or the procedures, without violating the norms of the culture. These cultures, therefore, tend to flourish when there is an agreeable climate, when the product is all-important, where the customer is always right, and when resources are available for all who can justify using them. Top management then feels able to relax day-to-day control, concentrate on resource allocation decisions, and the recruitment and placing of key people.

The climate for change to a task culture in museums has never been better. The product is becoming all important, the visitor is becoming the customer and, therefore, needs to be treated as such. However, the resources available are also being competed for by all departments within museums with a vigour that has become stronger as the resources have been reduced. Top

165

management may feel the easy way out would be to allow a task culture to evolve rather than actively implement it; this would need serious consideration and careful thought by any senior managers involved, for if all the components (except the resources) were not available then competition between top management and team leaders, using any available influence, would inevitably result in conflict within the museum or gallery. In either case, morale in the work groups would decline and the individual jobs become less satisfying. People will begin to change their psychological outlook and reveal their individual objectives. Such a state of affairs would necessitate rules, procedures, exchange methods of influence and the use of positional resource power by the managers to get work done. In short, the task culture often tends to change to the role or power culture when resources are limited or the total organisation is unsuccessful.

Task culture is difficult to control and inherently unstable by itself. It is likely that any task culture which evolves within museums at the present time could only do so for a short period while individual projects, with guaranteed funding, are undertaken. Senior museum managers should realise that such a culture would need to be changed immediately resources for the specific project had dried up. The task culture should always be the personal choice of those by whom it is operated, certainly at middle and junior management level. This is the culture which most of the behavioural theorists point towards, with its emphasis on groups, expert power, rewards for results and the merging of individual and group objectives. It is the culture most in tune with current ideologies of change, adaption and individual freedom. Task culture is very popular but is very difficult to control and should not be allowed to take hold if the resources are not available to give it its full head.

So, it is important for senior managers within museums to realise the inevitability of the task culture becoming predominant within an organisation. The large number of new museums created in the past decade, coupled with the considerable changes that are taking place within established museums, provide great impetus for task cultures to be created.

Senior managers within museums should understand that, as long as a task culture is relevant and useful it should be encouraged, but they should also guard against such a culture taking hold and continuing after its worth has been exhausted. This often happens a few years after a museum is founded. Resources are made available for the creation of a museum but there is often a predictable cycle where, following the opening day, resources are then reduced for a considerable period of time (five to ten years in many cases) and the museum merely 'ticks over' until it is redeveloped. The task culture which evolved to build the museum in the first place becomes irrelevant and counter-productive once the funds decline when the museum is up and running. Regrettably senior managers, without a knowledge of the changes that are needed, allow the task culture to perpetuate long after the short-term foundation of the museum has passed. It then, inevitably, goes wrong.

THE PERSON CULTURE

The person culture has the individual as its central point. If there is a structure or an organisation that exists only to serve and assist the individuals within it, or if a group of individuals decide that it is in their own interests to band together in order to follow their own inclinations (and that an office, a space, equipment, or even clerical and secretarial assistants would help), then the resulting organisation is a person culture. It would exist only for the people in it with no intentions of building any superior levels of management. Barristers' chambers, architects' partnerships, families, and small consultancy firms often have this type of culture.

Person cultures are rare because, usually, the identity of the organisation is stronger than the identity of any single individual. Organisations are usually created by the efforts of a strong character but, over a period of time, the strength of the organisation's character as a whole will probably become more powerful than that of the individual who created it. However, although it might be rare to find an organisation where the person culture predominates, within museums there are certainly individuals whose personal preferences are for this type of culture, but who find themselves operating in a more typical organisation. The stereotype of the research academic is of a person-orientated man/woman operating in a role culture. He/she does what he/she has to do, researches what he/she must, in order to retain his/her position in that organisation. But essentially he/she can build his/her own career, carry out his/her own interests, all of which may directly add interest to the organisation although that would not be the point of doing them. Subject specialists often feel little allegiance to the organisation but regard it rather as a place to do their own research with any accruing benefit to the main employer being of secondary importance. This is the case in museums, and there are many person-orientated members of staff within museums, in all sectors, carrying out their own specialised work. These people are not easy to manage. There is little influence that can be brought to bear on them. Being specialists, alternative employment is often available to them, or they have protected themselves by tenure, so that resource power in this context lacks potency. Position power, not backed up by resource power achieves nothing. Specialists are unlikely to bow down to other experts and therefore expert power will have little effect. Only the personal power of individual senior managers will produce results from person-orientated subject-specialists in museums; senior management should be aware that their personal methods of management (i.e., their force of personality) are possibly the only way in which subject-specialists with senior status can be effectively managed (see Chapter 7).

The person culture is, therefore, not likely to take hold in any museum as a total entity; nevertheless individuals (particularly subject-specialists occupying senior management positions) will take this type of culture upon themselves. The results for management need careful consideration.

DIAGNOSIS OF ORGANISATIONAL CULTURE

Having explored four possible cultures, and acknowledging that there are more, we need to be able to diagnose the culture of our organisation/department/group in order to determine whether it is weak and whether there is any room for performance improvement that can be initiated by managers. There are several reasons why all individuals, but managers in particular, should have a good understanding of organisational culture. As we know, where cultures are strong people feel good about what they do. Where the social information network (the grapevine) has generated widely shared values and beliefs about the museum or gallery and what it does, employees come to believe they are part of something important, and they take pride in this.

Managers must understand cultures in order to manage them, or change them. It is possible to look for evidence of the organisation's culture by observing the people within the organisation. As outsiders we should consider the following:

1 Analyse the physical setting of the organisation. It is possible to tell something about a museum's values by paying attention to its buildings, the materials used in its construction, the furnishings and even the colours used.

2 Look at written or published material compiled or released by the museum. Examine the content of annual reports, press releases, newsletters and magazines. What does the museum say about itself to its employees and to the general public? Strong cultures tend to make statements about their values and beliefs without being apologetic. Weak cultures use such communications to discuss performance in conventional financial form (balance sheets, income statements, and the like). They discuss the data itself, but avoid any mention of the people and beliefs which make it possible.

3 Pay attention to how the museum treats outsiders.

4 Talking with employees may reveal how they feel about their museums. Employees in museums are unlikely to know how the culture is defined. Where it is strong, they will be able to discuss what the values are. Where it is weak, their answers to questions will reveal disagreement and a lack of common ground. Questions should be asked about the museum's history, its success, the kind of people who work within it, the number of visitors who attend, and the nature of working conditions.

5 Investigation as to how employees spend their time in the museum is also useful. What people spend their time doing is an indication of what they think is important. In the case of a strong culture, one would assume that the activities of employees mirror the values of that culture.

It is easier to diagnose the type of culture base from inside the organisation as a manager or employee than it is from the outside as an onlooker. The key to inside observation is to disregard individual biases and beliefs; it is best not to evaluate – just to record. Usual conversations with colleagues within an organisation are likely to be far more revealing than formal meetings. Formal meetings may well obscure the real issues as a result of internal politics and manoeuvring. Four kinds of information that can be gathered to ascertain a cultural diagnosis from within a museum are:

1   An appreciation of the career progression paths taken by most employees in their gradual move through the hierarchy of the museum. The pathway to the top is a good guide to the culture of the museum. It should be expected that those who move up through the ranks have values and beliefs which are consistent with the norms of the culture. Whereas those who come in from outside may well have to adjust their own preconceived (and preheld) values and beliefs in order to coincide with the culture of the museum they are joining.

2   It is interesting to look at how long people stay in their jobs. This is particularly important in the case of middle levels of management. Where tenure in a position is of short duration there may be no incentive to participate in activities which have long-term life cycles, long pay-back periods, or high risks. Such a culture could stifle innovation.

3   A great deal of information can be gathered by looking at the material written by members of the museum and by listening to their conversations. Without wishing to advocate any sinister motive, managers should be aware that listening to the content of conversations can provide them with distinct pointers as to the state of the organisation generally. For example, it is useful to know who talks to whom, whether the conversations are about internal affairs and politics, or are genuinely concerned with responding to the needs of the visitor or changes in the environment that affects the museum. This is particularly important where a great deal of dialogue goes on between members of staff and could easily descend into mere gossip rather than effective problem-solving for the good of the museum and the visitor.

4   The traditions of the organisation, as has already been mentioned, have a bearing upon its culture. An investigation into the kind of myths and anecdotes that are communicated through the museum can add to the information already found in the diagnosis of the culture. Great pride is taken in organisations with traditions and young organisations quickly establish their own myths and anecdotes, if the culture is strong.

The assessment and interpretation of the culture within a museum can be undertaken relatively easily. This is necessary and should be the goal of every senior museum manager, for pointers will be given to likely future problems if the diagnosis is correct. Especially indicative of problems within an organisational culture are excessive concern with internal affairs and difficulties, too much attention to short-term issues and targets, indications of poor morale and swift turnover of staff, inconsistency in standards across departments, frequent emotional outbursts and excessive conflict between sub-cultures. All these are areas of concern to managers and they should be treated seriously.

ORGANISATIONAL CONFLICT

It is not possible for any organisation, or group of people, to exist in total harmony – conflict is inevitable at some stage or another. The objective should be for effective managers to exploit the inevitable differences of opinions, values, priorities, talents and personalities in order that the reasons for conflict are minimised and the aims of the individual (or group) are directed to coincide with the organisation. There is a dilemma for all managers in that it is difficult to have argument and competition without conflict and all three are inevitable. There is a human tendency which is certainly evident in museums, naturally to shrink from argument, competition and conflict but, as these are inevitable, the competent manager must learn to identify their causes and find solutions.

In all organisations there are individuals and groups competing for influence or resources. There are differences of opinion and values, conflicts of priorities and goals. There are pressure groups, lobbies, cliques, rivalries, contests, pressures of personality and bonds of alliance. Groups in organisations have different roles, different goals and different skills, and so have individuals. The blending of these differences into one coherent whole is the task of management. Such a blending may involve giving some groups priority over others, ignoring some preferences and accepting others, and curbing some initiatives whilst promoting others. By co-ordination of all these elements, and care in the management of their interaction, progress towards a resolution of conflict is made.

I agree with Charles Handy when, in his book *Understanding Organizations* he maintains that there are three manifestations of difference: argument, competition and conflict:

> Words have overtones, and although one cannot build definitions on over-tones, we do generally regard argument and competition in themselves as useful things, conflict as not. Argument and competition can be disruptive in which case they degenerate into conflict, or occasionally, they are banned because they are seen as symptoms or outcrop of conflict. Conflict can arise from other sources than argument or competition. In a sense the managerial dilemma could be seen as how to have argument and com-petition without conflict, how to prevent them degenerating into conflict, how to turn conflict where it exists into argument and competition.
>
> (Handy, 1976, p. 214)

One way to avoid the degeneration of argument into conflict is to encourage an openness in the discussion of differences. In museums this can be through regular discussion between supervisors and their subordinates or through a recognised machinery for the resolution of conflict, and an approach towards consultative management from the top downwards. Good managers encourage and practice openness in the discussion of differences. They are successful as integrators partly because the differences do not degenerate into political conflict. However, the expression of feeling in argument is commonly kept below the surface in the traditional way in which people in museums and galleries interact. Nevertheless, if the organisational culture will accept it, an open resolution of argument can be beneficial. Regretfully, deep-seated conflict or mistrust may be masked by elaborate politeness or even by the antagonistic ignoring of each other completely. If individuals are ignoring each other when they should be communicating, or communicating stiffly or formally when they should be involved in creative discussion and collaboration, productivity is affected.

Two conditions seem to be necessary in order to cause conflict. On the one hand there is a feeling that things are not as one would like them to be and, on the other, that someone should be blamed. Conflicts can thus arise in the personal anxieties and unhappiness of individuals in a way that might seem to the impartial observer to be quite unjustified. In some cases the target for dissatisfaction may be chosen unjustifiably. In serious cases the organisation itself, particularly its senior management, may be blamed for areas of dissatisfaction that do not, in fact, exist. Many areas of conflict may seem to be irrational, which is often a direct result of members of the organisation being bored or dissatisfied with their work and believing the organisation is not living up to their expectations; in such cases they often hold management responsible. With resource limitations being applied to museums so heavily at the present time, coupled in some cases with ineffective management and an employment situation which precludes individuals from seeking alternative work, such behaviour is commonplace. A basic cause of conflict is resentment of insensitive authority; this may often be the last thing that is actually mentioned when individuals are questioned on the reasons for their poor performance or irrational behaviour, but it is usually the cause.

Competition between individuals or groups (particularly competition for resources or career positions) can lead to areas of conflict being surreptitiously initiated without the knowledge of management. Such conflict exists whenever mutually exclusive goals, policies, resources or rewards are being sought simultaneously. This would hardly cause conflict if attaining one did not automatically exclude the attainment of others, or more than one was not being sought at the same time. As it is, competition and conflict are the inevitable results of a simultaneous desire for mutually exclusive goals.

In general, people compete in order to see their personal beliefs, values, goals and ideologies prevail, and they compete in order to win more freedom (or territory) in order to do as they please – remember the person culture? Such competition for power and influence is usually closed. Only a few people can achieve autonomy, make decisions they consider vital, and obtain all the resources they need. Hence the inevitability of conflict. Even though the majority of conflict may seem to us to be of a personal nature, it is often a result of inappropriate organisational structures. Correct structural design of the organisation can go a long way to alleviating inevitable conflicts resulting from normal arguments and competitiveness. However, the experienced manager should be able to reflect on differences in objectives and ideologies and identify areas that may cause conflict. This requires, as we have already discussed, a knowledge of the culture of the organisation or the culture of the groups/teams within it. Any person filling a role in one culture could be expected to take on the values of that group or organisation. He/she would then be just as likely as any other individual to come into the same kind of conflict of interest with people in other groups whose values are different.

If the conditions for conflict prevail and become an inevitable source of dissatisfaction a target will manifest itself as something, or someone, to blame. The manager will require skill in managing conflict in order to address these preconditions in a professional and effective way. Indeed, some varieties of conflict can be beneficial and turned towards the goals of the organisation. Obviously the most effective way of managing conflict is to prevent it ever arising, although this would seem to be an almost impossible situation to achieve. Conflict may be seen as a sign of ineffective management but this would only be true if it had become endemic in the organisation. The manager who is acting thoughtfully and sympathetically should suffer less conflict than the manager who has a dictatorial or non-consultative approach to his/her subordinates. The key is to encourage a situation where the organisation, and the individual, both have a face-saving remedy, and each goes part way towards the other's goals. In other words, if prevention has not been successful, specific techniques may be required. These can be summarised under the following headings:

- *Coercion:* individuals can be encouraged to stop their conflict behaviour. This may result in anger, or even more resistance to rational thought, and a tendency to revenge if there is little chance of retribution.

- *Procrastination:* putting off actually dealing with conflict a manager can hope that it will be forgotten. This is neglectful, inadequate and, eventually, liable to prove disruptive.

- *Arbitration:* playing for a compromise on one side or the other often leaves one party resentful at being a loser; the compromise achieved rarely satisfies all groups for long.

- *Persuasion:* the soft side of coercion. This puts the antagonists in an inferior position which is unlikely to be more than a short-term resolution.

- *Buying-off:* conflict can sometimes be resolved by offering individuals or groups incentives or motivators, particularly of a financial nature. This approach is unlikely to win the manager real respect and conflict may resume over the original object after the benefits of being bought-off have been forgotten.

172

- *Coalition:* mischievous managers often engineer intergroup conflict rather than conflict with the management or organisation generally. This may resolve (in the short-term) conflict within the organisation but creates more serious problems by forcing individuals to choose sides, creating a divisive feeling within the organisation.

All the above strategies are likely to be minimal in their effectiveness. They are no more than quick responses to problems which may appear to provide short-term relief but, invariably, store-up trouble for the future and may even ensure it is then worse. Nevertheless these are usually the first methods attempted by many inexperienced managers.

More effective strategies are required, examples of which are:

1 *Separation*
   If there are conflicts between individuals or groups, a peaceful existence may be ensured by keeping antagonists apart. This is often an effective solution but is difficult to apply in museums with relatively small numbers of staff and few opportunities for separating groups or individuals.

2 *Appeals*
   Conflicting individuals or groups may be allowed to take their dispute to a higher authority in the organisation, i.e., above the manager who is normally responsible for them. This may protect the antagonist from self-interest on the part of their immediate supervisor (and it also absolves him/her from any subsequent blame). Furthermore, because there is a prospect of getting a more objective resolution of the conflict from someone who is not emotionally involved, it may encourage the antagonists to deal more patiently and honestly with each other before taking the problem to a higher authority. This is an effective approach within museums.

3 *Mediation*
   This involves helping the antagonists to understand one another's position and to accept that, for the other, it has validity. It is sometimes possible to do this for colleagues or members of the manager's own team, but it is often the case that the supervisor is too closely involved to be properly detached and, as with the appeals procedure (above), antagonists might ideally be referred to some kind of 'ombudsman' elsewhere in the organisation.

4 *Opening the competition*
   If a win-lose competition has sprung up, a method of resolving such conflict might be to find extra resources or rewards, or transform the rules, so that all can win something. By turning the situation into a win-win competition rather than a win-lose situation, all parties will be able to achieve a goal. In the current economic and resource limited climate this method may not be possible very often, but it is worth trying.

The four strategies mentioned above can be regarded as having only medium effectiveness. They may not cure conflict totally but they can probably help the antagonists to cope with their situation. The aim of good management should be to find effective strategies that not only cope with the immediate problem but also lay the foundations for a collaborative climate in the future.

Three strategies can be identified with this aim in mind:

1 *Re-combining work groups*
   This is the strategy of moving individuals around, not so much to separate antagonists (though it may have that effect), but to give them the regular stimulation of learning to work with other people and breaking old habits. The hope is that this will make them more capable of accepting one another's differences as well as making previous priorities and hostilities seem less pressing. The task force system (or matrix organisation) is an example of re-combining work groups and has merit as an organisation design generally. In museums there is a tendency for individuals to spend considerable periods of time (in some cases whole careers) in a specialist department doing an expert function. Whilst this specialism may preclude a great deal of movement within museums, an attempt can usually be made to find alterative work of a similar nature within another department. Certainly if task forces are used within museums then senior museum managers will be able to shift individuals possessed of a potential for the generation of conflict into a task-based group for short periods of time.

2 *Finding a common goal*
   As the simultaneous pursuit of mutually exclusive goals is a source of major conflict it is obvious that management should encourage the setting aside of differences in favour of pursuing some higher goal that both parties can agree upon. This is particularly important in museums where resource allocation is limited and departments may not understand their own reduction of resources at the expense of increases elsewhere. The key to the necessary understanding is consultation between members of staff in order that the goals of the organisation and the goals of the group or department are discussed, understood and combined.

3 *Integrated bargaining*
   This is the attempt to negotiate a solution between antagonists so that both can gain something. The essence of this approach is that neither should be required to give up anything that is vital to them. It is the search not for compromise, but for a creative solution that satisfies both parties. Once again a consultative approach on the part of management goes hand in hand with this approach and points museums in the direction of less restrictive role cultures, and a less authoritative approach by management generally. There are many cases within museums where we have a unitary view which considers management and authority as being pre-eminent. Any attempt to contain or resolve conflict by such an approach in an authoritarian way will usually be doomed to failure.

An alternative is the pluralist view, which necessitates the recognition of the existence of many different interest groups with different objectives, influenced by different value systems and working within the power structure of the organisation. Conflict resolution should be seen as the outcome of a management approach that provides a system of checks and balances. Effectively, it recognises the legitimacy of all groups to pursue their claim. A trade-off in the form of negotiation ensures a degree of collaboration and may enable individuals and groups to achieve a degree of success due to their various objectives or goals. This may seem a win-lose situation for management but any point of agreement or settlement could be construed as a gain-loss for both sides.

The authoritarian view has traditionally looked at conflict as being something which is harmful and destructive to management's authority or control. However, conflict viewed on the basis of the pluralist approach may be seen as a series of interactions between individuals and groups which enable the organisation to progress forward. The interaction provides outcomes which enable stability to be achieved and which provide measures for satisfaction of the participants. In this way conflict may be seen as providing a measure of creativity. The existence of conflict processes, which allow conflict to be managed in this way, represents outcomes whereby the various sources of conflict are seen as legitimate and integral parts of the organisational system. Any manager who has dealt with labour relations issues can understand that such conflict is managed on the basis of consultancy and negotiation, the conduct of which is regularised to some extent by the existence of rules and procedures. It is unfortunately the case that other types of conflict are not handled in this same established way. In dealing with conflict, there is no real substitute for talking to people.

Negotiation is the essence of conflict resolution. An authoritarian or non-consultative style of management will not allow any meaningful negotiation to take place and continued conflict will be inevitable.

ORGANISATIONAL CHANGE

Change will have an increasingly profound effect upon the nature of power and authority in any organisation. In museums, however, specialisation has had (and will continue to have) dramatic effects on the nature of the superior–subordinate relationship. Rational 'legal' authority has given way to authority based on expertise. In museums this is as a result of the specialist nature of senior management positions, and has been compounded by innovations in technology over the past decade or so.

Museums, therefore have the dual problem of subject-specialists and technical innovations. Whilst the technical change is important, it must first be decided whether change is a good or bad thing. Undoubtedly, much of the work of museums has progressed for generations without any fundamental changes and there may be little requirement for change in some cases. However, as has already been discussed in this book, the culture, climate and environment within which museums exist is now changing at an ever-increasing rate. Add to this the technological innovations that have taken place in the past decade, plus the increases in competition from other similar venues, coupled with the decreases in funding in real terms from the variety of funding sources, and the problem begins to arise as to how inevitable change can be accomplished *without* bringing conflict. The reasons for change are therefore quite strong and, depending on the circumstances of each individual organisation, change is probably going to be inevitable in the next few years. The technology of museums may be changing, but so are the attitudes of the individuals employed within them. Changes are expected by museum employees, the public, and by those influencing the provision of resources – particularly funding. Change should be a positive thing, indeed, an essential thing if museums are to grow and develop, or even to keep up with the requirements of visitors and the innovations of competitors.

That change is required is becoming obvious to all with an interest in the future of museums in an ever-changing environment. That change will be difficult is known to all of those who have the task of its implementation, even with their limited training or experience. The influence of the lower levels in museums and galleries has become stronger as the decisions made by the upper echelons are seen to be ineffective. Add to this the influence of visitors, bureaucrats and politicians, and it can be seen that there is currently an extraordinarily important job to be done in managing change within museums.

Only the upper echelons of the museum profession (assisted by their governing bodies) will be able to force change before change is forced upon them. The question that cannot be answered is what nature these changes will take. Nevertheless, the impact of change on museums will be profound, particularly if change is forced upon museum management as a result of the action of subordinates. The leaders are also the led; superiors depend on their subordinates to get things done. If superiors assume an expandable amount of total control they can communicate regularly with subordinates, welcome opinions and take up suggestions; in other words, invite influence over themselves. At the same time, the involvement of subordinates in what is being done means that the superior's influence expands also, for they are more likely to do what needs to be done. The authoritarian method of leadership undertaken by a person who assumes a fixed amount of total control, and clings to what he/she perceives to be his/her rightful share, may look as if he/she is dominating everyone; in museums it is often the case that his/her actual influence on what is done by his/her subordinates may be very little. As a result others also act on this assumption, so that each group defends its share; conflict and minimal co-operation will prevail. I challenge the commonplace view that control is, and should be, unilateral – from the leader to the led. Leaders have always had greater control but the led now have greater control than ever before. The method of change, therefore, should be a consultative one; one in which deliberation is carried out by a broad cross-section of people within the organisation.

176

Change will require considerable adaptation on the part of the organisation and those within it. Not only will it increase the complexity of the relationship between the organisation and its environment but it will compound problems of maintaining internal organisation solidarity, of all types of co-ordination. Values and goals will become more diverse, more pluralistic and conflicting, and there will be a greater impulse towards attempted, but possibly unco-ordinated, rationality in organisation decision-making and operation. As a consequence, the problem of managing change can usefully be viewed as the problem of 'managing intelligence'; and this can have unique forms of organisational conflict associated with it.

Change demands that we develop an all-important, yet illusive, interdisciplinary ethos. The motivation of specialists usually comes from an identification with a body of knowledge and a methodology which may not be compatible with the need for the organisation to change goals and reorder priorities. Moreover, the motivational structure of experts can lapse into an identification with means, or techniques, rather than with ends.

Since one of the main concerns in museums is the problem of managing specialists, and what constitutes effective interaction between the expert and the policy-maker, it is important to study this issue further. There is a growing tendency for professionals in museums (particularly those at lower levels) to confuse policy making with professional parochialism. This, combined with a lack of comprehensive strategy at the top – the tendency to become tied with excessive detail rather than provide overall policy guidance – can cause considerable problems for the invention and implementation of new alternatives. The top often fails to grasp what it means to manage specialists. Above all, this increasingly important dimension should not be looked at merely as the problem of providing administrative support for the experts in the museum. The responsibility for setting new goals, for planning change, cannot be carried out effectively without some responsibility assumed by the top in establishing the method whereby knowledge of a strategy through which new policy alternatives will arise. What is required is a major involvement by senior managers in the defining of the criteria necessary to guide the organisation's management of its own intelligence. In industrial organisations this has come to be known as developing a corporate strategy. This means establishing a collaboration with specialists and devising a framework for systematically integrating their efforts.

The nature of change is such that there are increasing pressures in the socio-political-cultural environment of the museum for new forms of planned change which will make museums more responsive, both to their internal specialists and their external users. There is no doubt that change within museums is as vital to their future now as it has ever been. The effectiveness of change, the resolution of conflict and the understanding of culture within their organisations, is a fundamental task of senior managers in museums. The climate is forcing changes which require considerable expertise on the part of those senior museum managers. In its way, this book has tried to explore the depths of the theory which has enabled changes to be made in the business world over the past century or so. The crucial differences between museums and businesses makes the selection of criteria more difficult, but the message should remain clear. It is up to the chief executive (the museum director) to grasp the nettle and accept that his/her management skills are lacking. Any organisation is only as good as the person at the top of the team he/she has built around him/her. The time has come when museum directors the world over must stop blaming their staff, funding bodies, the public or whatever other scapegoat they wish to find, for the failure of museums to adapt to change. The very people who apportion blame are the reason for the problems which museums must now urgently solve.

13

Total Quality Management in museums and galleries

There are fashions in everything and it seems the management fashion of the 1980s and 1990s has been Total Quality Management (TQM). In some parts of the world, notably the USA, whole sectors of industry have become Total Quality organisations. In one instance a very powerful country has declared that its armed forces are now dedicated to Total Quality – whatever that may mean.

Up and coming museum managers and aspiring directors are no doubt learning the buzz words of TQM in order to make themselves more marketable to a new employer. I suspect that the governing bodies of museums all over the world are waiting for TQM to catch hold in the museum sector. In the UK we have the additional pressure of a government which preaches the words of quality (through its Citizens Charter and Chartermark initiatives) for everyone except itself. So, how have museums responded to this? Although I doubt whether more than a handful of museum people know about TQM they have unwittingly been putting many of its tenets into practice since before TQM was invented. This is because the concept of quality, or high standards, has always been part of the professional duty of people who work in museums. That desire to achieve high standards did not always cover the whole spectrum of work carried out in museums but, thankfully, in most cases the collections came first and quality in the management of them has always been good, if in many cases empirical and a little traditional. Nevertheless, the high standards of curatorial management of the collections have often been slow to pass across to other areas of museum work – particularly the interface with the users, visitors, customers or whatever other title you would like to give those people who use the services museums supply.

With our need to compete for business, museum managers now resort to tactics which have been well used in other production or service industries. They do this because they see a real risk of losing business if they do not. In previous years our predecessors did not have to worry much about caring for the visitor or, indeed, attracting the visitor in the first place. Until the advent of the independent sector nearly all UK museums and galleries had relied almost totally on financial subsidy by central or local government. This money was provided because museums and galleries were seen as important parts of the cultural and educational needs of society. No one was interested in how many visitors passed through the open door because 'visitor statistics are meaningless aren't they – what counts is the quality of the exhibition/collection not the number of people who see it'. This attitude was perfectly acceptable at the time and the result was that museum directors could afford the luxury of being carefree academics with a bias towards their collections. The visitors were, after all, something to be tolerated – a rather necessary evil which tended to get in the way of the objects and make superbly designed exhibitions rather untidy.

Exhibitions were designed not with the public in mind but with the reputation of the Director in mind. Plumbing, roofing, restrooms, shops and restaurants were all neglected in the cause of self-promotion by a few individuals. The public did not know any better and there was no imperative for the museum manager to do better. If quality was ever mentioned it was only in the context of objects or exhibitions. Generations of people had attended museums to be 'educated', to see things unavailable elsewhere, to be told things they could not find out anywhere else. There was no real competition to the role played by museums – especially not for the average person of moderate or poor means and education.

Then along came television, video cassette recorders and personal computers to fill the knowledge gap in an incredibly comprehensive way. The public now know a lot more than the museum manager gives them credit for. One of the things that has had a deep effect is that the public have become aware of the fact that knowledge is not something to grasp as soon as it is offered because there may be no chance to acquire it again, with the opportunity to learn gone forever. They can now acquire knowledge at a selective rate. They can choose the subject, the type of interpretation, the time, place and, most importantly, the medium. Their choices have been multiplied hugely in the space of just a decade or so. They also have more leisure time and more choices as to how they can spend that time. They are a generation of inheritors, with money in their pockets and a good life with little likelihood of serious conflict reaching them personally.

Suddenly the era of the entrepreneur is born – the undertaker, the person who takes risks and gets things done. These people see the opportunity in this new generation and invest in a future which will cater for them directly. They build sports and leisure centres, theme parks, safari/wildlife parks, computer games, video rental stores, CD machines and start to entice a post-war generation of baby boomers with all the things their parents could never dream of. As this revolution was going on museums clung on to the past – that was, after all, their business. Their directors were all of the previous generation and not only could they not see the whole revolution happening, those parts which were most evident (Carnaby Street, pop videos, Nintendo etc.) they disliked. Such was their parochialism that they continued to lead their institutions down the path of traditionalism long after other, equally prehistoric, industries had started to change. Their views were fixed, their minds set and the competition was not worthy of being noticed. A quality service didn't matter because the visitor was 'below the salt' anyway. No meaningful income was derived from the visitor so they could be ignored without any real effect on income.

These attitudes persisted until the mid-1980s when the competition, which had grown unimpeded by the museum industry, began to attract such an audience that the museums started to empty. Worse still, the local and national funding bodies started to reduce their funding and ask questions about value for money. Museums were never required to charge admission but it became clear that only the most precious could avoid this ultimate decline towards the commercial.

As soon as there was a mere breath of commercialism the visitor became a customer, and customers demand service. Suddenly the museum sector became a service industry and that required management which was not dedicated to the promotion of the individual but to the interests of the public and the growth of the industry. All these effects demanded an element of professional management that had been ignored before. Worse still, because of the generation still occupying the top management positions, that ignorance continued way past its sell-by date. The concept of management as a valid discipline was not only alien but also unpalatable to those in charge at that time. The idea of quality was unnecessary because the word could only be relevant to one thing – the collections.

What these managers were missing is what we need to learn – what, in the context of management, is quality? According to the British Standards Institute's BS4778, quality is, 'The totality of features and characteristics of a product or service that bear on its ability to satisfy stated or implied needs'. What this means is that, if you boldly tell everyone that you have a superb museum you had better ensure you have, because you are implying/stating that your 'product' or 'service' is of high quality. Well, you may believe that a 'superb museum' is one with fine collections, high curatorial standards and academic research, but your customers will expect clean toilets, adequate car parking, a good restaurant, facilities for the disabled, and a host of other services which have very little to do with the collections but are important to the public. The visitor's perception of quality and the curator's perception are bound to be different. The work of a curator might as well be the black arts for all the public know of it. The likes and dislikes of the visitor can only be learned, but curators are not going to absorb the psyche of the visitor, they must be taught to be receptive to the public's needs. Then, when curators talk about quality, they will know that there are a variety of 'qualities' some of which are important to the customer and others to the provider of a service. Neither can be neglected at the expense of the other and neither can be taken as being more or less important.

The concept is simple: museums are not filled with curators, attendants/ warders, administration/support staff, technicians, researchers etc.; visitors do not consist of adults, children, groups, readers, corporate guests etc. There are two categories of people in any organisation – suppliers and customers.

What is even more confusing is that the demarcation of staff and visitor does not necessarily mirror the terms 'supplier' and 'customer'. Within a museum or gallery there are internal customers amongst the staff and, wait for it, some of our visitors are suppliers. 'How so?' you cry! Well, in TQM-speak, this is what is called a 'quality chain' – a series of supplier/customer links which are inside and outside any organisation and can be broken at any stage of the quality process. If there is a failure to provide a quality service at any stage of the process this has a way of multiplying and causing failures and problems elsewhere. An example might help:

> A customer writes to your museum requesting a copy of a photograph in your photo collections. The order is quite specific down to the negative number, postage/packing and the cost of the print. The customer has placed the model order. Your photographic department's quality process has yet to be devised with quality in mind. The process being used is best described as 'the pot luck process'. Two weeks pass before the curator gets down to that particular pile of correspondence wherein which our model order lurks. However, the cheque was extracted on the day the letter passed through the post room and the finance department paid it into the bank immediately. The curator realises he has an order which is old and which has been paid for. There have been murmurings lately of the Director tightening up on this sort of thing, so he places a priority order with the lab for a print to be taken. Three weeks after the order came in, the print is despatched to the customer. Meanwhile, the customer is a bit annoyed to receive a bank statement showing her cheque has been cleared yet no order has arrived. But, not so fast, in the same post is an envelope with your museum postmark – that's alright then isn't it? No, not exactly; the envelope has no stiffening or 'do not bend' label and the photograph is folded. The image itself is blurred and out of focus. There is no receipt only a grubby compliments slip with a totally indecipherable signature.

What we have here is a lack of a quality process illustrating how failures can multiply into disasters. Let us look closely at the scenario.

Because quality was not a factor there were no systems in place to ensure a procedural process was followed when the enquiry first came in. The 'right hand' did not know what the 'left hand' was doing so the finance department did its job by cashing the cheque, but no cross-check was made with the curator.

The curator's main problem seems to be the management of his own time. Using a 'pile of papers' as a measure of when a response is required is quite common but totally unacceptable in a well-managed museum or gallery. There should be proper systems which set standards of quality for staff. If this had been in place the request in this example would not have gone unnoticed for two weeks. Because it took two weeks the curator was then panicked into having the work done urgently (with extra costs involved) and then sending it off without either checking the print properly or ensuring the packaging was fit for the purpose. To add insult to injury, this lack of quality was then manifested to the customer with a grubby compliments slip. A profound message has been sent to the customer – 'we do not care about a quality service and we don't mind who knows it'.

This may seem to be an example of the worst kind, but I am sure most readers will have experienced a similar lack of service from suppliers, whether museums or other organisations. The usual analysis of a failure like this would be that the checks and balances usually applied were not in place. Traditional management principles would point us towards this conclusion. They would say we needed Quality Control. Quality Control is something which is applied *at the end* of a process to ensure mistakes are not passed on to the customer. Plainly, in the case of our curator and his photograph order, this did not happen. Most management principles require an element of *control* at or during the process which provides the *output* to the customer. TQM is different in this crucial respect – it is concerned with *inputs*. In short, TQM checks that the process is correct at the beginning and then throughout, so that quality is guaranteed by the time the output is made.

This is easy to say but rather more difficult to put into practice. How do we achieve a sense of quality in *all* the people who work for our organisation? With difficulty when, in the past, we have always been prepared to put right our failures after the fact and hopefully before the customer became aware of our mistakes. What is more we have a tendency to be a little lazy over our attention to 'customer care' in museums – mainly because, until recently, we did not perceive that the 'customer' actually existed.

Our first thought should be to ensure that our work and the 'product we are manufacturing' (i.e., the service) meets the requirements which are set by management in consultation with those who have the task. What should those requirements contain? Well, they should look carefully at what is a quality output for that area of the work being done by the museum. Let's go back to our curator of photographs for a moment to see if he could have done any better. What were the quality requirements which should have been met in this example?

1 *Availability*
Quite simply – did the curator have the photographs in his collection which the enquirer was seeking? If not she should have been told politely and efficiently within a short time-scale. If they were in the collection he could proceed to supply them.

2 *Delivery*
If he has the product then he should be able to deliver it in a quality manner – quickly, safely and efficiently.

3 *Reliability*
The quality of the product should be good, not a blurred and out of focus image printed on a piece of paper which is the wrong size. The product

should be fit for the purpose and reliable. The customer expects reliability and will only buy from us again if she gets it.

4 *Maintainability*

If the museum has a reputation for poor quality, word will soon get around. In many senses this maintainability would directly refer to keeping a product working. A photograph, you might think, is not something which is affected by maintenance or the lack of it. In fact the photograph example allows us to consider another, equally important element of maintainability which is often forgotten. We are not only interested in providing a product which is intrinsically maintainable but we must also maintain our own reputation as a quality organisation and we do that by providing a quality service in everything we do – even when sending out a single photograph to an enquirer.

5 *Cost-effectiveness*

Everything we do should be cost-effective – not only for us but also for the customer. How can we do this for, you might say, if it is cost-effective for the customer it cannot possibly be cost-effective for the organisation? In fact, the customer expects value for money, a realistic price and a quality service. If all of these are supplied then the margins possible will provide a healthy profit for the product or service supplied.

The key is also for museum retailers and marketeers to be kept under control in our essentially service-orientated regime – they must be made to understand the needs of the customer and the museum's ability to meet these demands. With this knowledge they can grasp the essential difference between museums/galleries and the commercial/industrial sector. The ability of our museums and galleries to meet the demand of our visitors/customers whilst supplying a quality service requires a process of work which has quality at its root – i.e., Quality Assurance rather than Quality Control. This is the Quality Process and it involves the transformation of inputs into desired outputs. In the case of our photograph example, the input was the research request and the desired (although not achieved) output was a successful quality product being received by the customer.

The Quality Process turns the detection of problems *after* work has been done (i.e., Quality Control) into a pre-product element. We should be trying to ensure the controls are there *before* and *throughout* the whole process. If this is possible, quality is almost guaranteed.

This is the briefest of résumés of the TQM process but museum managers should be aware of the importance of quality and strive to ease systems into place which ensures that quality is a part of everything happening in their museum or gallery.

14

Conclusions for museum managers

During my research for this book the environment in which museums and galleries operate has moved further towards the commercial sector than at any time in history. The original aim in looking at the implications of management and organisation theory and their relevance to the museum context had been to examine any possible correlation between management knowledge as expressed by theorists over the past century, to discover how that knowledge was put into practice, and to draw parallels with the contemporary museum situation. Whilst still achieving this aim, the whole tenure of museum management has been shifted during the past few years. These shifts have been identified and provide even greater relevance to the findings in this book.

I have tried to separate this work into two distinct areas, the management of the individual within museums and the management of museums themselves. Both are key areas and I have examined their historical and contemporary contexts to ascertain the current position and, perhaps, direct thought to the future. I hope, too, I have helped the reader to modify his/her skills in these distinct and important areas.

In reviewing established management theory the general conclusion is that museums have been managed traditionally along the lines of scientific and classical principles. It is hardly surprising when it is realised that the majority of senior museum managers have little or no formal training in the disciplines of management; certainly not to a level equivalent to their qualifications as subject-specialists. Most job holders in such important posts have achieved their position as a result of their pre-eminence in academic or other subject-specialist fields, they have rarely been appointed as a result of a qualification in, or even a particular flair for, management. This is hardly surprising for their principle task is to lead institutions with a high proportion of subject-specialists with organisational objectives of a primarily academic nature. However, lack of formal management training, lack of knowledge of up-to-date techniques of management, and a certain unwillingness to learn, have resulted in approaches which are based more on learning acquired 'on the job' than on the proven research of others and, naturally, result in techniques that may be adequate but are certainly not optimum. Scientific Management is a natural method for academically orientated individuals, and Classical

Management is probably an intuitive aspect of learned behaviour. The consequence of this lack of specialist knowledge in management subjects is a predominantly out-of-date approach by many senior members of the museum profession to their primary task, that of managing their institutions.

In examining other, more recent, approaches to the management of individuals it can be seen that the authoritarian (and in some cases dictatorial) approaches used in many of the more prominent museums are no longer either appropriate or acceptable. Using such styles of management does not take into account the great social, cultural or perceptual changes that have taken place in recent years. Neither do these non-consultative approaches allow for the radical changes that have taken place in the attitudes of the workforce. They do not address the fundamental differences in the public's perception of museums, and they stifle the innovation so necessary in a leisure-orientated society which now provides the greater part of a museum's audience. A management style that advocates rigid rule-following and distinct pyramidal lines of reporting for all staff, will not provide the entrepreneurial flair and flexible decision-making which has become a prerequisite for the running of inspired and cost-effective institutions. The management of change is a craft that must be learned in the same way as any other discipline, yet the changes that have been forcing museums to radically alter their approaches to the majority of their functions have been handled with a distinct lack of positive attempts to acquire knowledge in this area. There have also been cases where management deficiencies, when categorically pointed out, have been ignored.

The organisational structure of many museums follows the traditional approach tending towards bureaucratic principles. Whilst bureaucratic solutions are proven and acceptable, they do not provide a management solution to the whole range of activities and disciplines found in most museums. However, they are found throughout the museum framework and are only deviated from in rare instances. In managing the organisation we looked at the seriousness of including an awareness of appropriate structures within museums with regard to other types of structure which have been developed to deal with similar organisations in the manufacturing and service sector. The appropriateness of structure is shown to be a primary reason for success or failure in organisations. We looked at the contrasting adhocracy as the direct antithesis of the more normal bureaucracy. We did this to represent the options open to museum managers in their attempts to contrive a more open system within the, necessarily confined, limitations of their current organisational situation. In so doing the 'matrix structure' within the entire organisation is shown to be more appropriate for dealing with temporary situations. Museums have a diverse set of criteria within their structures and this book proposes that a confined structure to deal with one area may not be appropriate for another. The example of collections management versus design/display illustrates this need for alternate solutions, but also highlights one of the fundamental inadequacies in museum management: when senior managers react by structuring their organisations in the same way for each eventuality.

The importance of a bias towards a flexible and consultative approach is pin-pointed by the realisation that the broad range of academic and personal experience within museums expands from skilled members of staff, qualified in highly specialist subjects, to lower graded workers occupying manual labour posts such as object cleaning. The styles of management, the design of specific jobs, and the division of labour, all require more than empirical judgement on the part of the manager. Work rotation, motivation and consistent/continuous training, backed by appraisal and counselling should be crucial elements of the general duties of museum managers. The appreciation of these fundamental skills has been lacking in the museum profession and requires urgent review.

Part of the realisation that a senior manager must also be a skilled specialist in management techniques is a hurdle that has yet to be tackled and the environment in which museums are required to operate is demanding action now. The commercial pressures on the museum sector are such that these basic skills must be added to subject-specialist attainment in order to provide a secure future for those museum professionals who seek to take up senior museum appointments in the future. The governing bodies of museums are setting criteria that contain many more non-curatorial priorities than has been the case in the past. To this end they require senior executive staff in whom they can lay confidence to not only preserve curatorial standards, but also to provide leadership in an extremely competitive environment. Competition has never been greater and audience attendance never more important. The days of quiet museums with a small devoted audience are no longer with us. The public are used to noise, bustle and vibrancy, and the skilled museum manager knows that these features bring vitality and excitement. This will, to some, smack of errant commercialism, particularly when its aim is to open wallets and purses, and rattle credit cards, but it is the key to future success.

Effective management includes knowledge about individuals within organisations and about the organisations themselves but, in an environment that includes customers, the consumer must also figure highly in the policy making process. There has been, and will continue to be, a distinct tendency to require 'commercial flair' as one of the peripheral attributes for the engagement of new museum directors; the shift in this direction is a source of concern to the curatorial and academic staff of many museums. This need not be to the detriment of museums if there continues to be a bias towards curatorial qual-ification and experience, and a realistic measurement of management knowledge as well. Danger arises if notice is not taken of the need for change in the approach of senior management to the acquisition of fundamental management knowledge. The controlling authorities in museums and galleries will be unlikely to allow the situation to continue indefinitely. It is likely that management expertise will be sought from outside the museum profession if that expertise does not manifest itself from within. This would be a retro-grade step for it would bring the heavy influence of commercialism into institutions that carry out a large number of functions that can never be commercial.

The ability of the museum manager to apply management techniques, organisational design and marketing impetus to an institution is constrained by curatorial sympathy born out of experience. This experience is primarily a knowledge of these very differences between the museum and the commercial context. Whilst museums can only benefit from an awareness of management and organisation theory/practice, they risk an undermining of their whole purpose if the distinctions between curatorial priorities and commercial potential are misaligned. The real skill is joining together commercial approaches and curatorial policy where each are mutually supporting and sustaining. The public face of many museums is only the tip of a giant research/preservation iceberg. In the past some museums have laid too great an emphasis on the 'hidden' aspects of their operation; it is not unusual for the staff involved in the public presentation aspects of a museum (i.e., interpretation, design, display and education) to be heavily outnumbered by their colleagues in research/ conservation departments. This may well be a wholly necessary division but thought should be given to the appropriate relationship between work done for the mass of visitors and effort required for the minority of researchers. Traditional emphasis has been placed on the collection rather than the consumer. The primary concern must always be with the long-term well-being of the collection but a change of emphasis may be necessary in order to win back a dwindling audience in such a way as to provide the resources necessary to carry out non-commercial work to an even higher level than current financial constraints allow.

Museums are non-profit making institutions. Any commercial activity resulting from significant management skill on the part of senior staff will eventually bring forth a greater ability to generate more financial resources for their non-commercial work. This, if nothing else, should give impetus to museum professionals to acquire the skills advocated in this book. I wish them well and I hope my efforts to crystallise needs and processes are of benefit to them.

Appendix: Code of Financial Practice example

1 INTRODUCTION

1.1 The purpose of this code is two-fold. First, it provides help and advice for staff in the Museum who have responsibility for the management of resources or the control of income and expenditure. Second, it lays down procedures to ensure that at all times the financial management of the Museum is conducted in accordance with the highest standards. However, staff must be aware that a serious breach of this code will lead to disciplinary action.

1.2 This code is determined by the Director of the Museum as Accounting Officer for funds provided by .... [herein would be inserted the name of the grant aiding body].

2 RESPONSIBILITY

2.1 The Director is responsible to the Trustees and the .... for the effective and efficient use of resources, the solvency of the Museum and for safeguarding its assets and collections. The Director is responsible for submitting for approval annual estimates of income and expenditure to the Board of Trustees.

2.2 The Director is responsible to the Board for preparing annual estimates of income and expenditure for consideration by the Board and for the management of resources within estimates approved by the Board. Within this code reference is made to the Director. Except when provided to the contrary, the Director may delegate functions but not his/her responsibility, to other staff.

2.3 The Museum Secretary is responsible to the Director for operational matters concerned with the collection of income and the commitment of expenditure. The Museum Secretary is also responsible for the compilation of all accounts and accountancy records of the Museum.

2.4 To assist him/her in discharging his/her responsibilities the Director is empowered to designate members of staff as Budget Managers. Budget Managers shall be responsible for the control and monitoring of expenditure within budgets allocated to them. The delegation to Budget Managers shall be in writing. Budget Managers are responsible to the Director for ensuring that the action they take is in accordance with this Code of Financial Practice.

3   THE BUDGET

3.1 *Preparation*
The Director is responsible for the preparation of annual estimates of income and expenditure. The annual estimates of income and expenditure shall be incorporated as part of the annual update of the Museum's ongoing 5-year Corporate Plan and shall be approved by the Board of Trustees and submitted to the ....

3.2 *Approval of annual estimates*
The Trustees shall not delegate the approval of the annual estimates of income and expenditure. The Board will be asked to determine, by resolution, the approval of the budget. The resolution shall specify the surplus or deficit that the Board is approving on the main account and any subsidiary accounts that the Museum may hold. If the .... cannot provide Grant-in-Aid at a level sought by the Trustees in consultation with the Ministry/Authority, then the Ministry/Authority will request a revision of the Annual Estimates. This request will be in writing.

3.3 *Authorisation*
Once the Board has approved the annual estimates of income and expenditure, the Director is authorised to incur expenditure in accordance with this Code of Financial Practice. The authorisation of the Director to incur expenditure is up to, but not exceeding, the amount specified in the Financial Memorandum.

3.4 *Admission fees and other charges*
The Trustees shall be responsible for determining the admission fees and other charges levied by the Museum in respect of its exhibitions and other services supplied to customers. The Board may delegate responsibility for determining fees and charges to the Director but shall review all fees and charges annually or at such lesser intervals as may be required.

3.5 *Monitoring*
The Director is responsible for presenting to the Board of Trustees at each of their meetings a report of actual income and expenditure in such form as may be determined by the Trustees from time to time.

3.5.1 Designated Budget Managers are responsible to the Director for the control of expenditure from the budgets allocated to them.

3.6 *Budget management*

Budget management responsibilities will be delegated by the Director to responsible managers (Budget Managers) in expenditure and income headings. Budget Managers will receive allocations for their areas of responsibility, after the approval of the annual estimates of income and expenditure by the Board of Trustees, together with various management targets which may be set by the Director. Responsibility Centres are the main aggregating centres of work into which the Museum is sub-divided for financial management purposes e.g., curatorial departments, administration/personnel, marketing and maintenance.

3.6.1 Budget Managers will be free to exercise virement between the heads of expenditure in their Responsibility Centres for sums up to a figure approved by the Director from time to time. The Museum Secretary will be notified of all such virements in an approved format.

3.6.2 Virements for sums greater than that approved from time to time by the Director must be submitted through the Museum Secretary for approval by the Director.

3.6.3 It shall be the duty of each Budget Manager to bring to the Director's attention any estimated shortfall in income or increase in expenditure that is not able to be contained within the approved estimates for that Responsibility Centre.

3.6.4 Responsibility Centres will not be able to retain savings against budget heads that arise through 'windfall' benefits (e.g., pay awards less than budgeted). These will accrue to the main Museum budget. Responsibility centres will not be able to carry forward underspendings of their budget allocation to the next financial year and therefore must prudently ensure that underspendings are identified in advance in order that they can be transferred to the main Museum budget.

3.6.5 Any proposal for additional expenditure that affects the estimated surplus or deficit approved by the Board of Trustees shall be submitted to the Director who may recommend action to the Board of Trustees.

3.6.7 Virement will not be permitted between revenue and capital budgets or between operational and purchase grant headings without prior approval of the Director who will seek permission of [grant aiding body].

3.7 *Audit*

All parts of the Museum may be subject to Internal Audit at any time. The Internal Auditor shall be appointed by the Director and has authority to visit all responsibility centres of the Museum to interview staff and to have access to all records relating to funds, assets and property of the Museum. The Internal Auditor will be responsible to the Museum Secretary and exceptionally, if dissatisfied with the action taken by the Museum Secretary in response to professional concern drawn to his/her attention by the Internal Auditor, then the Internal Auditor has a right of access to the Director who must communicate his/her concern to the Chairperson of Trustees. The Internal Auditor will collaborate and co-operate with the External Auditors to ensure that there is no unnecessary duplication of audit effort.

3.7.2 The primary objective of an Internal Audit is to review, appraise and report upon:-

(a) The soundness, adequacy and application of accounting, financial and other control.

(b) The extent to which systems of control ensure compliance with established policies and procedures.

(c) The extent to which resources are accounted for and safeguarded from losses of all kinds arising from fraud, misappropriation and other offences or waste, extravagant and inefficient administration, poor value for money or other causes.

(d) The suitability and reliability of financial and other management data.

(e) The extent that systems of control are laid down and operate to achieve the most economic, efficient and effective use of resources.

3.7.3 In addition to the work of the Internal Auditor there will be, from time to time, specific audits covering, but not limited to, such matters as special projects and contracts, Income Tax and Value Added Tax.

3.7.4 Auditors are entitled to receive such explanations as necessary concerning matters under review. Any records kept in Responsibility Centres must be retained for audit purposes for at least seven years.

3.7.5 In the event of any Budget Manager becoming aware of discrepancies or deviation from normal practice the matter should immediately be drawn to the attention of the Director.

4 BANKING

4.1 The Museum bankers are the [insert Bank name address here]. All funds due to the Museum shall be deposited in an account maintained with these bankers for the purposes of the Museum. No other account or funds associated with or maintained for the purposes of the Museum shall be established except with the authorisation of the Director.

4.2 The signatures for the authorisation of transactions in relation to this account shall be as approved from time to time by the Director. Authorisation for the expenditure of funds shall require two signatures from the following group of authorised signatures:

- The Director
- The Deputy Director
- A. N. Other
- A. N. Other

4.3 All arrangements with the Museum's bankers regarding the bank account and the issue of cheques are under the control of the Museum Secretary. All new cheques may be ordered from the bank only on the authority of one of the designated cheque signatories agreed by the Director. All cheques drawn on behalf of the Museum must be signed in a manner agreed by the Director.

5   BORROWING

5.1 Short-term borrowing for temporary revenue purposes shall be authorised by the Director within limits determined by the Financial Memorandum of the .... The Director shall report such short-term borrowing to the Board of Trustees at the earliest opportunity.

5.2 Borrowing for periods in excess of twelve months shall require the authorisation of the Board of Trustees and shall comply with any requirements of the Financial Memorandum of the ....

6   INCOME

6.1 *General*

6.1.1 The Museum Secretary is responsible for the collection of all monies due to the Museum and must approve the form of all receipt forms, books, tickets or other official acknowledgements of monies received. Any monies due to the Museum which are considered doubtful debts can only be written off in accordance with the provisions of this Financial Code.

6.1.2 Monies due to the Museum from external organisations or persons shall be requested on Museum invoices issued by the Museum Secretary. Responsibility Centres are not permitted to deal directly with invoicing unless agreed by the Museum Secretary.

6.2 *Grant-in-Aid*

6.2.1 The .... provides grants for three purposes. Virement between these grants is only allowed in accordance with the Financial Memorandum of the .... with .... approval. The grants provided include:
(a) Operating Grant-in-Aid
(b) Special Maintenance Grant-in-Aid
(c) Purchases for the Collection Grant-in-Aid

6.2.2 Operating Grant-in-Aid is provided for normal day-to-day running costs such as salaries and wages, consumables and supplies, maintenance of premises, administration, exhibitions and maintenance of exhibits.

6.2.3 Special Maintenance Grant-in-Aid is provided for maintenance projects which have been identified as outside the scope of regular maintenance provided within the Operating Grant-in-Aid.

6.2.4 Purchase Grant-in-Aid provides assistance with the purchase of objects for the nation and to add to the Museum's already extensive collections.

6.3 *Carry over of Grant-in-Aid*
In order to abide by Government regulations the Museum is not able to carry over Grant-in-Aid for operations or special maintenance from one financial year to the other. However, special permission has been given for Museums to carry over Purchase Grant-in-Aid from one year to the next as this acknowledges the difficulties Museums have in determining budgets for potential purchases for the collections and the relatively small sums provided for the purchase of objects against their realistic cost.

6.4 *Admissions, income and other charges*
The Museum Secretary shall collect all admission fees and other charges. All admission fees are payable in advance of admission and careful records will be kept of all concessionary admissions and complimentary admissions. The Museum Secretary will carry out spot checks on the admission procedures and maintain rules for admission staff in consultation with the Managing Director of the Museum's Trading Company [insert the name of the Company].

6.4.2 The .... Company shall, collect admission fees on behalf of the Museum and be reimbursed accordingly under terms agreed from time to time between the Museum Director and the .... Company.

6.5 *Collection of money and banking*

6.5.1 The collection of all monies due to the Museum is the responsibility of the Museum Secretary. All monies received must be paid promptly into the accounts office or where this is not practical, with the agreement of the Museum Secretary, paid directly into the Museum's bank account. Such money should be paid over gross (i.e., payments may not be made out of receipts) and to be accompanied by supporting documentation for audit purposes. For reasons of security it is not advisable to take cash to the bank at the same time each day or at the same time each week.

6.5.2 As a safeguard against misappropriation of income and to ensure that credit control procedures are applied, Budget Managers and others concerned with the generation of income should ensure that notification of the need for a sales invoice is rendered to the Accounts Department for all income due to the Museum as soon as the service has been agreed. The approval of the Museum Secretary is required for any departure from the Museum's invoicing system.

6.6 *Receipt books*

If a Responsibility Centre needs to issue receipts for sundry cash it should obtain an official receipt book from the Museum Secretary. Any monies received in this way must be paid over to the Accounts Department regularly and not allowed to accumulate. Adequate arrangements must be made for the safekeeping of all such money.

6.7 *Credit notes*

Requests for credit notes should be submitted to the Accounts Department and should be approved by the following *before* credit notes are actually raised by that Responsibility Centre. All requests to be agreed by the relevant budget holder. In addition the following authorisations are required:
(a) Request for credit notes of refunds up to £50 to the Museum Secretary
(b) Request for credit notes of refunds over £50 to the Museum Director.

6.8 *Bad debts*

The accounting system will credit Responsibility Centres with income when the invoice is prepared. If that income is not received this may be regarded as a central cost (i.e., bad debt), or the original credit may be reversed to the Responsibility Centre concerned. The Museum Secretary will decide which is most appropriate in the circumstances. The authority for writing off bad debts is as follows:
(a) For individual debts up to and including £500, the Museum Secretary.
(b) For debts in excess of £500 the Deputy Director or Director.
(c) In any case of bad debts the Director should be informed.

6.9 *Goods and services provided to other Museum Responsibility Centres*

6.9.1 When Budget Managers provide goods or services for other Museum Responsibility Centres a transfer request form should be used to transfer the appropriate charges. These forms can be obtained from the accounts department. They are pre-numbered and they are issue-recorded in the Accounts Department for audit purposes. Blank forms should not be photocopied to provide further supplies.

6.9.2 The issuing Responsibility Centre should issue on the form details of the goods and services provided and account or accounts to be credited. The form must be signed by the Budget Manager or his/her authorised nominee. The receiving Responsibility Centre should check the details on the form and enter the account code or codes to be charged. The form must be authorised for processing by the Budget Manager or an authorised nominee and sent to the Accounts Department without delay. Transfer requests should not be used to effect transfer of resources between Responsibility Centres where there has not been a provision of goods or services by one Responsibility Centre to another.

6.10 *Goods and services provided to outside bodies*

6.10.1 Where goods or services are provided by the Museum to individuals or outside bodies, an appropriate charge shall be made. The Accounts

Department shall issue invoices for such goods or services and Responsibility Centres must supply the information which will enable them so to do. Budget Managers shall not issue invoices unless agreed by the Museum Secretary.

6.10.2 An economic rate should be charged for any goods or services provided by a Responsibility Centre and the Accounts Department (which must be consulted before the price is agreed) shall advise on the appropriate rate. It is important that such income, once invoiced, is actually received. If Budget Managers have any suspicion that payment for any goods and services provided has not been received, or will be received after long delay and effort on behalf of the Museum, they should consult the Museum Secretary as soon as possible, before any more goods and services are provided.

6.11 *Disposal of items on inventory*

6.11.1 For the purpose of this paragraph, the term 'inventory' refers to any asset belonging to the Museum (excluding items which form part of the Museum's collections) which is essentially capital (i.e., has an excepted useful life of more than twelve months) as opposed to revenue in nature. Items of inventory can therefore be fixed or moveable and most commonly include equipment and furniture.

6.11.2 In cases where it becomes apparent that an item of Museum inventory needs to be disposed of, the following authorisation levels and procedures must be observed:-

Current replacement cost of asset to be disposed of is up to:

Value of Order	Authorisation
£3,000	Budget Manager or nominee
£3,000 to £10,000	Budget Manager
Over £10,000	Director or Deputy Director

It is the authoriser's responsibility to ensure that the decision to dispose of the asset is justified.

6.11.3 Details of all inventory items disposed of should be notified to the Museum Secretary.

6.11.4 Proceeds and costs of disposal are to be allocated to the Responsibility Centre which owned the asset disposed of.

6.11.5 If in cases where the asset is to be replaced, a trade-in allowance is accepted then the order for the replacement should be authorised in accordance with this Financial Code (7.3.3 and 7.3.4) based on the cost of the replacement *before* deducting the trade-in allowance.

6.11.6 These procedures apply to the disposal of all Museum inventory, whatever the source of their funding.

7   EXPENDITURES

7.1 *General*

The Director is responsible for all payments made by or on behalf of the Museum. The Director shall approve all payment procedures.

7.2 *Salaries and wages*

The Personnel Manager, under the supervision of the Museum Secretary, shall be responsible for the maintenance of personnel records and for the provision of relevant information to enable all salaries, wages, pensions and other emoluments to be paid. The Museum Secretary shall be responsible for ensuring such payments are made and for the maintenance of the related records, including those of a statutory nature.

7.2.2 All payments for salaries, wages, expenses and subsistence must be made by or arranged by the Accounts Department. All remunerative payments must be made through the Museum's own payroll system, unless an alternative arrangement has been agreed in writing by the Museum Secretary.

7.2.3 Payments are made in accordance with pay scales approved by the Board of Trustees and any backdated pay awards, for weekly or monthly paid staff are paid as soon as is practical and when approved by the Director on behalf of the Board of Trustees.

7.3 *Orders and contracts for goods and services*

7.3.1 It is a requirement that goods and services purchased by the Museum satisfy operational requirements and are obtained expeditiously and economically. Budget Managers are responsible for all orders issued by their Responsibility Centre.

7.3.2 Budget Managers shall ensure that purchases are made at the most favourable rate by obtaining estimates on the basis that the acceptance of any estimates other than the lowest is not permitted except in exceptional circumstances and in consultation with the Museum Secretary and/or the Director. The details of the circumstances shall be recorded in writing.

7.3.3 The procedures for obtaining estimates shall be as follows:

Value of Order	Requirements
Up to £3,000	The Budget Manager shall use good sense as to the need to obtain information in addition to an estimated price from a supplier.
£3,000 to £25,000	Three written quotations are required.
Over £25,000	Three competitive tenders in accordance with the tender procedures as set by the .... and the Museum, and a written contract in a form approved by Museum solicitors.

197

Tenders and multiple quotations are not required if any of the following conditions apply:

(a) The goods to be purchased are proprietary items and are sold at a fixed price.

(b) The price of the goods is controlled by Government regulation or trade organisation.

(c) The goods are only obtainable from a single supplier and there is no genuine price competition.

(d) Repairs where parts for existing plant and machinery are required or the product needs to be compatible with existing installations and the budget holder considers that this work should be carried out or provided for by the original supplier.

7.3.4 The arrangement for authorisation of orders shall be as follows:-

Value of Order	*Authorisation*
Up to £500	The Budget Manager or designated nominee. (The Budget Manager shall set an order value limit for each nominee and inform the Museum Secretary accordingly in writing).
£500 to £5,000	The Budget Manager.
£5,000 to £25,000	The Director or Deputy Director.
Over £25,000	Authorisation by any one signature from the group of authorised signatures after approval of the Trustees' Sub-Committee.

7.3.5 The arrangements for authorisation of orders to be paid for by the Museum's Purchase Grant shall be as follows:

Value of Order	*Authorisation*
Up to £999	The Museum Director.
£1,000 and over	The Museum Director with counter signature by the Chairperson of Trustees or his/her nominee.

7.3.6 Budget Managers shall be responsible for ensuring that the procedures prescribed by the Director for the receipt of goods and services are adhered to. If it is necessary to vary the procedures the authority of the Director or the Deputy Director shall be required in writing to authorise that variation.

7.3.7 The tendering procedure if required under 7.3.3 is outlined in Annex 2.

7.4 *Building works*

7.4.1 The principle stated in the preceding paragraphs (authorisation of orders) shall apply to any contracts entered into in relation to building works or the maintenance and service of building equipment. The Building Services Manager shall be authorised to enter into contracts not exceeding £2,000 for the provision of building services. Contracts between £2,000 and £25,000 shall require the approval of the Director or Deputy Director. Contracts in excess of £25,000 shall require the approval of the Board of Trustees.

7.4.2 The Building Services Manager shall use his/her best endeavours to ensure that a wide variety of contractors employed in building work are used at the Museum, by using an approved list of contractors which shall be maintained by the Museum. This approved list of contractors will take into account the financial viability, size and experience of the contractor and include systems to ensure security of contractors' staff working on Museum premises.

7.5 *Purchasing procedures*

7.5.1 Orders may only be placed by Budget Managers and such other persons as approved by the Director. The Museum Secretary will maintain a register of authorised purchasers together with specimen signatures. All orders shall be on Museum stationery which shall be uniquely and individually numbered and shall be placed through the Museum's financial accounting system and carry a prescribed authorisation signed by an authorised purchaser.

7.5.2 The current price, or an estimate of it, must be obtained before an order is placed and the details must be entered on the order. The person placing the order must ensure that the expenditure is a valid charge on the Museum and that adequate funds are available to meet the expenditure.

7.5.3 Budget Managers should be aware that occasionally firms offer gifts and inducements which overreach the acceptable limits of general available promotional handouts, e.g., diaries and pens or routine hospitality. Such offers must not be accepted and must be reported to the Museum Secretary immediately. Budget Managers are advised that the acceptance of gifts or inducements to influence purchasing decisions is a disciplinary offence. Orders must not be given to a firm which transacts business in this way.

7.5.4 Official Museum order forms must not, in any circumstances, be used for making personal purchases.

7.5.5 The policy of the Museum is not to pay for goods or services until deliveries have been made and found to be satisfactory for the intended purpose. However, under certain circumstances the supplier may be justified in requiring part or full payment in advance.

7.5.6 Orders must not be placed by telephone unless the circumstances are as a result of a matter of true urgency. The verbal order must include the number of the confirmatory official order form which must be used and issued on the same day and must be clearly marked as a confirmatory order.

7.5.7 Goods on inspection or approval. All requests for inspection copies of books, other published materials or any other goods must be routed via the Responsibility Centre which made the order except in the case of books which should be routed via the Library. Any invoices which are received by the Museum in relation to goods ordered on an inspection basis which are not the subject of a bona fide Museum Purchase Order will be the responsibility of the individual concerned.

7.6 *Contracts*

7.6.1 This paragraph applies to the contracts for services, works or supply of goods which provide for payment to be made in instalments against a certificate including partial staged or final performance against a specification.

7.6.2 The Museum Secretary shall ensure that a register is kept recording amounts due and payments made under such contracts.

7.6.3 All payments to contractors shall be made on a certificate signed in the manner determined by the Director. All payments to contractors on account of contracts shall be made in accordance with such contracts and the appropriate Budget Manager shall supply the Museum Secretary with details of the total amount of the contract, the estimated value of the work to date and of materials on site, the amount deducted by way of retention, VAT, liquidated and ascertained damages in respect of unsatisfactory work, the amounts previously paid and the amount now due for payment.

7.6.4 During the currency of a contract the Museum's Internal or External Auditors shall, subject to Health and Safety requirements be granted access to the contract works and may undertake such investigations as they consider desirable.

7.6.5 Any extra or variation to a contract may be specially ordered in accordance with the terms of the contract. All such extras or variations must be notified in writing to the contractor, provided that no such order shall be given which would incur expenditure in respect of additional work not covered by the tender unless such expenditure has been authorised by the Director or the extra costs can be funded by virement or by other sources of income.

7.6.6 On completion of a contract the appropriate Budget Managers shall produce to the Museum Secretary a detailed statement of the work under the contract and all vouchers, documents etc., showing full measurements, additions, deductions and omissions which shall be examined by the Museum Secretary before a final certificate is required under the contract to be issued to the contractor.

7.6.7 Claims received from contractors in respect of matters not clearly within the terms of any existing contract (for example, alleging breach of contract) shall be referred to the Museum's solicitors for consideration of legal liability and to the Museum Secretary before a settlement is reached.

7.7 *Coding certification and authorisation of invoices for payment*

7.7.1 Budget Managers shall be responsible for the validity and accuracy of invoices passed by their Responsibility Centres to the Museum Secretary for Payment. Authorisation of an invoice for payment by a Budget Manager or authorised signature shall be taken by the Museum Secretary to mean:-
(a) That goods and services have been received.
(b) That prices are correct.
(c) That the coding is correct and that adequate funds exist to meet the expenditure from the budget.
(d) That the expenditure was a valid and approved charge on the Museum.
(e) That calculations are correct.
(f) That, where appropriate, entries have been made in the Responsibility Centre inventory and stores records.
(g) That the invoice has not previously been approved for transmission to the Museum Secretary for payment and that the copy order has been properly marked off to prevent duplicate payment.
(h) That the invoice includes or excludes, as appropriate, a charge of Value Added Tax in accordance with the regulations of HM Customs and Excise.

7.7.2 Budget Managers must supply the Museum Secretary with the names, specimen signatures and authorisation codes of persons who they authorise to approve invoices for payment. A form is available for this purpose which allows Budget Managers to specify particular account codes and any expenditure limit imposed on such nominees. These forms must be signed by the Budget Manager and must be retained for reference in the Administration Department. The Museum Secretary must be notified without delay of any changes.

7.7.3 Invoices should not be certified for payment by the person authorising the order.

8   EXPENSES

8.1 Staff shall be reimbursed for actual expenses incurred whilst on Museum business within and subject to the current rates and regulations approved by the Museum which shall be based on .... expense rates. Museum staff are required to exercise economy and take advantage of special travel facilities when ever possible.

8.4 Persons requested to provide a service or attend an interview may be reimbursed for expenses actually incurred within the limits that apply to staff. They should be made aware, in advance, of the Museum's regulations, procedures and current rates of reimbursement by the Budget Manager concerned and the Budget Manager should take account the need for economy. Payment should be made by cheque and forwarded to the applicant by the Accounts Department.

9 PETTY CASH

9.1 Budget Managers may have a cash imprest, by arrangement with the Museum Secretary, to enable them to make minor purchases without the need to use the official ordering procedure. The Museum Secretary is responsible for determining the maximum held in any imprest after consultation with the Budget Manager. Imprests should not be used for travel or subsistence expenditure. Security of the imprest and the authority for purchases of a minor nature should be the responsibility of one person delegated by the Budget Manager. When responsibility for holding the petty cash is transferred, it must be balanced and handed to the Museum Secretary for verification and safekeeping. Budget Managers are to notify the Accounts Department of any such change in order that the procedure may be explained to the new holder by a member of the Accounts Department.

9.2 Petty Cash boxes must be kept locked and stored with an appropriate record in a secure place when not in use. Vouchers for petty cash dispersements must be obtained and forwarded to the Accounts Department when making claims for reimbursement.

10 INSURANCE

10.1 The Museum Secretary shall be responsible for arranging those insurances which are necessary and shall keep records of all insurances effected on behalf of the Museum and the property and risks covered thereby.

10.2 Prompt notification shall be given to the Museum Secretary of all new risks.

10.3 The Museum Secretary shall be given prompt notification of any fine, loss or other damage, accident or occurrence which may give rise to a claim under the Museum's insurances.

10.4 Every member of staff who receives expenses for driving their personally owned motor vehicle must, when required, produce the registration document, insurance policy and current certificate of insurance and Department of Transport Test Certificate to the Museum Secretary. Policies shall be comprehensive and cover use on official business of the Museum.

11   INVENTORIES/ASSETS REGISTER

11.1 An asset register shall be maintained by the Museum Secretary integral to the Museum's accounting system which shall serve the purpose of the Muscum's inventory.

11.2 Each Budget Manager shall be responsible for all inventory items of his/her Responsibility Centre and shall arrange for them to be periodically checked.

11.3 The Museum Secretary shall be informed of any deficiencies or surpluses which are revealed on inventory checks.

11.4 Disposals of items of inventory shall be in accordance with paragraph 6.11 of this code.

11.5 References to inventories and asset registers do not include items which are deemed to be part of the Museum's historical collections which are covered under separate codes.

12   VALUE ADDED TAX

12.1 The Museum Secretary shall maintain the VAT records for the Museum and shall make all VAT payments and receive all VAT credits as appropriate.

12.2 The Accounts Department provides VAT advice to Budget Managers in the Museum as requested. Budget Managers are advised in writing when specific changes take place which affect the Museum in general.

12.3 In general, most of the supplies made by the Museum may be regarded as falling within the scope of VAT. If Budget Managers are in any doubt they should consult the Museum Secretary.

ANNEX 1: CODE OF FINANCIAL PRACTICE – COMPLIANCE

The Code of Financial Practice is part of the rules and procedures of the Museum. It is therefore necessary that all Budget Holders are conversant with this Code and ensure any staff to whom they have delegated responsibility under the Code are also aware of its content and implications. In order to ensure understanding and compliance with the Code, Budget Managers are required to sign below that they have read the Code and understand it.

Annex 1 will be updated in line with any updates which are made to the Code itself and at any time when the Code is updated this should be read and signed again by Budget Managers.

Budget Manager   *Signature*   *Date*

ANNEX 2: RULES GOVERNING THE SEEKING OF TENDERS AND THE PROCESSING OF TENDERS

1 The Code of Financial Practice of the Museum require tenders to be secured for the purchase of goods or services costing in excess of £25,000.

2 Authorisation to invite tenders must be obtained from the Director or Deputy Director. The Building Services Manager is authorised to invite tenders for work falling under his/her responsibility.

3 Invitations to tender must give full specification of the goods or services required. The details must include delivery/completion dates and any special conditions.

4 Invitations to tender must indicate clearly the exact date and time for the close of tendering and must require all tenders to be returned to the Museum Secretary.

5 The instructions must make it clear that tenders are to be returned in a sealed envelope inside an outer envelope, itself marked 'tender enclosed'.

6 The Museum Secretary will ensure that the sealed tender envelopes are date and time stamped upon receipt and are kept in the Museum safe until the assigned time of opening.

7 At the appointed time, the envelopes containing the tenders shall be opened by the Budget Manager in the presence of the Director and Deputy Director. The tenders shall be recorded on a list which will be signed by the Director and Deputy Director.

8 If the contract to which the tender relates exceeds £100,000 the tenders shall be opened in the presence of a member of the Board of Trustees in addition to the Director and Deputy Director. The Board Member shall also sign the list recording the tenders received.

9 The tenders shall be considered by the responsible Budget Manager, who shall select the tender representing the best value for money.

10 The tender document shall be returned to the Museum Secretary together with a recommendation and brief rationale for the choice of supplier/contractor.

11 The Museum Secretary shall arrange for the rationale and recommendation to be placed before the Director, or in cases of emergency, be considered by the Deputy Director and the Building Services Manager.

12 With the prior agreement of the Director tenders may be evaluated by professional advisers appointed by the Museum. In such circumstances the procedures for receiving and opening tenders shall be as above. The recorded tender documents may then be passed to professional advisers for evaluation.

Glossary

This glossary comprises words which will be of use to the manager working in a museum or gallery. Most of the terms are general in nature although many have been specifically defined for the museum and gallery context. Italicised words are cross-referred elsewhere in the glossary.

ACAS abbreviation of *Advisory, Conciliation and Arbitration Service*.

accountability state, or quality, of being *accountable*.

accountable liable to be required by a specific person (or group of people) to report on and justify actions in relation to specified matters.

accrual an accrued expense or an accrued revenue.

accrual accounting making up accounts in which income and expenses are recorded at the time when they are incurred and not when they are actually received or paid.

action-centred leadership leadership that is achieved by carrying out the actions that are expected of a leader. The phrase is associated with the work of *John Adair* (born 1934) who held that leadership can be learned and is not simply a quality that certain people are born possessing.

adhocracy the opposite of *bureaucracy*.

administrative management theory an approach to developing general principles of management in which attention is concentrated on formal organisation structures. This theory was particularly influenced by the views of Henri Fayol.

Advisory, Conciliation and Arbitration Service (ACAS). This is the body charged by government with the general duty of promoting and improving industrial relations in the UK. Its advisory service provides advice and practical assistance on any aspect of industrial relations, including recruitment and selection, payment systems and incentive schemes, the formulation and operation of effective systems of workforce planning, communication, consultation and collective bargaining.

amortise to pay off a loan gradually or to put aside money periodically in order to pay off a loan.

annualisation the process employed by government of financing an organisation on an annual basis. For example, national museums and galleries are funded with *grant-in-aid* which is available for a twelve month period and may not be carried over.

Area Museum Councils (AMCs) regional support organisations for museums and galleries, funded variously by the *Museums and Galleries Commission* and local authorities etc.

arms length principal principal defined by Lord Redcliffe-Maude in a report *Support for the Arts in England and Wales* for the Gulbenkian Foundation (1976) wherein distancing of government from the policy of arts and cultural organisations was defined. It has since become a basic tenet of British Government Arts Policy.

Army Museums Ogilby Trust charitable trust with links to the *Ministry of Defence*, to support Regimental and Corps museums in the United Kingdom.

Arts Council (The) independent body funded by Government to support the visual, performing and fine arts. An Executive *non-departmental public body*.

Associate of the Museums Association (AMA) a class of membership of the *Museums Association* following an examination being taken or a workplace development programme being completed.

Association of American Museums (AAM) the professional and institutional association for North America.

Association of Independent Museums (AIM) a UK national organisation supporting independent museums.

attendant a security guard in a museum or gallery, see also *warder*.

audit (noun) critical examination and analysis of accounts performed by an independent person in order to assess their accuracy and, often, to detect fraud. Also a critical examination and analysis of an activity by an independent person performed to check the efficiency of the activity and, often, to check security.

audit (verb) to perform an *audit*.

auditor one who performs an *audit*.

authoritarian management a managerial style characterised by the practice of authoritarianism and, usually, belief that human relations are irrelevant to getting work done, but people are necessarily indolent, self-centred and uncooperative, and that people require strong direction and control if discipline is to be maintained. See McGregor's *Theory X*. Under authoritarian management people are motivated basically by fear of losing their jobs.

authoritarianism reliance, by a person, on unquestioning acceptance of his/her directives coupled with an aversion, by him/her, to consulting people before formulating directives that they must carry out. Authoritarianism fits naturally into an *autocracy*.

authority a person who makes decisions, gives opinions, judgement or information or takes action that affects others people is said to have authority if the people affected believe that, if asked, he/she could justify his/her actions in terms that they are willing to accept.

autocracy a power structure in which one person (an *autocrat*) clearly has and exercises power over all others in an organisation.

autocrat one person who exercises power over all others in an *autocracy*.

autocratic management synonym for *authoritarian management*.

awareness a knowledge of what is going on in a manager's relationships with other people, why they are behaving in a particular way and what the manager's influence is having on their behaviour.

balance sheet a statement of the financial position of an organisation on a specified day. It shows the total value of the organisation's assets, liabilities, provisions, contributed capital and reserves. The value of the assets should equal the sum of the values of liabilities, provisions, contributed capital and reserves, and this is the sense in which the statement 'balances'.

below-the-line not taken into account when computing a specified kind of profit.

benchmark originally a mark made by a skilled craftsman on the bench to determine a specific reference point. Now used for any carefully described or measured object with which others are compared.

best-fit a system where a number of variables are put together concerning the leader, the led, the task, and the context on a scale between 'directive' and 'consultative' to find the 'best-fit' for any particular situation.

break-even analysis computing costs and revenues for different volumes of production in order to determine the break-even point.

break-even chart a chart on which two curves are plotted: The expected sales revenues from the production of various quantities of a product and the costs (fixed and variable) of producing those quantities. The curves intersect at the break-even point.

British Association of Friends of Museums (BAFM) the national association for volunteers and Friends groups within museums and galleries.

broadening the process of preparing a middle manager for a top management position by means of job rotation so that he/she acquires a broader outlook.

budget a plan expressed in financial terms: a summary of planned financial expenditures and receipts over a period or related to an activity.

budget centre the smallest section of a firm for which a budget is prepared and a system of budgetary control.

budgetary control control which is based on the use of budgets for various activities and comparison of actual performance with budgeted performance.

budgeting the process or activity of preparing budgets.

bureaucracy defined by Max Weber as an organisation in which 1) the regular activities are distributed in a fixed way as official duties, 2) jobs are arranged in a hierarchy with each job holder's authority to command and to apply various means of coercion strictly defined, 3) there are written documents to govern the general conduct of the organisation (Gerth and Wright Mills, 1958).

business plan synonym for *corporate plan*.

capital   a stock of money, possessed by an organisation which may be invested from time to time in assets in order to earn income but which is intended not to be diminished.

capital budget   a document showing the extent and timing of an organisation's proposed capital expenditure over a future period. The revenue that the expenditure is expected to produce, the cost of capital to be used for the expenditure and the net profit that will result.

capital budgeting   the process of choosing from possible investment projects the ones that an organisation will invest money in.

capital goods   manufactured or constructed objects that have a long useful life and are used to assist in the production of, but are not incorporated in, other goods. Capital goods include machinery, tools and buildings.

capital investment   investment in *capital goods*.

capital rationing   a situation in which an organisation has only a limited amount of money available for capital expenditure.

capital structure   the way in which the capital of an organisation is divided among various sources.

cash budget   a statement of the estimated totals of cash that will be received and paid by an organisation during each of a number of future periods (months, weeks etc.).

cash book   a record of payments and receipts.

cash flow   the pattern and extent of payments and receipts of cash by an organisation over a period.

cash flow statement   a statement of an organisations actual or projected cash in-flows and out-flows measured at suitable intervals over a period.

chain of command   see *line of command*.

chair of trustees   an individual appointed to preside over a Board of Trustees and regulate it by choosing who is to speak and by ensuring adherence to rules and procedures. In the case of national museums the appointment of a trustee is made by the Prime Minister or other Secretaries of State, the trustees then elect a Chairperson.

channel of distribution (or distribution channel)   a series of enterprises, or types of enterprises, involved in transferring ownership of goods from producer to ultimate consumer.

classical management   often called the 'process school' because it uses management as a process and examines the component parts of the process separately. Has its roots in writings of Henri Fayol.

closed-loop control system   a control system in which there is *monitoring feedback* and the information about the deviation (e.g. the difference between the actual and desired states of the controlled condition) is used within the *control system* to change the controlled condition in a way that reduces deviation.

collections   the assets owned (or otherwise held against specific policies) by museums and galleries, and which relate to their primary objectives of preserving and interpreting the heritage.

collections management   similar to *stock control* in commerce or business. The activity, process or study of ensuring the collections of a museum or gallery are catalogued, accessioned, controlled, preserved and conserved to a satisfactory standard.

communication   transmission of information, ideas, attitudes or emotions from one person or group to another person or group. Transmission of data from one machine to another.

company secretary   official of British registered company who has certain legal and administrative responsibilities laid down by the Companies Acts.

comparative management   study of the practice of management in different cultures or countries in order to determine widely observed basic principles as well as cultural differences.

competence   state or quality of being able to take specified action without referring to other people or without gaining special authorisation or without violating rules about who may take that action. Also the quality of having the necessary ability, training or experience to undertake a specified task.

comptroller and auditor general   UK public official responsible for auditing the accounts of Government Departments (including national museums), presenting an annual report to the Public Accounts Committee of the House of Commons.

consultative management   a managerial style which is characterised by consulting subordinates about decisions that will affect them while making it clear that their views are for information only and will not necessarily influence the decision. Often forms part of the paternalistic management style.

consumer   someone who, or organisation that, consumes specified goods – i.e., buys them but does not directly use them for manufacturing other goods or for resale at a profit.

contingency   something that may happen but is not certain to happen.

control system   a subsystem of an *open system* in

which activity is directed towards maintaining, or affecting in a prescribed way, the value of some parameter of the output of the system. The parameter affected is called the 'controlled condition'.

core running costs the costs incurred by museums and galleries to carry out their core functions. The core usually being the curatorial elements and their support.

corporate identity characteristic, or uniform, style of design adopted by an organisation in all forms of visual communication with the public.

corporate image the image that people usually have of a particular organisation.

corporate plan the document which describes the forthcoming activities, changes and targets to be achieved by an organisation over a future period of time.

corporate planning the activity, process or study of planning changes in the corporate strategy of an organisation over a future period of time (also known as 'strategic planning').

corporate objective an objective which is to be achieved by an organisation (also known as 'corporate goal'.

corporate strategy the general nature of organisations relationships with its environment.

cost a measure, for the purposes of accounting, of the cash value of whatever an organisation has parted with (or is liable to part with) when making an expenditure. In financial accounting, a cost that has been incurred is usually called an expense.

cost accounting the systematic measurement, analysis and recording of the costs incurred by an organisation or by particular activities, processes or departments of an organisation and estimation of costs to be incurred in the future or the costs that would be incurred in given circumstances.

cost centre a location, person, item of equipment or other division of an organisation for which costs may be ascertained and which is used for the purposes of cost control.

cost of sales the expenses incurred in producing or acquiring goods that have been sold.

cost-benefit analysis (CAB) providing a basis for choosing between two or more investment projects by assigning monetary values to the benefits that would arise from the projects but would not be in the form of cash.

craftsman a worker in a particular occupation who possesses a whole range of manual skills and knowledge and who uses his/her own initiative and judgement to decide how to carry out his/her work.

critical activity an activity on a *critical path*.

critical event an event on a *critical path*.

critical path an unbroken sequence in a network going from the start event to the end event and having a lower total float than any other path between those points.

critical path analysis (CPA) activity or process of finding the critical path in a network finding ways of reducing the time taken by the critical path and using the critical path for control purposes.

curatorial sympathy the ability to apply commercial management principles in a museum and gallery context. An awareness of curatorial issues.

customer a person who receives goods or services from an organisation providing goods or services. The term is well known in retailing but disliked in museums and galleries. Recently a synonym for *visitor* in museums and galleries.

data processing (DP) systematically operating on data in order to produce new data according to established rules or to extract information or to revise the data.

data processing system a group of machines and of procedures for using them in order to carry out some task of data processing.

database a large, comprehensive, central or otherwise significant collection of data; especially when carefully organised and recorded so that information may be derived from it by using electronic data processing.

decision theory the part of mathematics that deals with ways of analysing decision-making problems and provides methods for making optimum decisions.

decision tree a diagram of a sequence of decisions, each of which involves choosing between a known number of alternatives and depends on the results of the previous decisions.

decision-making the process or activity of selecting from among possible alternatives, a future course of action.

delegate (noun) someone who represents other people at a conference or convention.

delegate (verb) to entrust to another or to entrust part of one's authority to another while retaining responsibility for that person's exercise of authority.

delegation assigning work, responsibility and authority so that subordinates can make maximum use of their abilities.

democratic management a management style where decisions are made after discussion. Synonym for *participative management*.

department one of a number of distinct parts of

an organisation; usually recognisably distinct because its activities are the responsibility of a single manager.

department head the manager of a department of an organisation, see also *keeper*.

Department of National Heritage UK Government Department responsible for policy practice concerning sport, culture, the arts, broadcasting, the national lottery, the millennium fund, and museums and galleries. The Department funds some national museums and galleries, the *Arts Council* and the *Museums and Galleries Commission*.

departmentation (or departmentalisation) the aspects of organising which consists of specifying that parts of the organisation are to be departments.

depreciation the systematic estimation of how much the *cost* of a *fixed asset* has expired.

distribution channel synonym for *channel of distribution*.

division a department of an organisation; especially a large department e.g., curatorial division.

donor someone who makes a gift or grants some power.

double-entry book-keeping a method of recording transactions (almost universally applied in business accounts) in which each transaction is recorded as a credit in one account and a debit in another account.

down-grading the movement of an employee to a job that has fewer responsibilities and/or involves less skill and/or lower status and/or, especially, has a lower rate of pay.

earned income in the case of grant-aided museums and galleries the income earned by the Trustees through their own entrepreneurial or commercial efforts. Admission revenue or retailing. Defined in the Income Tax Acts as remuneration from an office or employment, pensions given in respect of past service in an office or employment, payments made on termination of an office or employment, income 'immediately derived' by the recipient from carrying on his/her trade, profession or vocation.

economics a social science concerned with describing and analysing the use of scarce resources in the production and distribution of goods and services for consumption by individuals and groups.

economies of scale reduction of the cost of producing something achieved by increasing the quantity produced.

entrepreneur a person who is skilled at identifying new products (or sometimes new methods of production) setting up operations to provide new products, marketing the products and arranging the financing of the operations.

entrepreneurial of, relating to, or characteristic of, *entrepreneurs*. The UK Government expects museums and galleries to have an 'entrepreneurial approach' to their work.

established task the tasks assessed as being the activities necessary to be carried out to fulfil the objective of the organisation. Usually determined by an *establishment audit*. Used by Government to assess the work of National Museums.

establishment audit a critical examination and analysis of the activities of an organisation to determine the activities necessary for the organisation to carry out its objectives.

establishment of staff the number of staff required to carry out the objectives of an organisation.

estimates a term used by some Government Departments to describe the budget round for the coming financial year.

event in project network techniques (e.g., *critical path analysis*) an event is a specific accomplishment that occurs at a recognisable point of time.

exception report deviation from a plan that is presented to someone practising *management by exception*.

expense the outlay of cash and the calculation for accounting purposes of the cash value of money which has been spent or is committed to spend in exchange for goods, services or labour.

facilities management planning, installation and operation of an organisation's electronic data processing equipment by another specialist firm.

feedback part of the output of a system that is used to evaluate the performance of the system. In *communication* the process of 'listening'.

Fellow of the Museums Association (FMA) senior class of membership of the *Museums Association* or members who have practised in the profession for a minimum number of years (usually eight).

fellow an individual in a senior class of membership of a professional institute. In some institutes a member who has practised the profession for a minimum number of years is qualified to become a fellow. In others an examination has to be taken or a thesis submitted.

financial accounting activity or process of systematically recording and analysing information in monetary terms relating to the transactions of an organisation, primarily in order to provide information to people other than the management of the organisation.

first-line supervisor a manager who is responsible

for the activities of a number of subordinates, none of whom manage anyone else.

fixed assets an asset of an organisation that is not a current asset and is intended to be used by the organisation for a period of time (usually longer than a year). Fixed assets are often described as 'property, plant and equipment'.

fixed cost a cost that is incurred during the production of goods or services by an organisation and is the same whatever quantity or service is produced over a wider range of quantities or services.

fixtures and fittings items attached to the structure of a building but not forming part of it.

flexible working hours (FWH) an arrangement under which each employee of an organisation may choose the times at which he/she starts and finishes work each day to suit him/her self. In most arrangements of this kind, an employee must be at work during one or more periods of 'core time' (e.g., 10.00 a.m. to 4.00 p.m.) and must work for a minimum number of hours in each week or month.

forecast (noun) a result of *forecasting*.

forecast (verb) to give a statement of what is likely to happen in the future, based on considered judgement and analysis.

forecast outturn a financial statement of what is to be the likely 'outcome' at the end of a financial year based on the information available at the time the forecast is made.

forward plan synonym for *corporate plan*.

franchise an arrangement by which a retailer is given an exclusive or conditional right to sell specific goods or services within a specified area.

friend term used to describe support societies in museums and galleries 'Society of Friends of ....'.

function a group of related activities that contribute to the performance of work by an organisation (such as, the curatorial function), i.e., all activities relating to curating the collections of a museum or gallery.

functional organisation organisation into departments according to function.

Gantt chart a graphic representation on a time-scale of the current relationship between actual and planned performance; especially one which uses a standard set of symbols invented by an American industrial engineer, Henry Lawrence Gantt (1861–1919).

general manager a manager who determines and implements the broad objectives of a whole organisation, determines the resources to be made available for obtaining those objectives and has significant responsibilities in more than one major field of activity (usually working through managers who specialise in single fields of activities). A general manager is especially concerned with the formulation and interpretation of policy and within long term planning.

general management the work performed by *general managers* or the general manager within an organisation.

goal a desired result of activity by an individual or an organisation. The end result of a plan. A state which an individual, consciously or unconsciously strives to achieve.

goal setting process of establishing what a person or an organisation should achieve at some time in the future.

grade the recognised standard specification of quality. A description for the positions in the hierarchical structure of employment.

grant a sum of money paid by a grant giving organisation (a charity or trust) in order to aid another organisation (e.g., museums and galleries).

grant-in-aid the term used by Government Departments to describe money voted by Parliament to Executive *non-departmental public bodies*. This would be for *core running costs* in the case of museums and galleries.

grievance an aspect of conditions of employment that is thought by an employee to hurt him/her or cause him/her injustice and which he/she complains about.

grievance interview an interview which is intended to provide an opportunity for an employee to state fully the nature of a grievance to someone who is responsible for attempting to resolve the grievance.

grievance procedure the way in which an employee who has a grievance can seek redress to it. In Great Britain every employee must be given a written statement of the Grievance Procedures to be followed in his/her employment.

gross cash flow the sum of *net profits* (after tax has been paid) and the amount of *expense* determined as *depreciation* of an organisation over a period (sometimes known as *cash flow*).

gross income the amount of revenue received by an organisation over a period. In museums and galleries the gross income would include *grants* and *earned income*.

gross profit sales revenue (or net sales) from selling specified goods over a period minus the expenses incurred in acquiring or manufacturing the goods. The expenses incurred in selling the goods and any indirect costs are not subtracted from revenues when calculating gross profit. Also this figure expressed as a percentage of sales revenue (also known as *gross profit margin*).

gross profit margin   the ratio of the *gross profit* acquired by an organisation over a specified period from the sale of a specified product to its sales revenue for that product during the same period (usually expressed as a percentage).

gross working capital   the total value of the current assets of an organisation.

group appraisal   *performance appraisal* of a person carried out by a group of three or more of his/her superiors working as a team.

group dynamics   area of study concerned with the nature of groups of people, their patterns of development and their relationships with individuals and other groups.

group interview   a selection interview at which two or more applicants for a job are interviewed simultaneously – often conducted as an informal conversation.

group selection   selection of persons for employment by observing a group of candidates performing an exercise in, for example, problem-solving.

group-decision method (or group decision-making, or group problem-solving)   a method of solving a problem affecting a manager and some or all of the group of people he/she manages, in which the manager states the problem to a meeting of the group and asks the group to decide on the solution.

guided practice   counselling and guidance for workers as part of their training and ongoing development. Demonstrations for inexperienced staff members to discover how other elements of work within the organisation are carried out.

halo effect   phenomenon found during *performance appraisal* in which a person's impression of one characteristic of someone is so strong that it affects his/her impressions of that person's other characteristics.

Hawthorn studies   a long series of observations of people at work carried out at the Hawthorn factory, near Chicago, of the Western Electric Company from 1927 until 1932.

hidden agenda   the matters that are important to an individual at a meeting but which he/she cannot discuss or deal with, either because the matters are not a formal agenda for the meeting or because they are personal emotion matters relating to the meeting (e.g., intense dislike of another member of a committee).

hierarchy   an arrangement of the positions in an organisation into ranks so that the holder of a position in one rank is responsible to the holder of a position in the next higher rank for the performance of his/her job.

human relations management   see *Hawthorn studies*.

human relations school   an approach to the theory of management of organisations that emphasises the individual worker's need for satisfactory relationships with other members of his/her work group and his/her need to participate in decisions that effect his/her work. This approach developed from the *Hawthorn studies*.

human resources management   see *personnel management*.

hygiene factor   an aspect of a job that can contribute to the dissatisfaction but not the satisfaction of the job holder according to the *motivation-hygiene theory*.

hygienic management   a management style characterised by a provision of high wages, employee benefits, good working conditions and good supervision in the belief that workers will therefore have high morale and will work harder.

ICOM   abbreviation for International Council of Museums, the international organisation for museum professionals. Part of UNESCO and based in Paris, France.

imprest   a sum of money given to someone by an organisation (originally by a Government) to spend on its behalf for specified purposes. An 'imprest system' is that of controlling *petty cash*.

incentive   something that urges a person on to achieve some goal.

incentive payment   part of an employee's remuneration that is related (according to a known rule) to the degree to which he/she has achieved an objective desired by his/her employer.

income   revenues of a person or an organisation over a period. See also *earned income*.

income and expenditure account   a *profit and loss account* of a non-profit making body.

independent museums   museums which are not predominantly grant aided by central or local government and are usually vested in charitable trusts or companies limited by guarantee.

indirect cost   a cost of an expenditure on goods, services, or labour used by, or benefiting, a number of activities, products or *cost centres* where the extent for the use for each individual purpose cannot easily be measured. Also, a portion of such a cost that is associated with a particular activity, process or cost centre. Also the total amount of such apportioned costs associated with a particular activity, product or cost centre.

induction procedure (or induction programme) activities taking place when a new employee joins an organisation of which the objectives are to acquaint the individual with the organisation and his/her colleagues and to ensure that all the organisation's records and rules concerning the employee are complete. A briefing on the organisation's rules and procedures and health and safety information is also given.

industrial relations relations between trade unions and employers or between an employer and the unions representing his/her employees.

inflation a continuing increase in the general level of prices in an economy.

inflation accounts accounts prepared in a way that shows the affect of inflation on the value of fixed assets and identifies the increase in value of stocks caused by inflation.

information retrieval activity or process of obtaining specific required information from a store of data.

information technology (IT) technology relating to the transmission and storage of information.

information theory the general mathematical theory of the transmission of information.

internal audit an *audit* (of its accounts or one of its activities) performed by employees of an organisation who report to the senior management of that organisation.

interview (noun) formal face-to-face meeting between people in which one person supplies information to another or others; especially so that a person's suitability for a job can be assessed (selection interview); so that one person can present a complaint (grievance interview); so that a person's progress can be assessed (appraisal interview).

interview (verb) to meet with someone and ask him/her questions in an interview.

inventory the detailed list of goods or articles in a particular place or of the assets of someone or the collections of a museum or gallery. See also *stocktaking*.

job (noun) the collection of tasks, duties and assignments that an employee is employed to perform. A piece of work. A single item of work, complete in itself, performed by a person, or by an organisation or by a machine (especially a computer); especially, a piece of work that is separately identified for purposes of accounting, costing, or paying wages.

job (verb) to do small pieces of work for a variety of customers. To buy and sell securities as a 'jobber'.

job analysis activity or process of examining a *job* in order to prepare a *job description* and/or a *job specification*. The process may also determine the actual need for the job.

job costing practice or activity of allocating costs to specific jobs or items of production.

job cycle the complete sequence of operations that a worker has to perform in order to complete a unit of his/her output.

job description a statement of the purpose, scope, organisational relationships, responsibilities and tasks which constitute a particular *job*.

job design process, or activity, of deciding on the tasks and responsibilities to be included in a particular job and of deciding on the methods to be used for carrying out those tasks.

job enlargement training and encouraging employees to perform a range of jobs related to the ones they hold so that personnel can be used more flexibly. Assigning additional tasks to an employee in order to make his/her job more varied and interesting.

job enrichment changing features of a job other than compensation, physical working conditions and the essential tasks of the job in order to increase the job satisfaction of the person performing it.

job evaluation establishment of the relative worth of a number of jobs (not employees) in an organisation by considering for example, their complexity, the amount of training or experience required, how much the organisation would suffer if they were done badly and so on. See also *establishment audit*.

job factor an identifiable, measurable requirement the job holder must contribute, assume or endure in a specified job.

job holder the person who is employed in a specified position in an organisation.

job rotation transferring an employee from one job to another at a similar level in an organisation in order to give him/her experience before promotion.

job satisfaction the gratification (in the sense of mental pleasure following from the satisfaction of needs, desires or hopes) that a person derives from the job that he/she is employed to perform.

job security any form of promise to, or belief by, a person that there is a low probability that his/her employment in a particular job will be ended.

job sheet form used by a worker to record the jobs he/she has been engaged on, the quantity he/she has produced and the time spent on each (also known as a 'time sheet').

job specification a description of the personal characteristics required for performing a job. A job specification normally states the type of employee required for a job, in terms of skill, experience and special aptitudes, and summarises the working conditions found in the job. See also *personnel specification*.

job title   the name given to a particular job.

joint consultation   discussion between the representatives of *management* and the employees of an enterprise of matters of common interest, especially the way that plans for the future of the enterprise will affect its employees. Matters that are normally the subject of negotiation between trade unions and employers (such as pay and conditions) are normally excluded from joint consultation.

joint consultative committee   a committee established for the purposes of joint consultation.

keeper   department head in a national museum, usually (but not always) a curatorial position.

key event   synonym for *milestone*.

key results analysis   the activity of identifying the areas (usually between five and eight of them) of a manager's job that are crucial to the success of the job in the organisation and of quantifying the results that the manager must achieve in each area.

label   a slip attached to something and carrying identifying information. Also an interpretive description of an object within a museum or gallery collection.

labour cost   a cost that relates to the expenditure on remuneration of employees within an organisation. Included with this cost would be costs for pensions, superannuation and national insurance.

labour turnover   the rate at which employees leave an organisation usually measured by the ratio:

number of employees leaving during the year

average number of employees during that year

(also known as 'personnel turnover').

laissez-faire **management**   a management style where group members work on their own and the leader is much the same as other group members.

law of diminishing returns   a frequently observed phenomenon that when output depends on several inputs (such as labour, machines and materials) and some of the inputs are constant, then, beyond a certain limit, increases in the other inputs that result in smaller and smaller increases in output.

law of the situation   a phrase used by Mary Parker Follett (1869–1933), an American political and business philosopher, to describe the action that must be taken because of the circumstances that exist and not because a superior has given an order to a subordinate.

lay off   to cease to employee someone, usually temporarily, especially because of a) a contraction of business or, b) a strike in part of the organisation.

learning curve   a graph that shows improvement in the performance of a task, by an individual or a group, as it is repeated and more is learned about it.

liability   an obligation, especially an obligation to pay money.

limited company   a company whose members are required to contribute capital to the company but only up to a known limited amount agreed between member and company. No further contribution can be required even if the company is unable to pay its debts.

limited liability   a liability or possible liability that is limited in extent to a definite amount – especially the liability that a member of a *limited company* could have for paying the company's debt.

line of command   the sequence of people in an organisation through whom instructions from the chief executive pass before reaching a particular employee (also known as *chain of command*).

line manager   a member of an organisation who is responsible for the success or failure of a section of the organisation in performing part of the principle work of the organisation.

line relationship   relationship between two members of an organisation, one of whom may issue instructions and delegate authority to the other.

line responsibility   responsibility of, or similar to that of, a *line manager*.

local authority   a corporation consisting of members elected by the inhabitants of a particular area, but independent of national Government of the country, with powers to provide certain services in that area and the power to raise money by taxation (often called an 'authority').

local authority museums   UK museums and galleries which receive Grant-in-Aid from local authorities. Also museums and galleries which are part of local authorities.

London allowance   synonym for *London weighting*.

London weighting   a payment made to employees who work in London, which is in addition to the pay they would receive if they did the same job out of London and is intended to compensate for the additional cost of accommodation and travel in London. See also *London allowance*.

long-range planning   the activity, process or study of preparing plans that cover long periods (usually five years or more).

long-term costings the activity, process or study of preparing plans that cover estimates of the cost of an organisation over long periods (five years or more).

manage to carry out the task of ensuring that a number of diverse activities are performed in such a way that a defined objective is achieved – especially the task of creating and maintaining conditions in which desired objectives are achieved by the combined efforts of a group of people (which includes the person doing the managing).

management the process, activity or study of carrying out the task of ensuring that a number of diverse activities are performed in such a way that a defined objective is achieved, especially the task of creating and maintaining conditions in which desired objectives are achieved by the combined efforts of a group of people (which includes the person carrying out the management). Also a group of people within an organisation who are primarily concerned with the management of the activities of that organisation.

management accounting preparation and analysis of financial information about an organisation's operations for use *within* the firm to assist in the formulation of policy and in day-to-day control of operations (see also *forecast outturn*).

management audit a systematic, detailed examination of the quality of *management* in an organisation in order to suggest improvement.

management by exception technique of carrying out the control function of management by paying attention only to deviations from a plan.

management by objectives (MBO) a systematic procedure for planning the work of managers in an organisation which is characterised by collaboration between each manager and his/her superior in analysing the manager's tasks and establishing quantified objectives to be achieved by the manager within specific time limits.

management science application of scientific techniques, research and results to problems of management. Virtually synonymous with *operational research* although it is sometimes suggested that Management Science is concerned with general theories while operational research is concerned with solving particular problems.

manager a person who has been appointed to carry out a job of *management*. Also a person who undertakes such jobs as a profession.

managerial effectiveness defined by W. J. Reddin (1971) as 'the extent to which a manager achieves the output required of his/her position'.

managerial grid a representation of managerial styles on a two-dimensional grid. The dimensions are concern for production (horizontal axis) and concern for people (vertical axis). Each dimension has nine possible ratings from one (low) to nine (high).

managerial structure the established relationships between managerial positions in an organisation, usually described in terms of responsibility and authority.

managerial style the way in which a manager characteristically conducts his/her dealings with his/her subordinates (sometimes called 'management style').

margin synonym for *profit margin*.

mark-up the difference between the selling price of a *product* and its cost to the seller, especially when the seller calculates it as a standard percentage of the cost.

mark-up pricing setting of prices at which goods are to be sold by applying a standard mark-up to the cost of the goods.

market research systematic and objective research for, and analysis of, information concerning the actual or potential markets or *products*.

market segment a group of buyers within a market for a *product* who can be identified as being especially interested in a particular variant of the product.

market share the ratio of an organisation's sales of a *product* (either the number of units sold or the value of sales) during a period in a specified market to the total sales of that type of product during the same period in that market.

market value the market value of something (a *product* or service) at a particular time is the price that any buyer might reasonably be expected to pay for it at that time if he/she was able to make a considered judgement of its value and was not influenced by any special relationship with the seller.

marketing the activities of an organisation that concern acquiring and maintaining markets for the organisation's *products* and for ensuring that the organisation's output reaches those markets.

materials the goods that a manufacturer buys for conversion into manufactured products. Also the value of a manufacturer's stock of unconverted materials.

materials management activity, or study of planning, organising and controlling the flow of an organisation's materials at all stages between the organisation's suppliers and its store of finished goods.

materials requisition   a document which authorises and records the issue (from a *stock*) of materials of use.

matrix structure   see *task force*.

measured day work (MDW)   *payment by results* in which a fixed bonus is paid to a worker whenever his/her performance is at or above a predetermined level.

measured work   work for which standard times have been set using techniques of work measurement.

media planning   activity or process or choosing the media that are to carry specified advertising.

merchandise   goods that an organisation has bought with the intention of reselling them without altering their physical form.

merchantable quality   in English Law, goods are of 'merchantable quality' if they are fit for the purpose or purposes for which goods of that kind are commonly bought.

merit increase   an increase in pay given to an employee if his/her performance satisfies some criterion.

merit payment   in addition to a standard time rate for a particular type of work in an enterprise that is paid to individual workers because of their special skills or responsibilities.

merit rating   assessing an employee's performance and personal qualities – usually so that his/her pay can be determined.

method study   systematic recording and critical examination of existing and proposed ways of performing tasks involving human activity in order to develop and apply easier and more effective methods and reduce costs (also known as 'motion study').

microfiche   a sheet of photographic film on which a number of microcopy images have been recorded in a standard format (also known as a 'fiche').

middle manager   a manager in an organisation who is not a *first-line supervisor* and is not in a *general management* position. Also a person in an organisation with the same status as middle managers in that organisation.

middle management   the middle managers in an organisation.

milestone (or milestone event)   an event picked out as particularly important when applying a *project network technique* (also known as a 'key event').

Ministry of Defence   UK Government Department responsible for the Armed Forces and defence. The Department also funds six major service museums (Royal Air Force Museum, National Army Museum (National), four Navy

museums) and indirectly funds over a hundred regimental museums.

model   a representation of a system.

monitor   to observe or measure continuously the activity or output of a system in order to discover variations from a planned or normal state.

monitored control system   a synonym for *closed-loop control system*.

monitoring feedback   in a *control system*, transmission of information about the control condition along a separate path provided for that purpose, comparison of the information with information about the desired state of the control condition and production of information about differences between actual and desired states.

motivate   to create circumstances in which a particular individual will acquire *motivation* to behave in a particular way.

motivation   the causes of particular behaviour by an individual – especially causes (e.g., emotions) related to the internal state of the individual. The process or study of motivating people to behave in a particular way.

motivation-hygiene theory   the view, advanced by an American Psychologist, Frederick Hertzburg (born 1923) that an employee derives job satisfaction from two separate sources: hygiene factors and motivators.

motivator   an aspect of a job that can contribute to the satisfaction but not the dissatisfaction of the job holder according to the *motivation-hygiene theory*.

museum director   a member of staff of a museum or gallery who has authority over all other members in determining the conduct of the organisation. Similar to chief executive.

museum registration   a phased scheme of minimum standards whereby museums in the UK can become registered with the *Museums and Galleries Commission*.

museum secretary   the head of administration and finance in a national museum, (similar to a *company secretary* in business).

Museum Training Institute   the industry lead body for the museum and gallery industry with a remit to provide standards and competencies for the training of individuals in the museum and gallery profession.

Museums Association – the (MA)   the professional and institutional membership body for the UK.

Museum Documentation Association (MDA)   an organisation, primarily funded by the *Museums and Galleries Commission* and charged with setting and maintaining documentation standards within museums in the UK. Also acts as an impartial source of advice to museums on cataloguing, documentation and information technology matters.

Museums and Galleries Commission – the (MGC) independent committee appointed by Government as advisers and to be the watching brief on museums and galleries. Also funds *Area Museum Councils* and the *Museum Documentation Association*.

national museum one of nineteen UK museums, defined by the *Museums and Galleries Commission*, which receive Grant-in-Aid directly from the Government.

negotiate to discuss with someone with whom one has a difference or dispute possible terms for the settlement of the difference or dispute. To transfer something to someone in such a way that he/she is the undisputed owner of it. To deal with an event, a problem, or a difference with someone. To proceed successfully.

negotiating machinery the institutions for conducting negotiations between employers and trade unions and the rules governing such negotiations.

net (adjective) after specified deductions have been made. Not subject to any further deductions. From which no deductions may be made; as in 'net price' (a minimum price). Sold at net prices.

net (verb) to gain as a net amount. To compute a net amount.

net assets total assets of an organisation less current liabilities. This is equal to the capital employed. Total assets of an organisation less current liabilities, debt capital, and any other long-term loans and provisions.

net cash a phrase used to announce that no cash discounts or credit will be given.

net cash flow net profit (after payment of Corporation Tax) of an organisation over a period. See *cash flow*.

net current assets difference between the values of an organisation's total current assets and its total current liabilities at a particular time.

net income the *net profit* of an organisation over a period measured after deducting payments of Corporation Tax, interest on debt capital, and (usually) preference dividends.

net operating income the profit made on an organisation's main operations over a period. It is made up of the net sales minus cost of sales and other operating expenses.

net present value (NPV) the net present value of an investment project is the present value of the sequence of cash in-flows associated with the project minus the present value of the sequence of cash out-flows associated with the project.

net profit a financial gain which is achieved by an organisation over a period or from a particular activity which is measured after allowing for all expenses and lost costs incurred during the period.

net profit margin the ratio of *net profit* acquired by an organisation over a specified period from the sale of a specified product to the revenues it received during that period from the sale of a product (usually expressed as a percentage).

net realisable value the price at which something could be sold less the expenses of selling it.

net revenue synonym for *net profit*.

net sales (or net sales revenue) total invoiced charges for the sale of goods or services over a period less cash discounts taken by customers, the value of returns by customers and any other allowances.

network a diagram used in project network techniques that represents the component activities and/or events in a project and shows their interrelationship.

non-departmental public body (NDPB) an organisation (e.g., museum or gallery) independent from Government but relying for Grant-in-Aid from a Government Department and, in the case of museums and galleries, have its collections vested in trustees by Government.

non-profit-making operating under rules which require all income to be applied to future activities of the same type (usually charitable) and forbidding distribution of profits to, for example, suppliers of capital (the term is not to be taken literally: a non-profit-making organisation may make profits for its own purposes but not in order to enrich others).

non-profit organisation an organisation (museum or gallery) which has as its intention not to make a profit, usually to break even, at the end of a financial year.

object (noun) term used in museums and galleries to describe items within their collections.

objective (adjective) expressing or involving the use of facts without distortion by personal feelings or prejudices.

objective (noun) the desired result of some effect or activity.

objective function a function linking values of variables in a system to values of the performance measure for the system.

objective test a test consisting of questions to be answered by the testee in which each question has only one correct answer. Thus the opinion of the person marking the test does not influence the rating he/she gives the testee.

obsolescent becoming *obsolete*; nearly *obsolete*.

obsolete no longer in use; disused; outmoded.

occupational psychology the study of psychological problems associated with work which arise in connection with, for example, vocational guidance, design of aptitude tests, personnel selection, training, work study or ergonomics. (Also known as 'industrial psychology'.)

open system a system of regularly interacting components whose activity is largely concerned with converting material or energy taken in from outside the system into some output or export that is returned to the environment.

open-door policy attitude taken by a manager or supervisor that any of his/her subordinates who have a problem can feel free to come to discuss it at any time.

open-loop control system a control system without monitoring *feedback*. An open-look control system is not affected by the actual state of the control condition.

operating grant *grant* given to a museum or gallery for the purpose of offsetting the operating expenses of that museum or gallery (see *purchase grant*).

operating profit profit derived by an organisation over a period from its normal operations.

operational research (OR) the activity, process or study of applying scientific methods (especially mathematical) to the solutions or problems involving the operation of a system.

operations management application of the principles and techniques of production management to the management of non-manufacturing organisations.

operator a person carrying out a job in a mechanistic manner without any managerial responsibility.

opportunity cost the value of some course of action which one could take but does not. For example, the opportunity cost of holding cash in a current account instead of investing it in securities (because it is thought necessary to have the money instantly available) is the value of the interest that is forgone (sometimes called 'cost').

organisation the act or process of organising. A result of organising; a set of definitions of positions which are intended to enable the position holders to work together to carry out certain tasks. Also the group of people holding positions in an organisation.

organisation chart a chart which shows one or more aspects of relationships between positions in an organisation, usually showing the way responsibility is allocated.

organisation and methods (O&M) the body of knowledge concerning data processing systems, including ways of arranging flows of work, methods of performing tasks and the design and use of data processing equipment.

organisation theory the body of knowledge about *organisational behaviour* and *organisational structure*.

organisational behaviour the behaviour of people when they are acting as members of organisations.

organisational change change in the organisation's structure or in the usual forms of organisational behaviour in a particular organisation.

organisational climate the points of view, particularly on how employees should be treated, that are common to most senior people in an organisation.

organisational culture the feelings of the majority within an organisation, their aspirations and thoughts about the organisation make up its 'culture'.

organisational structure the established pattern of relationships between members of an organisation.

output the product of an activity. The quantity produced by a person, a machine, a factory, or some other unit in a period of time.

Parkinson's Law the aphorism 'work expands so as to fill the time available for its completion' written by an English author, historian and journalist, Cyril Northcote-Parkinson (born 1909).

participative management a managerial style characterised by extensive use of the *group-decision method* and in which each person is given wide opportunity to exercise discretion in his/her work. The style represents a complete contrast to *authoritarian management*. People practising participative management usually believe that people can be emotionally committed to doing jobs well. They would accept McGregor's *Theory Y*.

passing off falsely representing that goods being offered for sale are those of a particular producer or dealer e.g., by unauthorised use of a brand. Falsely representing to be an institution by naming another organisation with a similar or identical name.

paternalism managerial style characterised by a belief that subordinates are necessarily less mature and less capable of looking after themselves than their bosses – i.e., treating one's subordinates as children.

paternalistic management a managerial style

(especially when practised throughout an organisation) characterised by provision of a wide range of valuable rewards for employees in a belief that employees will work well out of gratitude, and out of fear that they could lose the important benefits if they did not work well.

Pay As You Earn (PAYE) system for collection of UK income tax under which an employer deducts tax from all remuneration he/she pays to employees and sends the tax to the tax collector.

payment by results (PBR) a payment system in which a worker's earnings are related to the work he/she has done and to other factors within the control of the worker.

peer goal-setting activity of setting personal objectives (as in *management by objectives*) by groups of people of similar status in an organisation.

performance appraisal assessment of how well an employee does his/her job; especially an assessment carried out as part of an organisation's formal procedure in which regular assessments are made, records kept of the results, and action taken to improve performance.

performance indicator the measure that is used to evaluate performance of an organisation, a department within an organisation, or an individual carrying out a job.

performance measure the measure that is used to evaluate alternative plans for the operation of a system in an *operational research* problem.

performance review in a system of *management by objectives*, the regular meeting between a manager and his/her boss to agree a new job improvement plan.

performance standard the result that is to be achieved in each key area in a *key results analysis*.

period of account in UK Revenue Law, the period of time between one balance sheet date and the next.

personnel all or a group of the employees of an organisation.

personnel management activity, function or study of helping managers in an organisation to make the best use of the human resources of the organisation (see also *human resources management*).

personnel specification see *job specification*.

Peter Principle the aphorism that 'in a hierarchy every employee tends to rise to his/her level of incompetence'. Named after a Canadian educationalist, Lawrence Johnstone Peter (born 1919).

petty cash a fund of cash held by an organisation and used to make small payments.

piece rate the amount to be paid for each unit of output in a *piecework* payment system.

piecework payments system used especially for direct workers in which an employee's earnings are proportional to the number of units of output produced by him/her.

plan (noun) a projected course of action that is designed to lead to desired results (as in *forward plan*).

policy principles and objectives which guide decision-making on particular matters and which express broad intentions or attitudes. A general outline plan of action. A document setting out the terms of a contract of insurance.

policy-making the activity or process of deciding on *policy* to be followed in the future.

position a collection of tasks and duties within an organisation the performance of which requires the service of one person.

position description *job description* especially one relating to a managerial or senior job.

position of authority a position in an organisation of which the occupant (whoever it may be) automatically has authority.

post (noun) a position, the job someone is employed to perform.

post audit a critical review of the way in which a project was carried out, undertaken when the project is complete.

potential assessment (or potential review) assessment of an employee's future career in any organisation. Procedure for regularly assessing the future careers of all employees in an organisation.

power capability of a person to influence other people to act in accordance with his/her intentions (usually within specified limits). A person may acquire power from many different sources; the commonest kind derives from authority and the acceptance of that authority by the people who are to be influenced. A person may have power over someone because he/she is skilful in making effective threats (e.g., a blackmailer) or because he/she is able to exert general influence over people to make them follow him/her (e.g., a religious leader).

power structure the distribution of power within an organisation.

power-expert the power that accrues to an individual in an organisation by virtue of him/her being an expert at a particular subject.

power-personal the power which is given to a person within an organisation by his/her colleagues as a result of his/her character, personality, or charisma.

power-position a position in an organisation of

which the occupant automatically has power.

power-resource the power that is attributed to a person within an organisation because of the resources he/she controls.

preventive maintenance work undertaken on plant, machinery or equipment that has not developed any faults in order to prevent the occurrence of faults (e.g., lubrication, painting, replacement of parts). Work undertaken on artefacts and objects within museum and gallery collections in order to conserve and preserve them before any deterioration in their condition has taken place.

Privy Council a body, consisting of an unlimited number of people (at present about 300) appointed by the Crown, which has the power to legislate by issuing orders in Council on a wide variety of matters (notably in relation to foreign and commonwealth affairs). Royal Charters, which are held by a number of museums and galleries are submitted to the Crown by the Privy Council.

product a result of production; an *output*. An item or a class of identical items that an enterprise offers for sale – extended to mean a type of service that an enterprise offers to its customers (as in museums and galleries).

product manager an employee of an organisation who is responsible for developing and promotion of one or more of the organisation's products (but not all of them).

product planning activity or process of specifying future new products within a known product line for an organisation. The emphasis in product planning is on identifying what would be profitable for the organisation to sell. The emphasis in product planning in museums and galleries would centre on best use of the museum and galleries collections allied to needs of the *visitor*/user.

production the act or process of producing. Synonym for *output*.

production control activity or process of ensuring that an organisation produces planned quantities of its products (*outputs*) according to a specified design, to a specified quality, at planned costs.

production management management of all aspects of an enterprise concerned with transforming materials into finished products. Although the techniques and principles of production management were developed within a context of manufacturing, they are applicable to organisations with other kinds of 'products' (e.g., enterprises providing services such as museums and galleries). The term 'operations management' is sometimes used to emphasise the general applicability of the discipline; 'manufacturing management' is used to emphasise application to manufacturing enterprises.

production planning activity of deciding the processes and operations, and their sequence, to be used to manufacture an organisation's product in required quantities to a specified design and of specified quality. The activity may include deciding the layout of production facilities, designing tools and specifying work methods (also known as 'process engineering' or 'process planning').

productivity *output* per unit of input. For example, output per man hour or output per £ of investment.

profit an excess of revenues over associated expenses for an activity or over a period, or for a particular transaction.

profit and loss account (**P&L account**) account recording the *profit* or loss made in the period from one balance sheet date to the next and how much of any profit has been appropriated to, for example, payment of dividends.

profit centre a part of an organisation that is regarded as having its own financial targets to achieve and has the manpower and material resources necessary to achieve those targets.

profit margin (**or margin**) synonym for *profit*. Ratio of *profit* to *revenue*.

profit plan a forecast, made at the beginning of an accounting period, of an organisation's *profit and loss account* for that period. It is based on a forecast of sales for the period and on budgets which show the planned cost of operations necessary to achieve those sales. See also *forecast outturn*.

profit planning the process or activity of drawing up a *profit plan*.

profitability quality or state of being *profitable*.

profitable producing benefits; especially in the sense of creating additional wealth. Yielding a *profit*.

pro forma invoice an invoice sent when payment is required before goods will be despatched.

programme a plan – especially when expressed in very general terms. A schedule. An important category of the activities of an organisation with a common purpose. Especially one identified for purposes of *programme budgeting*. A group of activities with a common purpose carried out within an organisation especially when incidental to the main activities of the organisation or existing only for a defined period.

programme budgeting an approach to the formulation of plans (especially budgets) for an organisation in which attention is concentrated on the organisation's objectives and the organisation's activities are grouped into programmes where each programme is concerned with achieving a single objective. Budgets and other plans are set out for each programme (rather than for departments of the organisation) and the accounting information required to control activities is analysed according to programmes. Sometimes called a *corporate plan*.

project a proposal or scheme. A piece of research. An activity (or usually a number of related activities) carried out according to a plan in order to achieve a definite objective within a certain time and which will cease when the objective is achieved.

project management the study, or the body of knowledge concerning the management of projects.

project manager a manager who is responsible for the successful completion of a single project.

project network technique any of a group of methods describing, analysing, planning and controlling *projects* and which involve the use of *networks*.

psychometric testing a system of analysing the profile of an individual or the necessary attributes an individual will need to carry out a specific job. A scientific analysis using a questionnaire to determine the suitability of an applicant for a job.

public relations (PR) Activity, practice or study of efforts to bring about a favourable estimation of an organisation by the public in general or by particular people who are important to the organisation.

public sector central Government, local authorities and the public corporations that run nationalised industries (including public museums and galleries).

purchase grant *grant* given to a museum or gallery for the specific purpose of purchasing items for the collection of that museum or gallery (see *operating grant*).

purchase order a written order from an organisation for goods (and sometimes services) that it wants to buy. Often on a preprinted form incorporating information about acknowledgement, delivery and payment.

quality circle a group of between four and ten individuals who work for the same supervisor or foreperson and who voluntarily meet together, usually for an hour each week, to identify, analyse and solve work-related problems.

quality control activity, process or study of ensuring that the output of production processes conforms with the prescribed standards.

quantitative management the application of scientific techniques, research and result to the problems of management. Synonymous with *operational research*.

quasi autonomous non-governmental organisation (quango) similar to *non-departmental public body*.

recruitment obtaining employees for an organisation.

recruitment advertising advertising of which the objective is to inform people of the existence of a job and to persuade suitable candidates to apply for it.

redundancy quality or state of being redundant. A person who is redundant.

redundancy payment a payment that an employer is required by statute to make to an employee who is dismissed because of redundancy.

redundant surplus to requirement. Used to describe an employee who is no longer required because the work he/she does is no longer necessary to his/her employer. Sometimes, and in some countries, called 'retrenchment'.

reference a statement about one or more aspects of a specified person's character or behaviour or of the way that a specified organisation usually conducts its business which has been given by someone named by the person or organisation at the request of a person who intends to employ, do business with, or extend credit to the person or organisation.

regional arts associations (RAAs) regional organisations supporting the performing, visual and fine arts organisations with money variously supplied by the *Arts Council*, local government etc.

resource a material or an abstract quality that a person or organisation uses to perform work (e.g., tools, stock, time, employees). Something one can turn to in case of need, especially financial backing.

resource aggregation summation, period by period, of the resources available or required for a project.

resource allocation process, or study, of scheduling activities and resources required by those activities given limits on the availability of resources.

responsible having responsibility for the performance of a specified task. Having an obligation to a specified person or a group of people to perform a specified task or job. Synonym for *accountable*. Trustworthy; able to answer for one's conduct and obligations.

responsibility   obligation, of a person, to perform some task (or to see that others perform it) in a way that satisfies criteria laid down by another person or group of people. Also a task that a person must perform under an obligation of that type. Synonym for *accountability*.

restrictive practice   a practice adopted by workers which serves (as they see it) to protect their employment but which employers think prevents improvements in methods of work.

retention   a part of the charge for work done by a contractor that is not paid until sometime after the work is completed so that deductions can be made if the work turns out to be faulty.

return   the value that results from the use of something, especially the money that is produced by using or investing a sum of money, often expressed as a percentage of the sum invested. A formal or official report, especially one compiled regularly and giving statistics that has been ordered by an authority. Merchandise that has been returned as unsatisfactory or surplus.

return on investment (ROI) (or return on assets)   ratio of net income of an organisation over a period to the average value during that period of the operating assets of the organisation.

revenue   an amount of money or other valuable benefits received or receivable by an organisation. Synonym for *sales revenue*.

revenue account   a *profit and loss account*, especially of an investment trust or a company specialising in buying and selling real property.

risk   the probability of failure or loss associated with a particular course of action.

risk analysis   estimating the probability distribution of each factor affecting an investment project and then simulating the possible combinations of the value of each factor to determine the range of possible outcomes and the probability associated with each possible outcome.

risk manager   an employee of an organisation who carries out *risk management* for that organisation.

risk management   the process, activity or study of reducing the *risk* of loss to an organisation, particularly loss caused by accident.

role   a set of expectations of how the occupant of a particular position in an organisation ought to behave. Specifically the function performed by a person in the organisation.

salary   a fixed regular payment to an employee for work done.

salary administration   activities concerned with fixing and sometimes paying salaries in an organisation.

salary structure   the principles, rules and procedures by which the salaries of an organisation's employees are determined.

sales revenue (or revenue or sales)   the total amount of money (or a measurement in monetary terms, of the total value of property or services) receivable by an organisation in exchange for goods or services of specified kinds supplied by the organisation during a specified period.

scalar principle   a principle, often followed when organising, that each member of the organisation should have one and only one superior (apart from one chief executive) who has no superior within the organisation but may be responsible to people outside it. The idea is that if a subordinate (a) has a superior (b) who in turn, is the subordinate of superior (c) then (c) should have no direct authority to issue directives or control the activities of (a).

Scientific Management   the principles of management relating mainly to the management of production work, that were formulated by an American Engineer, Frederick Winslow Taylor (1856–1915). Also known as *Taylorism*. Taylor's views were extended and developed by his colleague Henry Lawrence Gantt (1861–1919) and by the Industrial Engineers, Frank Bunker Gilbreth (1868–1924) and Lillian Evelyn Moller Gilbreth (1878–1972) who laid down the foundations of the modern science of *work study*.

self-actualization   making the most of one's potentialities; becoming all that one is capable of becoming.

sensitivity analysis   analysis of how errors in one or more estimates will affect the conclusion drawn from the estimates.

seven-point plan   a list of questions arranged under seven headings that serve as a checklist for assessing people for employment. The list was devised by British occupational psychologist, Alec Rodger (born 1907).

severance pay   compensatory payment to an employee who has been dismissed because of circumstances beyond his/her control. See also *redundancy*.

sitting next to Nellie   learning how to do a job by watching another person doing it. A skill, the ability, innate or acquired, which enables someone to perform a task proficiently.

skills analysis   a technique of method study, used in analysing jobs in order to train people to perform them, in which particular attention is paid to the way the worker interprets sensory information (touch, sight etc.) and uses it to guide his/her actions.

skills inventory   summary of the skills possessed by employees of an organisation.

222

span of authority synonym for *span of control*.

span of control number of subordinates to whom a manager delegates his/her authority, or who are responsible to a manager.

span of management synonym for *span of control*.

staff audit critical examination of the *establishment of staff* within an organisation to determine the optimum number of staff required to carry out the objectives of the organisation.

standard a level of individual or group performance defined as adequate or acceptable.

standard costing the process of determining *standard costs* of producing something under specified conditions.

standard costs a pre-determined cost of using some resource (such as labour or materials) in the production of something by a manufacturer which, according to the person who estimated it, is the cost that would be incurred if production were carried out under specified conditions.

status the status of an individual is the evaluation of him/her, relative to others, that is made by a specified group of people (or by society generally). The status of some attribute of people (such as job title, size of personal wealth, type of physique, or nature of political views) is the evaluation that a group would normally give to a person with that attribute if they new little else about him/her.

statutory audit an *audit* carried out to satisfy legal requirements.

stock a quantity of something that is kept or stored for use as the need arises. In museums and galleries the *collections* are the organisation's 'stock'.

stock control activity, process or study of ensuring that quantities of stocks (e.g., of materials, supplies or finished goods) are such that a satisfactory service level is maintained whilst *stock-holding costs* are minimised. See also *collections management*.

stock level (or inventory level) the magnitude of a *stock* of something.

stock turnover the ratio of the sales revenue of an organisation for a period to the average value of its stock-in-trade (or stocks of finished goods) during that period. The ratio of the total quantity of a stock-keeping unit issued during a period to the average quantity of the item held in stock during that period.

stocktaking measuring the quantities of items of *stock* that an enterprise has in order to obtain an accurate list of it (also known as 'physical inventory' or *inventory*.

stocking-holding cost the cost incurred because a *stock* of something is kept for a time.

strategic decisions made for the future policy of the institution and will determine what is to be done next, rather than what is being done at the present.

strategic plan a plan which sets out general methods or policies for achieving specified objectives; especially a plan of future corporate strategy (also termed a *corporate plan*).

strategic planning the activity, process or study of preparing strategic plans (also known as *corporate planning*).

strategy a general method or policy for achieving specified objectives.

strike manual a book giving details of procedure to be carried out during a *strike*.

strike refusal by a group of employees to carry out their assigned work in order to bring pressure on their employers to change some aspect of their working conditions.

subordinate a member of an organisation who is in a position below that of a second member (called a 'superior') if the *superior* has power over the subordinate by virtue of the authority attached to the position the superior holds.

subsidise to reduce the price of something by paying a subsidy. To assist an organisation or an industry by paying subsidies.

subsidy a payment to a producer of goods or a provider of services which is made either in order to reduce the cost of those goods or services to a defined group of consumers or in order to enable the recipient to continue in a business that might otherwise be unprofitable.

succession plan a document that shows, for each management position in an organisation (or each position above a certain level): the name of the present job holder; estimated date he/she will leave; name and experience of person (from within the organisation) who will succeed him/her, or note that no one in the organisation can replace him/her.

succession planning activity of drawing up *succession plans*.

superior a member of an organisation is a superior of a second member (called a 'subordinate') if he/she has power over the *subordinate* via virtue of the authority attached to the position the superior holds.

superordinate synonym for *superior*.

supervisor a manager whose main role is to ensure that tasks specified by others are performed correctly and efficiently by a defined group of people, especially when none of those people are themselves managers.

supplies goods used by an organisation but not incorporate in its final product.

suspense account a ledger account which records transactions that are not yet complete, e.g., payments in advance or unidentified receipts.

systems analysis activity, process or study of critically examining the ways of performing frequently occurring tasks that depend on the movement, recording or processing of information (i.e., data processing) by a number of people within an organisation.

tactic method adopted for achieving a minor objective within the context of a strategic or *corporate plan*.

tactical decisions those which affect the day-to-day work of the organisation and are usually made as part of an evolving process of management.

task a requirement for the exertion of human effort leading to a recognisable achievement.

task analysis systematic analysis of the behaviour acquired to carry out a repetitive job in order to identify areas of difficulty and to devise appropriate methods of training people to perform the job.

task force a small *ad hoc* group of managers (say four to six) in an organisation whose objective is to make a concerted determination of the course of action to be taken in a critical area of the organisation's activities. Task forces are a feature of organisations that have a system of management by objectives, where they are formed to examine how corporate performance can be improved. They are usually temporary.

Taylorism synonym for *Scientific Management*.

tender (noun) a formal, unconditional offer, specifically of something that will discharge a debt or obligation. A formal offer to perform work (which has been specified by the person or organisation to which the offer is put) at a fixed price. An unconditional offer to buy something at a particular price

tender (verb) to proffer something unconditionally, especially something intended to discharge a debt or obligation.

the 80/20 law (or principle, or rule) a widely observed phenomenon that if an organisation has a large number of products then 80 per cent (in number) of the products account for only 20 per cent of its sales revenue from all products, or that 80 per cent of a person's time will result in only 20 per cent productive results.

Theory x and y a set of assumptions about human behaviour that D. McGregor considered to be implicit in much managerial policy and practice.

time off in lieu (TOIL) time taken off by an employee in lieu of hours worked on a previous occasion.

time-and-motion study synonym for *work study*.

top management loosely, the chief executive of an organisation and managers close to him/her in the organisation's structure.

total quality management (TQM) a term used to describe a modern management theory wherein quality extends throughout the management process. It has been referred to as 'the totality of features and characteristics of a product or service that bear on its ability to satisfy stated or implied needs'. TQM is concerned with the quality of inputs as well as the quality of outputs (i.e., *quality control*).

trading account a statement of the gross profit of an enterprise for a period. It usually includes a summary of the major categories of revenues and expenses.

trading company a merchant; in the case of museums and galleries usually a limited liability company formed in order to trade and covenant its profits to the museum (a charity). Charities may not trade.

trading down introduction, by an organisation of new products that are distinctly cheaper than the products it has sold in the past. In museums and galleries the term could be used for exchanging objects in the collections for other objects of lower value or interest.

trading up introduction, by an enterprise of new products that are distinctly more expensive than the products it has sold in the past. In the museum and gallery context trading up would be exchanging objects in the collection for objects of greater value or interest. A practice carried out by postal museums with their philatelic collections.

trust obligation, enforceable in equity, to deal with property, over which one has control, for the benefit of some person or persons who are entitled to enforce the obligations. The person who is under the obligation is called the 'trustee' and the person who will benefit from it is called a 'beneficiary'.

trust deed a deed which sets out the terms of a trust.

trustee one to whom property is entrusted to be administered for the benefit of another.

turnkey contract an arrangement by which a client commissions a specialist firm to arrange the design and construction of a complex project and leaves all decisions to the specialist firm until the project is complete and he/she can 'turn a key' to set it working.

turnover sales revenue for a period. The ratio of sales revenue for a period to the average value of a class of the organisation's assets during that period.

two-tier board a group of people who are responsible for the conduct of an organisation and are divided into two committees. In museums and galleries this works by having a 'management board' consisting of full-time employees of a museum and gallery who are responsible for the museum or gallery's day-to-day operations and a 'supervisory board', usually a board of trustees, responsible for protect-ing the interests of the organisation's 'owners', the public. Usually, the management board is appointed by, and may be dismissed by, the supervisory board. The supervisory board, in the case of national museums is appointed by the Prime Minister or a Secretary of State and in local authority museums and galleries by local councillors and the independent sector by the board itself.

ultra vires latin for 'beyond power', that is, outside the competence or legal authority of someone or some body of people.

unfair dismissal dismissal from employment that is deemed to be unfair by an industrial tribunal. The employer has to show that the dismissal was not unfair.

unit price the price charged for goods expressed as a price per unit of measurement.

unit pricing an instance or the activity of quoting *unit prices*.

university museums museums and galleries which are part of UK universities.

value the amount of money for which something could be sold.

value added the difference between the sales revenue that an organisation gets from selling its product and the cost to it of the materials used in that product. (Also known as 'added value'.)

value analysis consideration of the function of all parts of the design of one of the organisa-tion's products to see whether any changes in materials, manufacturing methods, or design would increase the product's value to the organisation. The increase in value may arise because the product can be improved and its sale increased or because the cost of producing it can be reduced or both.

visitor a user of museums and galleries. See also *customer*.

voucher a document which explains why a payment was made.

wage (often used in plural) regular payment to an employee for services or work done. Especially payment in cash for manual work paid at weekly intervals.

warder a security guard in a museum or gallery, see also *attendant*.

wholesale (adjective) of, relating to, or engaged in *wholesaling*.

wholesale (verb) to act as a *wholesaler*.

wholesaler a person or organisation that buys goods and resells them to buyers who will either: resell the goods for profit, or use the goods to facilitate the production of other goods, or incorporate them in other goods they produce, or use them for personal consumption but not in a household (e.g., in a hotel or hospital).

wind up to arrange the affairs of a company or trust so that its dissolution can take place.

work purposeful activity.

work sharing reduction by a group of workers of the amount of work each of them does in order to avoid laying off some workers. Hence, when work is short, everyone suffers a loss of earnings to the same extent.

work simplification a programme for improving methods of working based on involving all workers in an organisation in a search for better methods of doing their jobs and applying common sense rather than sophisticated techniques of methods studies.

work study activity or process of systematically examining, analysing and measuring methods of performing work that involves human activity in order to improve those methods (in the USA, usually called 'motion and time study').

work-shedding concentrating on 'key activities' and shedding work which will not produce results. Based on *the 80/20 law* which states that 80 per cent of results can generally be attributed to 20 per cent of effort.

work-to-rule a form of industrial action in which employees remain at work but apply any regulations relating to their work strictly or interpret regulations in such a way that the amount of work done is limited.

working practice the way in which a particular kind of work is normally arranged, especially the number of workers usually engaged on the work or their qualifications.

World Federation of Friends of Museums (WFFM) the international support group for friends and volunteers of museums and galleries.

write down to decrease the value of fixed assets and record in an account by deducting an amount of depreciation.

zero-based budgeting the practice of justifying budgeted expenditure in relation to the performance to be achieved without reference to pre-existing plans or achievements.

This glossary is intended to assist the manager in museums and galleries to get to grips with the terminology and jargon of management. Many of the definitions have arisen through the usage of these words within this book but others have been included to provide the reader with a comprehensive dictionary of terms. In order to do this I have leaned heavily on an excellent book, which I commend to the reader, which has provided many of the definitions contained herein. This is *A Dictionary of Management* by Derek French and Heather Saward published by Pan Books in 1975, ISBN No. 0-330-28512-2.

Useful addresses

All telephone and fax numbers are given as UK numbers.

American Association of Museums
1225 I Street NW
Suite 200
Washington DC 20005
USA
Tel: 0101 202 289 1818
Fax: 0101 202 289 6578

Area Museum Council for the South West
Hestercombe House
Cheddon Fitzpaine
Taunton
TA2 8LQ
Tel: 01823 259696
Fax: 01823 413114

Army Museums Ogilby Trust
(AMOT)
2 St Thomas Centre
Southgate Street
Winchester
Hants
SO23 9EF
Tel: 01962 841416
Fax: 01962 841426

Arts Council of England
14 Great Peter Street
London
SW1P 3NQ
Tel: 0171 333 0100
Fax: 0171 973 6590

Association for Business Sponsorship of the Arts
(ABSA)
Nutmeg House
60 Gainsford Street
Butler's Wharf

London
SE1 2NY
Tel: 0171 378 8143
Fax: 0171 407 7527

The Association for Information Management
(ASLIB)
Information House
20–24 Old Street
London
EC1V 9AP
Tel: 0171 253 4488
Fax: 0171 430 0514

Association of British Transport and Engineering
Museums
John Liffen (Secretary)
c/o The Science Museum
Exhibition Road
London
SW7 2DD
Tel: 0171 938 8089
Fax: 0171 938 9736

Association of County Councils
Eaton House
66A Eaton Square
London
SW1W 9BH
Tel: 0171 235 1200
Fax: 0171 235 8458

Association of District Councils
26 Chapel Street
London
SW1P 4ND
Tel: 0171 233 6868
Fax: 0171 233 6551

Association of First Division Civil Servants
(FDA)
2 Caxton Street
London
SW1H 0QH
Tel: 0171 222 6242
Fax: 0171 222 5926

Association of Independent Museums
(AIM)
c/o Watling Chase Community Forest
Shenley Park
Radlett Lane
Shenley, Herts
WD7 9DW
Tel: 01923 852641
Fax: 01923 854216

Association of Leading Visitor Attractions
4 Westminster Palace Gardens
Artillery Row
London
SW1P 1RL
Tel: 0171 222 1728
Fax: 0171 222 1729

Association of Local Government
26 Chapel Street
London
SW1P 4ND
Tel: 0171 834 2222
Fax: 0171 834 2263

Association of Metropolitan Authorities
35 Great Smith Street
Westminster
London
SW1P 3BJ
Tel: 0171 222 8100
Fax: 0171 222 0878

Audit Commission
1 Vincent Square
London
SW1O 2PN
Tel: 0171 828 1212
Fax: 0171 976 6187

Biology Curators Group
(GCG)
c/o Townley Hall Art Gallery and
Museums
Townley Oark
Burnley
BB11 3RQ
Tel: 01282 424213

British Association of Friends of
Museums
(BAFM)
31 Southwell Park Road
Camberley
Surrey
GU15 3QG
Tel: 01276 66617

British Council
10 Spring Gardens
London
SW1A 2BN
Tel: 0171 930 8466
Fax: 0171 839 6347

British Standards Institution
(BSI)
389 Chiswick High Road
London
W4 4AL
Tel: 0181 996 9000
Fax: 0181 996 7400

British Tourist Authority
(BTA)
Thames Tower
Black's Road
London
W6 9EL
Tel: 0181 846 9000
Fax: 0181 563 0302

Charities Aid Foundation
(CAF)
48 Pembury Road
Tonbridge
Kent
TN9 2JD
Tel: 01732 771333
Fax: 01732 350570

Charity Commission
St Albans' House
57/60 Haymarket
London
SW1Y 4QX
Tel: 0171 210 4477
Fax: 0171 210 4545

City and Guilds Institute
1 Giltspur Street
London
EC1A 9DD
Tel: 0171 294 2468
Fax: 0171 294 2400

Commonwealth Association of Museums
P O Box 30192
Chinook Postal Outlet
Calgary
Alberta T2H 2V9
Canada
Tel and Fax: 00 1 403 938 3190

Companies House
55–71 City Road
London
EC1Y 1BB
Tel: 0171 253 9393

Contemporary Arts Society
(CAS)
20 John Islip Street
London
SW1P 4LL
Tel: 0171 821 5323
Fax: 0171 834 0228

The Council of Museums in Wales
The Courtyard
Letty Street
Cathays
Cardiff
CF2 4EL
Tel: 01222 225432
Fax: 01222 668516

Crafts Council
44a Pentonville Road
Islington
London
N1 9BY
Tel: 0171 278 7700
Fax: 0171 837 6891

Department of National Heritage
Heritage and Tourism Group
2–4 Cockspur Street
London
SW1Y 5DH
Tel: 0171 211 6384
Fax: 0171 211 6319

East Midlands Museums Service
Courtyard Buildings
Wollaton Park
Nottingham
NG8 2AE
Tel: 0115 985 4534
Fax: 0115 928 0038

English Heritage
Fortress House

Saville Row
London
W1X 1AB
Tel: 0171 973 3000
Fax: 0171 973 3001

English Tourist Board
(ETB)
Thames Tower
Black's Road
London
W6 9EL
Tel: 0181 846 9000
Fax: 0181 563 0302

Geological Curators' Group
c/o Geological Society of London
Burlington House
London
W1V OJU
Tel: 0171 434 9944

Group for Costume and Textile Staff in Museums
State Apartments and Royal Ceremonial
Dress Collection
Kensington Palace
London
W8 4PZ
Tel: 0171 937 9361

Group for Education in Museums
(GEMS)
63 Navarino Road
London
E8 1AG
Tel: 0171 249 4296

Group for Museum Publishing and Shop
Management
Ashmolean Museum
Oxford
OX1 2PH
Tel: 01865 278010

Group of Directors of Museums and Galleries
in the British Isles
c/o Lindsay Institute
Hope Street
Lanark
M L11 7LZ
Tel: 01555 661331 (ext. 272)
Fax: 01555 665884

Guild of Taxidermists
Art Gallery and Museum
Kelvingrove

Glasgow
G3 8AG
Tel: 0141 305 2671
Fax: 0141 305 2690

Industrial Society
48 Bryanston Square
London
W1H 7LN
Tel: 0171 262 2401
Fax: 0171 706 1096

Institute of Leisure and Amenity Management
ILAM House
Lower Basildon
Reading
Berks
RG8 9NE
Tel: 01491 874222
Fax: 01491 874059

Institute of Management
Management House
Cottingham Road
Corby
Northants
NN17 1TT
Tel: 01536 204222

Institute of Marketing
Moor Hall
Cookham
Maidenhead
Berks
SL6 9QH
Tel: 01628 524922

Institute of Personnel and Development
IPD House
35 Camp Road
Wimbledon
London
SW19 4UX
Tel: 0181 971 9000

Institute of Professionals, Managers and
Specialists Museum Staff
75–79 York Road
London
SE1 7AQ
Tel: 0171 928 9951
Fax: 0171 928 5996

International Council of Museums
(ICOM)
Maison de l'Unesco

1 rue Miollis
7572 Paris
Cedex 15
France
Tel: 00 331 47 34 0500
Fax: 00 331 43 06 7862

Library Association
7 Ridgmount Street
London
WC1E 7AE
Tel: 0171 636 7543
Fax: 0171 436 7218

London Federation of Museums and Art Galleries
BT Museum
145 Queen Victoria Street
London
EC4V 4AT
Tel: 0171 248 7444

MGC/Science Museum PRISM Fund
Science Museum
Exhibition Road
London
SW7 2DD
Tel: 0171 938 8055
Fax: 0171 938 9736

MGC/V&A Purchase Grant Fund
Directorate
Victoria and Albert Museum
London
SW7 2RL
Tel: 0171 835 1766

Midlands Federation of Museums and Art
Galleries
c/o Mr Iain Rutherford
Museums, Arts and Heritage Officer
Worcester City Museum and Art Gallery
Foregate Street
Worcester
WR1 1DT
Tel: 01905 723471

Museum and Exhibition Design Group
4 Crown Yard
Southgate
Elland
Yorks
MX5 0DQ
Tel and Fax: 01422 375680

Museum Documentation Association
(MDA)

Lincoln House
347 Cherry Hinton Road
Cambridge
CB1 4DH
Tel: 01223 242848
Fax: 01223 213474

Museum Ethnographers Group
Manchester Museum
Manchester
M13 9PL
Tel: 0161 275 2634

Museum Professional Group
(MPG)
c/o Godalming Museum
109a High Street
Godalming
Surrey
GU7 1AQ
Tel: 01483 426510

Museum Training Institute
(MTI)
1st Floor, Glyde House
Glydegate
Bradford
BD5 0UP
Tel: 01274 391056
Fax: 01274 394890

Museums and Galleries Commission
(MGC)
16 Queen Anne's Gate
London
SW1H 9AA
Tel: 0171 233 4200
Fax: 0171 233 3686

Museums and Galleries Disability Association
(MAGDA)
11 Eastgate Street
Winchester
SO23 8EB

Museums Association
(MA)
42 Clerkenwell Road
London
EC1R 0PA
Tel: 0171 608 2933
Fax: 0171 250 1929

Museums North (Northern Federation of
Museums and Art Galleries)
Arts Libraries and Museums Dept

County Hall
Durham
DH1 5TY
Tel: 0191 383 4478
Fax: 0191 384 1336

National Art Collections Fund
(NACF)
Millais House
7 Cromwell Place
London
SW7 2JN
Tel: 0171 225 4800
Fax: 0171 225 4848

National Association of Decorative and Fine Arts
Societies
(NADFAS)
8 Guildford Street
London
WC1N 1DT
Tel: 0171 430 0730
Fax: 0171 242 0686

National Campaign for the Arts
(NCA)
Francis House
Francis Street
London
SW1P 1DE
Tel: 0171 828 4448
Fax: 0171 931 9959

National Council for Vocational Qualifications
(NCVQ)
222 Euston Road
London
NW1 2BZ
Tel: 0171 387 9898
Fax: 0171 387 0978

National Heritage Memorial Fund
(NHMF)
10 St James's Street
London
SW1A 1EF
Tel: 0171 930 0963
Fax: 0171 930 0968

North of England Museums Service
House of Recovery
Bath Lane
Newcastle upon Tyne
NE4 5SQ
Tel: 0191 222 1661
Fax: 0191 261 4725

North West Museums Service
Griffin Lodge
Cavendish Place
Blackburn
BB2 2PN
Tel: 01254 670211
Fax: 01254 681995

Northern Ireland Museums Council
185 Stranmills Road
Belfast
BT9 5DU
Tel: 01232 661023
Fax: 01232 683513

Science and Industry Curators Group
(SICG)
Hampshire County Museums Service
Chilcomb House
Chilcomb Lane
Winchester
Hants, SO23 8RD
Tel: 01962 846304
Fax: 01962 869836

Scottish Museums Council
(SMC)
County House
20–22 Torphichen Street
Edinburgh
EH3 8JB
Tel: 0131 229 7465
Fax: 0131 229 2728

Scottish Museums Federation
Ettrick and Lauderdale Museum Service
Municipal Buildings
High Street
Selkirk
TD7 4JX
Tel: 01750 20096
Fax: 01750 23282

Social History Curators Group
Tyne and Wear Museums
Blandford Square
Newcastle upon Tyne
NE1 4JA
Tel: 0191 232 6789

Society of Archivists
Information House
20–24 Old Street
London
EC1V 9AP
Tel: 0171 253 4488/5987
Fax: 0171 253 3942

Society of County Museum Directors
c/o The Yorkshire Museum
Museum Gardens
York
YO1 2DR

Society of Decorative Art Curators
Leamington Spa Art Gallery and
Museum
Avenue Road
Leamington Spa
Warwicks
CV31 3PP

Society of Museum Archaeologists
c/o The Museum of London
London Wall
London
EC2Y 5HN
Tel: 0171 600 3699

South East Federation of Museums and
Art Galleries
c/o The Museum of Kent Life
Lock Lane
Sandling
Maidstone
Kent
ME14 3AV
Tel: 01622 763936

South Eastern Museums Service
Ferroners House
Barbican
London
C2Y 8AA
Tel: 0171 600 0219
Fax: 0171 600 2581

South Midlands Museums Federation
Banbury Museum
8 Horsefair
Banbury
Oxon
OX16 0AA
Tel: 01295 259855

South West Federation of Museums
and Art Galleries
Cheltenham Art Gallery and
Museums
Clarence Street
Cheltenham
Glos
GL50 3JT

Touring Exhibitions Group
29 Point Hill
Greenwich
London
SE10 8QW
Tel and Fax: 0181 691 2660

United Kingdom Institute for Conservation
(UKIC)
6 Whitehorse Mews
Westminster Bridge Road
London
SE1 7QP
Tel: 0171 620 3371
Fax: 0171 620 3761

Visual and Art Galleries Association
c/o The Old School
The High Street
Witcham
Ely
CB6 2LQ

Volunteer Centre UK
Carriage Row
183 Eversholt Street
London
NW1 1BU
Tel: 0171 388 9888
Fax: 0171 383 6448

Welsh Federation of Museums and Art Galleries
Ceredigion Museum
The Colisseum
Terrace Road
Aberystwyth
SY23 2AQ

West Midlands Area Museum Service
Hanbury Road
Stoke Prior
Bromsgrove
Worcestershire
B60 4AD
Tel: 015278 72258
Fax: 015278 76960

Women, Heritage and Museums
(WHAM!)
Institute of Archaeology
31–34 Gordon Square
London
WC1M 0PY
Tel: 0171 387 7050 (ext. 4938)

World Federation of Friends of Museums
(WFFM)
Secretariat of Presidency
4 rue Auguste Dorchain
75015 Paris
France
Tel: 00 33 1 43066183
Fax: 00 33 1 43066242

Yorkshire and Humberside Federation of
Museums and Galleries
Abbey House Museum
Kirkstall
Leeds
LS5 3EH
Tel: 0113 275 5821

Yorkshire and Humberside Museums Council
Farnley Hall
Hall Lane
Leeds
LS12 5HA
Tel: 0113 263 8909/3902
Fax: 0113 279 1479

Bibliography

Advisory, Conciliation and Arbitration Service (1983) *Induction of New Employees*, Advisory Booklet No. 7, ACAS, London.

Adair, J. (1973) *Action Centred Leadership*, McGraw-Hill, New York.

Adair, J. (1983) *Effective Leadership*, Gower, Aldershot.

Argyris, C. (1957) *Personality and Organization*, Harper and Row, New York.

Baker, R. J. S. (1972) *Administrative Theory and Public Administration*, Hutchinson, London.

Bakke, E. W. (1953) *The Fusion Process*, Labor and Management Center, Yale University, New Haven, Connecticut.

Bakke, E. W. and Argyris, C. (1954) *Organizational Structure and Dynamics*, Labor and Management Center, Yale University, New Haven, Connecticut.

Barnard, C. I. (1938) *The Functions of the Executive*, Harvard University Press, Cambridge, Massachusetts and London.

Beardshaw, J. and Palfreman, D. (1986) *The Organization in its Environment*, Pitman, London.

Bennis, W. G. (1966) 'Organizational development and the fate of bureaucracy', *Industrial Management Review* (MIT) Spring issue.

Bestermann, T. and Bott, V. (1982) 'To pay or not to pay', *Museums Journal*, 82(2).

British Standards Institute (1978) *Quality Vocabulary: Part 1 International Terms*, (BS4778), (ISO 8402, 1986), BSI, London.

Burns, T. and Stalker, G. H. (1961) *The Management of Innovation*, Tavistock, London.

Carzo, R. and Yanouzas, J. N. (1969) 'Effects of flat and tall structures', *Administrative Science Quarterly*, 14, 178–91.

Child, J. (1972) 'Organizational structure, environment performance: the role of strategic choice', *Sociology*, 6, 1–21.

Child, J. (1973) 'Predicting and understanding organization structure', *Administrative Science Quarterly*, 18, 168–85.

Child, J. (1977) *Organization: A Guide to Problems and Practice*, Harper and Row, New York.

Cossons, N. (1970) 'McKinsey and the museum', *Museums Journal*, 70(3).

Cossons, N. (1973) 'The Ironbridge Project', *Museums Journal*, 72(4).

Court, P. (1982) *The Systems Approach to Management Services Projects*, Management Services, London.

Cowling, A. G. and Mahair, C. J. B. (1981) *Managing Human Resources*, Edward Arnold, London.

Cribbin, J. J. (1984) *Effective Managerial Leadership*, Amacom, New York.

Cuthbert, N. (1970) *Management Thinkers*, Penguin, London.

Dandridge, T. C., Mitroff, I. and Joyce, W. J. (1980) 'Organization symbolism: a topic to expand organizational analysis', *Academy of Management Review*, 5, 77–82.

Deal, T. D. and Kennedy, A. (1982) *Corporate Cultures*, Addison-Wesley, Reading, Massachusetts.

Delbecq, A. L., Shull, F. A., Filley, A. C. and Grimes, A. L. (1969) *Matrix Organization: A*

Conceptual Guide to Organizational Variation (Wisconsin Business Papers No2), Bureau of Business Research and Service, Graduate School of Business, Univeristy of Wisconsin, Madison, Wisconsin.

Donaldson, L. (1985) *In Defence of Organization Theory – A Reply to Critics*, Cambridge University Press, London.

Drucker, P. F. (1990) *Managing the Non-Profit Organization*, Butterworth-Heinemann, Oxford.

Emery, F. E. (Ed.) (1969) *Systems Thinking*, Penguin, London.

Fayol, H. (1949) *General Industrial Management*, Pitman, London.

Fisch, G. G. (1961) 'Line-staff is obsolete', *Harvard Business Review*, Sept/Oct, Cambridge, Massachusetts.

Fopp, M. A. (1984) *The Museum Framework in Great Britain*, The City University, London.

Fopp, M. A. (1986) 'The science of management', *Museums Journal*, 85(4).

Fopp, M. A. (1988) *Museum and Gallery Management*, The City University, London.

French, D. and Saward, H. (1975) *A Dictionary of Management*, Pan Books, London.

Galbraith, J. K. (1969) *Organization Design: An Information Processing View*, Sloan School of Management Paper No 425–69.

Galbraith, J. R. (1973) *Designing Organizations*, Addison-Wesley, Reading Massachusetts.

Galbraith, J. R. and Nathanson, D. A. (1978) *Strategy Implementation: The Role of Structure and Process*, West Publishing Company, St Paul, Minnesota.

Gerth, H. H. and Wright Mills, C. (eds) (1958) *From Max Weber: Essays in Sociology*, Oxford University Press, London.

Hage, J. and Aiken, M. (1967) 'Relationship of centralization to other structural properties', *Administrative Science Quarterly*, 12, 72–92.

Haire, M. (1966) 'Biological models and empirical histories of the growth of organizations in modern organization theory', *Psychological Bulletin*, 66(4).

Hall, R. H. (1963) 'The concept of bureaucracy: an empirical assessment', *American Journal of Sociology*, 69, 32–40.

Hall, R. H. (1972) *Organization's Structure and Process*, Prentice-Hall, Englewood Cliffs, New Jersey.

Handy, C. B. (1976) *Understanding Organizations*, 2nd edn, Penguin, London.

Harrington, A. (1960) *Life in The Crystal Palace*, Jonathan Cape, London.

Healey, J. H. (1956) *Executive Co-ordination and Control*, Ohio State University Press, Colombus, Ohio.

Hunt, J. (1975) *Managing People at Work*, Pan Books, London.

Januszczak, W. (1986) 'A Tate a tete', *Guardian*, 25 September.

Kaufman, H. and Seidman, D. (1970) 'The morphology of organizations', *Administrative Science Quarterly*, 15, 439–51.

Koontz, H. (1966) 'Making theory operational: the span of management', *Journal of Management Studies*, 3, 229–43.

Koontz, H., O'Donnell, C. and Weihrisch, H. (1980) *Management*, McGraw-Hill, New York.

Kuhn, T. (1969) *The Structure of Scientific Revolution*, University of Chicago Press, Chicago, Illinois.

Lawrence, P. R. and Lorsch, J. W. (1967) *Organization and Environment: Managing Differentiation and Integration*, Harvard University, Cambridge, Massachusetts.

Leavitt, H. J. (1972) *Managerial Psychology*, University of Chicago Press, Chicago, Illinois.

Lewis, G. D. (1983) 'The training of museum personnel in the United Kingdom', *Museums Journal*, 83(1).

Lewis, G. D. (1984) 'Museums in Britain: 1920 to the present day', *Manual of Curatorship*, Butterworth and Museums Association, London.

Likert, R. (1959) 'A motivation approach to a modified theory of organization and management theory', in M. Haire (ed.), *Modern Organization Theory: A Symposium of the Foundation for Research on Human Behaviour*, Wiley, New York.

McGregor, D. V. (1960) *The Human Side of Enterprise*, McGraw-Hill, New York.

McWhinney, W. H. (1965) 'The geometry of organizations', *Administrative Science Quarterly*, 4, 356–57.

Mayo, E. (1945) *The Social Problems of an Industrial Civilization*, Harvard University Press, Cambridge, Massachusetts.

Merton, R. K. (1980) *Organizations*, March, Simon and Guetzkow, New York.

Mintzberg, H. (1981) 'Organization design: fashion or fit?', *Harvard Business Review*, 59.

Museums and Galleries Commission (1987) *Museum Professional Training and Career Structure – Report by Working Party*, HMSO, London.

Museums Association (1979) *Information Sheet – Careers in Museums*, Museums Association, London.

Oakland, J. S. (1989) *Total Quality Management*, Butterworth-Heinemann, Oxford.

Payne, R. and Pugh, D. S. (1976) 'Organizational structure and climate' in *Handbook of Industrial and Organizational Psychology*, Rand McNally, Chicago, Illinois, pp 1125–1172.

Perrow, C. (1970) *Organizational Analysis – A Sociological View*, Tavistock, London.

Pettigrew, A. M. (1973) *The Politics of Organizational Decision-Making*, Tavistock, London.

Pettigrew, A. M. (1979) 'On studying organizational cultures', *Administrative Science Quarterly*, 24(4), November.

Pugh, D. S. (1970) *Writers on Organizations*, Penguin, London.

Pugh, D. S. (1971) *Organization Theory, Selected Readings*, Penguin, London.

Pugh, D. S., Hickson, D. H., Hinings, C. R. and Turner, C. (1968) 'Dimensions of organization structure', *Administrative Science Quarterly*, 13(1), June, pp. 65–105.

Redcliffe-Maud, J. (1976) *Support for the Arts in England and Wales*, Gulbenkian Foundation, London.

Reddin, W. J. (1971) *Effective MBO*, Management Publications, London.

Rodger, A. (1952) *Seven Point Plan*, National Institute of Industrial Psychology, London.

Schein, E. H. (1965) 'Management and the worker – summary of the work of Roethlisberger and Dickson', *Organizational Psychology*, Prentice Hall, Englewood Cliffs, New Jersey.

Selznick, P. (1980) *Organizations*, March, Simon and Guetzkow, New York.

Shirley, R. C., Peters, M. H. and Adel, I. El-Ansary (1981) *Strategy and Policy Formation*, John Wiley, New York.

Simon, H. A. (1967) *The Changing Theory and the Changing Practice of Public Administration*, McGraw-Hill, New York.

Simon, H. A. (1957) *Administrative Behaviour*, Macmillan, New York.

Simon, H. A. (1976) *Administrative Decision-Making*, The Free Press, New York.

Singleton, H. R. (1966) 'The Leicester course', *Museums Journal*, 66(3).

Smith, A. (1971) 'The postgraduate course in gallery and museums studies, University of Manchester', *Museums Journal*, 71(3).

Stansfield, G. (1967) 'Museums in the countryside', *Museums Journal*, 67(3).

Stewart, R. (1985) *The Reality of Organizations*, Macmillan, New York.

Strong, R. and Cossons, N. (1985) *Lectures to the Tourism Society*, The Tourism Society, London.

Tannenbaum, A. S. (1968) *Control in Organizations*, McGraw-Hill, New York.

Tannenbaum, A. S., Kavacic, B., Rosner, M. and Vianello, M. (1974) *Hierarchy in Organizations*, Jossey-Bass, New York.

Taylor, F. W. (1903) 'Shop management', *Transactions of the American Society of Mechanical Engineers*, 24, 1337–1480.

Taylor, F. W. (1911) *The Principals of Scientific Management*, incorporated in F. W. Taylor (1947) *Scientific Management*, Harper and Brothers, New York.

Taylor, F. W. (1912) *Scientific Management*, Testimony to the House of Representatives Committee, Washington DC.

Taylor, F. W. (1947) *Scientific Management*, Harpers and Brothers, New York.

Thomas, J. M. and Bennis, W. G. (1972) *Management of Change and Conflict*, Penguin, New York.

Thompson, J. (1972) 'A Bradford project in community involvement', *Museums Journal*, 71(4).

Thompson, J. (1980) 'Cities in decline: museums and the urban programmes 1969–1979', *Museums Journal*, 80(4).

Thompson, J. (ed.) (1992) *Manual of Curatorship*, Butterworth and Museums Association, London.

Torrington, D. and Hall, L. (1991) *Personnel Management – A New Approach*, Prentice Hall, London.

Vickers, G. (1965) *The Art of Judgement: A Study of Policy-Making*, Chapman and Hall, London.

Voak, J. (ed.) (1986) *Report of the Board of Trustees October 1983 – March 1986*, Victoria and Albert Museum, London.

Weber, M. (1938) *The Theory of Social and Economic Organization*, Bedminster Press, New York.

Weber, M. (1968) *Economy and Society: An Outline of Interpretive Sociology*, Bedminster Press, New York.

Whyte, W. H. (1956) *The Organization Man*, Simon and Schuster, New York.

Woodward, J. (1958) *Management and Technology*, HMSO, London.

Woodward, J. (1965) *Industrial Organizations: Theory and Practice*, Oxford University Press, London.

Worthy, J. C. (1950) 'Organization structure and employee morale', *American Sociological Review*, 15, 169–179.

Index